The Way of Rest

CHERYL SCANLAN

The Way of Rest
Copyright © 2025 by Cheryl Scanlan

This is a discipleship companion book, drawing from the truth of Scriptures, personal biographical details of the author's life, as seen through the author's eyes, and the experiences of God's people through the ministry of Promised Land Living®. Where necessary or requested, names have been changed to respect privacy.

All rights reserved. No part of this book may be reproduced in any form without permission from the author. The author would delight in receiving an email with a story of how God is using the stories, frameworks and tools from the book in your life or someone you are discipling. To request permission, send your stories or to contact the author, email TWOR@promisedlandliving.com.

First paperback edition September 2025

Cover photo and cover design by David Scanlan
Co-authored by Brianna Scanlan
Graphics used with permission from Promised Land Living®, www.promisedlandliving.com
Edited by Diane Moser and TWOR Collaborative
Typesetting by Euan Monaghan

Softcover: ISBN 978-0-9844689-5-9
Kindle: ISBN 978-0-9844689-6-6
Audio: ISBN 978-0-9844689-7-3

Unless otherwise noted, all Scripture quotations are taken from The ESV® Bible (The Holy Bible, English Standard Version®), © 2001 by Crossway, a publishing ministry of Good News Publishers. Used by permission. All rights reserved. Scripture quotations taken from The Holy Bible, New International Version®, NIV®. Copyright © 1973, 1978, 1984, 2011 by Biblica, Inc. Used with permission of Zondervan. All rights reserved worldwide. www.zondervan.com

Corem Deo

Dedication

To those who have grown weary in doing good.

Table of Contents

Foreword vii
Endorsements ix
Acknowledgments xv

Introduction 1

Chapter One: The Journey is Too Long 5
Chapter Two: Still Small Voice 30
Chapter Three: Listening 55
Chapter Four: Interlude 74
Chapter Five: Abiding in the Vine 83
Chapter Six: Responsibility and Relationships 105
Chapter Seven: Desert Lies 129
Chapter Eight: Identity 150
Chapter Nine: Skandalon 171
Chapter Ten: Shadow of the Almighty 187
Chapter Eleven: Community 207
Chapter Twelve: Shalom 234

Appendix A: Listening Styles 249
Appendix B: Barriers 251
Appendix C: Shift Bookmark 254
Appendix D: Timeline 255

Foreword

WHEN CHERYL SCANLAN asked me to write the foreword to The Way of Rest, I didn't hesitate—because I didn't have to think twice about the profound impact her teachings have had on my own life. Cheryl is a dear friend, but more importantly, she has been a guide who helped me find peace and clarity when my own faith journey felt heavy and exhausting.

If you're picking up this book, you might already know what it's like to feel "off" in your walk with Christ. You love Jesus deeply, yet you sense there's something missing—a quiet ache that the abundant life promised feels somehow elusive. I've been there. Before embracing Cheryl's approach, I carried burdens that weren't mine, believing my faith required constant striving. It felt noble, but it was unsustainable and unfulfilling.

Cheryl gently and deftly showed me a different way—one that transformed my understanding of rest. She invited me into the profound simplicity of living from Christ's completed work rather than endlessly working for His approval. Through her guidance and the principles found in this book, I discovered that true rest isn't passive inactivity but a vibrant, freeing posture of the soul. It was a revelation for me because I held the belief, and bought the lie, that rest was selfish.

One of the most powerful aspects of The Way of Rest is Cheryl's transparent, heart-rending sharing. Throughout these pages, Cheryl bravely opens up about her own struggles and vulnerabilities—moments of exhaustion, illness, relational abuse, doubt, and pain. Her courage in revealing these deeply personal experiences creates a safe and authentic space for readers. Cheryl's vulnerability isn't merely inspiring; it's transformative, gently dismantling our defenses and inviting us to step into our own vulnerability with hope and trust.

In The Way of Rest, Cheryl shares the wisdom she has gained through decades of discipleship, hardship, coaching, and renewal. Her voice throughout these pages is one of compassion and authenticity, grounded in her own lived experience. She has spent hours with others listening to their heart cry beneath their words. She understands weariness because she has walked through it herself, emerging with powerful insights that she now generously offers to us. Her focus is on the reader as she curiously asks, "what is happening for you as you hear my story?"

I encourage you to approach this journey slowly, as I did. Savor it. Allow yourself to unwind from the pressures and expectations that have accumulated over years of faithful but exhausting service. Cheryl's gentle invitation to explore rest is more than theoretical—it's life-changing.

May you find, as I did, that in these pages you are not merely reading words and learning paradigms but encountering a profound truth: you can indeed live freely, joyfully, and abundantly from a place of divine rest. Cheryl's heart, expressed with vulnerable clarity, is a testament to the powerful peace Christ longs to give each of us.

Welcome to this journey—I pray it changes your life as beautifully as it changed mine. Shabbat Shalom!

Roy Moore
Friend & Vice Chairman, Come And See Foundation

Endorsements

In Cheryl Scanlan's The Way of Rest, *she invites us into a conversation with Christ where we learn to tune out the confusing clamor around us and abide instead in the beauty and power of his voice. Rather than casting her shadow over us, Cheryl brings us tenderly into the light of his love, where we discover for ourselves his sabbath rest and learn to incorporate the healing and humility of listening, of abiding, of surrendering. Through her writing stocked with vivid imagery and compelling stories, God takes what Cheryl describes as her "two loaves worth of grace and mercy" and multiplies it abundantly so our souls are left satisfied and refreshed. As each chapter unfolds, Cheryl creates in us a longing for more of Christ's gentle yet powerful presence precisely where we find ourselves right now.*

ELIZABETH A MITCHELL
(Cheryl's discipler mentioned in Chapters 1, 4, and 10)
Chief Development Officer, Awana International
Author of *Journey for the Heart* & *Morningside*

This book met me like a trusted friend—honest, unhurried, and anchored in truth. Cheryl doesn't offer trite answers or polished formulas; instead, she opens the pages of her own journey with a sacred willingness to walk us through her pain, her weariness, and the intimate process that led her to a new and deeper place of rest.

The Way of Rest is more than a book—it's a lifeline for those who love God but find themselves bone tired. It's for the leaders, the caregivers, the ministry hearts and marketplace builders who've been faithfully pouring out but quietly asking, "Where is the abundant life?"

Cheryl's voice is tender, steady, and trustworthy. Through every page, she becomes a companion for the soul—a guide who has lived what she teaches. This is a field guide to your Promised Land—restoring the heart song of God's people, a song of shalom, and mapping the way from striving to abiding.

Read it slowly. Let it minister. Let it sing.

DAVID ROSEN
Founder, Progress Rose
Coach, Builder, and Marketplace Global Minister

I found myself coached, taught, loved, and encouraged while reading Cheryl Scanlan's powerful book, The Way of Rest. *With the heart of a seasoned spiritual and professional coach, Cheryl courageously shares her flaws, failures, and joys — inviting readers into a path of authentic Christian living. Her vulnerability is a gift, offering hope to those seeking to overcome personal limitations and disappointments. The Way of Rest is a refreshing guide for anyone longing for a deeper, more genuine walk with God. Well done, Cheryl!*

OS HILLMAN
Author, President, Marketplace Leaders, Author of *TGIF Today God Is First*

When the first disciples experienced the risen Christ, they didn't recognize him. They doubted. They were afraid, They were confused. They had no category for Him. And he tenderly opened the Scriptures and their minds to understand that the cosmos has been changed by his resurrection.

What if, as contemporary Christians, we need to experience Jesus beyond our categories? When we, often despite a rich experience of faith, find ourselves perplexed and feeling hollow, perhaps Jesus is gently inviting us to expand our ability to see Him.

Through rich personal stories, careful reflection on Scripture, and a time tested approach, Cheryl brings all of the resources of her sharp mind and tender heart to the pages of this book. She echoes Jesus' words and resurrection actions and guides the reader step by step to recognize His presence with us in ways not previously apparent. She invites us to experience Jesus' life—an eternal kind of life—in resurrection joy and transformation!

ZANE CREAMER

JourneyMates Board of Trustees, Renovaré Institute Faculty Member
Eastertide, 2025

The Way of Rest is a beautifully written invitation to step away from striving and rediscover soul-deep rest through a genuine relationship with God. With vulnerable stories and thought-provoking questions, the author guides readers to embrace their identity as a place of rest rather than performance. This book peels away religious pressure and gently offers grace, strength, and renewed purpose for the weary. It's a powerful reminder that God's love is most clearly experienced when we stop striving and simply receive His care.

This book is a powerful tool for anyone needing rest for their body, mind, and spirit—an invitation to stop, breathe, and experience the deep, sustaining rest that comes from knowing God is for us. I know, because it brought me back to the place of rest I had lost.

RITA MAYELL

SR Strategist Samaritan's Purse, Author of *5'2" Giant, One Ordinary Man Who Changed the World*

In The Way of Rest, *Cheryl has managed to produce a work that is both personally honest and transparent. The lessons are theologically sound, practical for all, applicable in all, and edifying to all. Believers today are in great need of resources like this that encourage and guide the soul to engage with God, step out in faith on His Promises, and trust Him to do a deeper work that we all truly long for…painless, NO…worth it, ABSOLUTELY!*

I recommend this book to all who desire to go higher up and further in.

CHUCK MILIAN

Former Senior Pastor and Founder/Director Luke 2:52 Mentoring

The Way of Rest offers hope to Christians feeling weary or stuck despite their daily engaging in spiritual routines. Cheryl's transparency and the shared stories may be near to home and will encourage a deeper relationship with the Lord. Learning to become more self-aware by listening to the Holy Spirit and surrendering control helps to release burdens, fears, and lies that prevent living the abundant life that God promises us in John 10:10. Cheryl's practical "7 Step Shift" tool promotes transformation, and she emphasizes the importance of community through "Promise Land Living."

DEBI ZAAS

Former Director of Navigators Life and Leadership Coaching
Currently Navigators Life & Leadership Mentor Coach

Calling all lovers of Jesus who feel stuck, dry, weary, or at the end of their rope—you're not alone. We've all been there. The good news is that there is a way forward. It's called The Way of Rest. *Cheryl doesn't just write about it; she lives it. Take her hand and let her guide you, as she has so many others, into a deeper, more life-giving relationship with Jesus than you ever imagined. I've taken the journey, and it has made all the difference.*

STEPHANIE GUTTIERREZ

Missionary Care Manager, Modern Day Missions
Co-Executive Director, Footrock (retreats for pastors and missionaries)

Is your work never ending? Are your relationships draining you? Do your kids not always appreciate you? Is your spouse not seeing you or your point of view? Are you demanding too much of yourself? Are you weary of performing? Maybe you're caring for everyone but yourself. Maybe it's time to enter God's rest. The promised land was not just for weary travelers thousands of years ago. It's a place you can go to today. It's a place where you'll find life giving love. It's a place where you'll be seen. It's a place where you can slow down. It's a place where you'll hear God's voice. It's a place you can call home. Cheryl Scanlan does a masterful job leading you there because she's been there and she's taken many weary travelers there as their guide. If you're unsure how you can travel to this life-giving place, Cheryl is waiting to show you the way. Be sure to take the journey with her. You'll find your true home.

GREG LEITH

CEO, Convene, www.ConveneNow.com

The Way of Rest *is more than just a book; it's a sacred invitation. From the very first page, Cheryl writes with raw honesty and grace, warmly ushering you into a quiet place beside Jesus. Her vulnerability and wisdom pave a gentle path for readers to rediscover rest—not merely as a concept, but as a way of life.*

Cheryl shares her journey back to rest with profound authenticity. Through her words, practical steps, and inspiring stories of transformation from others, she offers more than encouragement—she provides a true companion for the road. Having had the privilege of walking this journey alongside Cheryl, I am deeply grateful for her guiding signposts of grace and presence, now made accessible to many more.

As someone engaged in cross-cultural missions, I find this book to be a rare and refreshing gift. It speaks directly to the weary hearts involved in difficult kingdom work, cutting through noise and busyness to nourish the soul with living water. The Way of Rest *will not just bless your life; it will become a cherished companion you turn to time and time again.*

KEISA CAPERS
Co-Founder Capture the Nations

"If you are a global worker feeling "off in your faith," this book will transform your life and ministry if you embrace it. I've personally walked through the Promised Land Living journey that this book unpacks, yet its pages revealed even more areas where God is inviting me to go deeper. From the introduction to the very last page, I found myself identifying places where I could experience greater freedom, trust, and intimacy with the Lord. This book is both a gentle guide and a powerful catalyst for those longing to live from a place of true rest and purpose. It doesn't just offer insight, it speaks directly to the heart of those who serve cross-culturally and are yearning to reconnect with the One who called them. Whether you're on the field, returning home, or somewhere in between, this book is a much-needed companion to help you walk in renewed identity and hope. I highly recommend it. Your soul will thank you!"

KATHY MAURER
Co-Founder, Capture the Nations

Acknowledgments

To all those who have journeyed with us in the Promised Land and willingly shared their discoveries of the seemingly impossible, thank you.

To friends and foes alike whom God has used to shape my heart so that it beats to His drum only, bless you.

To Elizabeth and Kris, who gave me a model for how to receive and then share the love of Christ, you passed the baton well.

To my immediate family, who willingly allowed our story to be used to minister to others who may be unable to articulate these common ailments of man that we will overcome with God, your bravery and respect for our journey is deeply appreciated.

And to you Brianna, may our relationship and the journey we took together in writing this letter of delight – our offering to the Lord – honor His gift of rest which transcends generations, crosses cultural boundaries, and fulfills the deepest longings of the heart. Together, we invite you, the reader, into His holy rest *today*.

Cheryl,
You once told me you didn't want to write a book.
You would rather it be written on the hearts of the people you love. You just so happened to write one on the heart of someone who writes. Thank you for showing me the way of rest.
Bri

Introduction

PICTURE YOURSELF IN a canoe on a navy-blue lake, still as glass, looking up at a snow-capped mountain. A cool breeze pricks your ears, but the sun is warm on your back. The silence around you is so complete that you quiet your breathing to blend with it. The air smells clean, almost as though you can sense the snow and stone thousands of feet above you. You lean back on the warm, woven cane seat and turn your eyes into the tranquil blue of a cloudless sky.

Imagine there is nothing you have to do, nowhere you have to be. There is no to-do list, and time has stopped. You know where all your loved ones are, and they know where you are. You feel your body begin to relax. The quiet is a comforting blanket now, a pleasant weight over your limbs and belly. Your mind slows its spinning until all it is concerned with is tracking a speck of an eagle soaring on the currents of the atmosphere against the blue. If you sink your eyes into it, past the bird, there is no end to the blue. Beyond that, you envision stars, but night and all its mysteries feel far off and imaginary.

Rest. Can you taste it?

I wonder, what keeps you from being able to fully rest with me in the canoe? How do we access this rest? To-do lists are shouting demands. Family members are making bad choices. The world is teetering on its axis as record-breaking catastrophes strike more and more often. Global powers play hard at their chess game as we, the common people, serve as the pawns in their conquests. The world is unstable. The needs around us are profound. Tending to our own needs has been delayed for the day we have more time. And here I am asking you to explore rest with me? Yes. This invitation is one that I believe is profoundly important. Each time I sit down to write, it is with prayer and a deep sense of responsibility towards you and your well-being that I ponder how to invite you into this open space of Holy Spirit-fresh air.

We don't need to travel to a remote cabin on a lake to experience it, although I would certainly enjoy that. I desire that through the journey we take together in this book you encounter Jesus in a new way and experience His light burden and easy yoke in place of the crushing burdens you have bravely shouldered for so long.[1]

Welcome. I am so glad you came.

I don't mind if you're tired. You don't need to have all the answers here.

Maybe you are exhausted from caring for everyone else. Welcome.

Maybe you need some of that care. Welcome.

Maybe you have been one of the many wounded by the church. I am sorry; welcome.

Welcome to the qualified, the unqualified, and the semi-qualified with imposter syndrome.

All you need to participate in this journey is a beating human heart. Jesus sees you; He came for you; He died for you; He loves you. I invite you to ponder, savor and digest what you will encounter. You may find you want to pause periodically. You can take as much time as you need.

The way of rest requires transforming by the renewing of our minds, a conscious and purposeful neural rewiring.[2] This wiring begins to change when we encounter something different than we expected and our former ways of interpreting don't make sense anymore. The schemas our brains make about the way the world works are being challenged.[3] When you expect shame and reproach, but someone gently offers grace, something loosens inside. When our right brain encounters another right brain,[4] glorious transformation becomes available to us.

---

[1] Matthew 11:28-30
[2] Romans 12:2
[3] Thompson, Curt. *Anatomy of the Soul: Surprising Connections between Neuroscience and Spiritual Practices That Can Transform Your Life and Relationships.* Carol Stream, Il, Saltriver, 2010.
[4] Thompson, Curt. *Anatomy of the Soul: Surprising Connections between Neuroscience and Spiritual Practices That Can Transform Your Life and Relationships.* Carol Stream, Il, Saltriver, 2010.

We then have an opportunity to respond and cooperate with God in this mysterious process of sanctification. To assist with the process of being made holy and whole, I will tell you story after story of people encountering God, and I will share a tool we can use to consciously facilitate this rewiring. In doing so, our eyes begin to see God more and more like He is and less like the god of our imagination. I believe that the more we see Him and participate in His love for us, weary one, the more His love can free us. This is the journey I'm inviting you into. And if you will go with me, I pray that you will experience the rising up as if on eagle's wings, being able to run and not grow weary, walk and not faint.[5]

You have been fighting the good fight. You have served Jesus. You know about obedience, and you know about washing feet. Maybe you have grown weary in doing good even though you know about the verse that tells you not to,[6] so you try hard to overcome your fatigue with more doing. The abundant life feels contrived right now. I know you're fine, so you say. I know you know you have everything you need in Christ.

But you're tired.

This book is for followers of Jesus who are feeling "off" in their faith. They know there is something more, but they can't quite grasp it. They keep bumping up against themselves or others. They may feel lonely and unseen or misunderstood. They want someone to walk with them. They want a companion to see them. They want a path to follow out of fatigue and weariness. They want to make sense of betrayal. They want assurances that the pain will be redeemed. They want to hear from someone who is living what they believe. They want to know where the abundant life is. They want to know that what they have believed all these years is still true (even though they know it is, they are tired by their own doubt). Some have checked themselves out of ministry altogether but haven't yet checked in with their Great Physician – maybe they don't know how, or they're afraid they will find they disappointed Him or that He will have yet another job waiting for them to do. Is any of this resonating for you?

---

5   Isaiah 40:31
6   Galatians 6:9

You love the Lord; you love the Lord's people, but you are just bone tired.

I see it. I see it in the halls of my church, in the groups that we run at Promised Land Living®, and even in my closest friends at times. And in my most raw and honest moments, I have seen it in myself. He has ministered to me deeply there. I see the extra breath before you step up into that room. The extra coffee cup in your hand and the puffiness under your eyes give you away. You can't quite hide the soul weariness behind them, something deeper than sleep or days off can fix. The very way you walk reveals the invisible burden on your shoulders. You are needed again. And you keep pouring out; you keep giving. Or maybe you are pulling away from everyone and everything, emotionally and/ or physically and have decided all you can do is sideline yourself.

Let this book be an invitation to you to bury your head in His chest. It took me a long time to learn how sweet that place is. Nestled. Reassured. Reminded. Let go of how you think you are supposed to be. He extends His hands to remind you what a yoke that is easy and light feels like.[7] So many well-meaning people and traditions have added weight to your yoke. Obligations and shame, comparisons, and expectations have accumulated.

You are battling those powers and principalities, the forces of darkness, with every phone call, meeting, and inconvenient time set aside for a lonely soul. You are being the hands and blistered, aching feet of Jesus. You have long passed the point that you didn't know how you were going to keep going. I wonder what has kept you going.

There will be time to learn how to fight in a new way, but for now, let me help you put your sword and shield down. Let Jesus take the weight of them; feel His hands over your hands, and let their heaviness crash to the ground at your feet. He will fight for you; you need only to be still.[8]

---

[7] Matthew 11:28-30
[8] Exodus 14:14

CHAPTER ONE

The Journey is Too Long

*"A bruised reed He will not break, and
a smoldering wick He will not quench."*
MATTHEW 12:20A

FLORIDA THUNDERSTORMS HAVE a particular knack for sneaking up on a person. I was covered in baby spit-up, my hair was frizzy, and I was already breathing hard when the rain fell on us suddenly as I lugged Michael's car seat in one arm and my Bible in the other across the parking lot towards a brown building. Wrong building. Back across the parking lot, as steam rose from the asphalt. My arms were burning, my back was aching, and rainwater was slowly soaking into the floral pastel fabric over my shoulders. I thought about how my New York friends would laugh if they could see Cheryl Scanlan, the CEO of a multimillion-dollar company, now being "mommy" so awkwardly just 4 months later. But the days of heels and power suits were behind me now.

I was new to Florida, new to Protestantism, and new to this church with a colicky newborn son. I was determined to go to this MUMS group (Mothers Uplifting Mothers) if only to get Tom off my back; he was worried I was spending too much time home alone since the move. We were late despite my best efforts, because Michael had blown out his diaper not once but twice that morning and then spit up all over me and his last clean, nice clothes.

When I finally, gracelessly, busted through the correct door, I could hear the speaker sharing something about parenthood. However, as my eyes quickly scanned the room, I felt I didn't belong there. They were beautiful, and I was covered in spit up. I froze for a second, very aware of my wet clothes cooling and sticking in the air conditioning, and then bolted for the car.

But before I could make it out of the building, I felt the gentle hands of two women at my elbows. Without a word, they guided me back inside. One took Michael and began to sway and bounce with him, and the other laughed as she gave me some Kleenex to dab my hair. Then the women began to share stories about their own babies and blowouts. I felt tears well up but not with embarrassment and frustration this time. I was relieved to be welcomed as I was, not as I was trying to be. My soul felt soothed by the speaker, Elizabeth's voice and her tender and compassionate understanding of womanhood and motherhood.

I felt quite drawn to her.

I choose to share this story here because these are the women who would introduce me to Jesus with their gentle, quiet, unconditional love, who would show me a way that was different than the fear and rigidity of my religious background. They showed me what He was like when His voice was still new and unfamiliar to me.

Jesus has a way of rest for us that reverses the straining and futile dynamic of the world's approach to productivity. We live from this rest by listening to His voice and abiding in His love and finished work. In this abiding, we release what is not ours to carry, replace lies with truth, and allow Him to recalibrate our relationships with others. This is the path we will walk together.

Rest is not just a nice benefit that we can access through Christ. It is not just good for our minds and bodies; it is our very position in Christ. We are encouraged to remain immovable in that position in Christ. It is central to our relationship with Him and our walk as His followers through this world.

In Rabbi Abraham Joshua Heschel's book, *The Sabbath*, he succinctly states, "Labor is a blessing, toil is the misery of man."[9] Scripture tells us that our labor is not in vain. Encouraging. Yet distinguishing that which is labor and that which is toil is a journey of discovery that each

---

9   Abraham Joshua Heschel. *The Sabbath*. 1951. New York, Ny, Farrar, Straus And Giroux, 2005.

believer embarks on as they seek to live the abundant life promised to us by Jesus in John 10:10. This abundant life is not something that happens to us. No, this life we will explore together is something that happens within us as we are sanctified and made to be more like Jesus.[10]

While labor began in the garden, toil was introduced at the fall. Sin brought thorns, sweat of the brow. The land would still nourish the body, but the soul would ache under the duress of the exile from Eden. Centuries later, the Lord brought a portion of creation back to a place of laboring in Him. The Israelites, brought out of Egypt and the brick-making business as slaves, entered the Promised Land described as a land flowing with milk and honey. God promised that the land would supply not only nourishment but abundance. This promise, however, was contingent upon the Israelites keeping His statutes and carefully observing His judgments.[11] Soon, the Israelites forsook God by seeking satisfaction and security apart from God. They hewed for themselves broken cisterns that could not hold water,[12] and created idols out of wood that could not save them.[13] Toil had once again replaced their labor.

I do not fully understand it, but I do observe that God fiercely defends rest.[14] The Sabbath is rest from conquering. The Sabbath is rest from surviving. The Sabbath is rest from toil, and that rest comes from a posture of humility that declares, "He is the great I Am, and I am not." One such story of His defense of rest demonstrates how fervently He feels about this subject: the Israelites were exiled to Babylon one year for every year of rest they denied the ground as set forth in the law.[15] A second and very sobering story helps us understand why Moses was not allowed to enter the Promised Land: he struck the rock rather than speaking to the rock as God commanded in Exodus 17:6. Early on in my walk, I found this to be a harsh discipline for Moses. However, 1 Corinthians 10:3-4 helps us to understand what God was protecting:

---

10 Philippians 1:6, Hebrews 10:14, 2 Peter 3:18
11 Leviticus 25:19
12 Jeremiah 2:13
13 Isaiah 44:15
14 Genesis 2:2-3, Exodus 20:8-11, Exodus 23:11, Leviticus 25, Deuteronomy 12:9-10, Matthew 11:28-30
15 2 Chronicles 36:20-21

"They all ate the same spiritual food and drank the same spiritual drink; for they drank from the spiritual Rock that accompanied them, and that Rock was Christ."

That rock was Christ, and Christ was struck once for all.[16] Moses did not take God at His word: whether in anger or doubt, and God made it clear that He could not allow him to enter the land as a result. God's design for rest is non-negotiable.

The Sabbath has always been there from the beginning of creation when God rested on the 7th day.[17] Everything in the Old Testament is a picture of what was to come through Christ. When Jesus came, He became our Sabbath. Our rest is now contingent upon Jesus' perfect obedience, not our own. The One who lives within us is our Sabbath. Christ is your Shabbat; Shabbat is in you. Now we work *from* that place of Sabbath rest, instead of being oriented toward future rest. Jesus said "It is finished," and we are done striving. We have to train to live from this rest,[18] to think from this rest, to experience life from this rest. How do we remain there? This is the focus of our journey: remaining in this rest.

∞ Working From Rest ∞

At any given moment we are working *for* our rest or *from* our rest.

God's rest is our inheritance. When we work for our rest, we are denying the inheritance that has already been given to us. In the life that is intended for us, we work from the Holy Spirit's empowerment and our position in Christ. Our position is not something we are trying to earn, gain, or prove anymore. But when we get caught trying to earn again, we begin to toil, and when we toil we get tired. We thirst. We

---

16 Romans 6:10, Hebrews 10:12
17 Genesis 2:1-3
18 Train used here as Strong's 3809 "Paideia" as used in 2 Timothy 3:16
"Strong's Greek: 3809. παιδεία (Paideia) -- the Rearing of a Child, Training, Discipline." *Biblehub.com*, biblehub.com/greek/3809.htm.

turn to other things—props, artificial dependencies, and find no water. We stay tired. But the Father's heart calls us back to rest.

We start wandering when we forget who we are and Whose we are. I named my ministry "Promised Land Living®" because the ministry is focused on helping Christians who have a relationship with the Lord but for a myriad of reasons are still functionally wandering in the desert. There is no joy in the desert; there is no rest in the desert; we are surrounded by death in the desert. But Promised Land rest is waiting for us.

The world is demanding. The world is insatiable in its quest to consume our time, our talents, our energy, our hearts, our minds. This world is, for now, under the merciless power of the father of lies, who is hell-bent on destroying. But God... He has overcome. As Christians, we are all citizens of Heaven living as foreigners in a place with different values, but we forget or were never fully taught the customs and culture of the Kingdom.[19] The axioms of the world tell us we are alone. Strive to survive. Work for love. But we get to leave that system behind and live from Shabbat rest in Jesus.

When Jesus sat down at the right hand of the Father, He rested from all His work. We now rest in His finished work on the cross. Yes, there is work for us to do, but that work happens *from* our confessed and declared Shabbat rest in Christ.[20] This is different from observing a Sabbath day rest; this is a heart at rest every day, the kind of heart that is willing to take God at His word, moment by moment. My entire ministry exists to help followers of Jesus live from a Sabbath rest in Christ every day: Every conversation, every marriage, every relationship, every decision.

In this work I, too, get tired. I, too, forget. I am not inoculated from slipping into a toiling state. But each time, I get to return to rest, training to become more and more dependent on the One who is in me. We do not need to be frightened when we find ourselves toiling. God shows us the path back to rest. But sometimes it takes us a while, sometimes years, to recognize that we are living from something other than the One who is living in us. The One who lives within us is our Sabbath rest.

---

19 Ephesians 2:19, Philippians 3:20
20 Hebrews 3, 4

∞ Weary Travelers ∞

At 8 pm one evening in the spring of 2021, I crash-landed into the recliner in my bedroom after my last call. I was exhausted. Everything was aching, my right foot was dragging, and my tongue was thick and useless. I wasn't sick, but I was just so worn down that the inflammation in my body was starting to imitate some of the neurological Lyme symptoms I used to have. I smelled the laundry detergent on the pillowcase and immediately started to drift away into sleep, regardless of the fact I was still in my day clothes. Tom walked into the room and asked me if I needed anything. I did, but I knew that even the effort of trying to form a response would take too much energy and further escalate the symptoms.

I was running so hard. My clients were high-ranking business leaders. I knew how that world worked, and I respected the rules. I gave all my strength daily to coach my clients and run my rapidly expanding ministry. I was doing what had to be done. My spirit was willing, but by the end of the day, I would ask my legs to carry me, and they would quite literally give out.

You may, like me, know what it means to not truly have had a vacation for twenty years. To this day, unplanned health-related cancellations mean that I always have make-up client sessions during every scheduled vacation time I have planned. Some of the things we carry just come with us to another location.

The exhaustion I had was body, mind, soul, and spirit.

I'm going to introduce a few more very different stories of weariness, all highly functioning people, all on journeys that had become too long.

Keisa started out very quiet. She didn't say more than 5 words during the first 3 or 4 Promised Land Living (PLL) group meetings. She had just left a leadership role of 12 years with another ministry because of a clash in values, and she was trying to start a nonprofit. She brought with her a heavy load of exhaustion and disappointment. Being in good company with a group of cross-cultural ministers, Keisa felt more at home and understood. She identified with the weariness of every member of this group as just a part of life, something you "suck up," something you don't talk about until it's too late. This group shouldered the weight of the reality that "the harvest is plentiful, but the workers are few."[21] At first, it was even a little uncomfortable for Keisa to receive ministry because she was so used to being the one pouring out.

But as she sat quietly absorbing the words from the coach and the community, God was ministering to her heart. She felt He was inviting her to relax. When she shared this with people close to her, they laughed, because historically she had been anything but relaxed. How did she find permission to relax? She experienced an important mindset shift from the Lord. She stopped doing *for* God, but began to *be with* Him, and from there started doing *with* Him. She felt she was responsible to "make it happen," but He showed her, "this isn't your ministry [it's Mine]."

She shared, "Slowing down to hear Him is just as important as doing the work. In fact, that *is* the work." She cut her working hours in an act of trust so that she had time to rest, and something unexpected happened. She reported that things still got done, sometimes nearly miraculously, in a shorter amount of time. She has time to be creative now, and that energy flows back into her work. She has become unburdened. She found rest.

Chris joined our group the first night with a bright, full smile and an easy laugh, but he was deeply lonely. He was highly successful professionally, and he developed an easy surface rapport with most anyone he met. But his charisma was a persona. No one really knew him. He had developed a face and a role that people liked. This front was well respected within his spheres of influence, but it was exhausting to maintain, and it was very isolating for his soul. He was tired. He realized that the pattern he had set for himself was no longer sustainable, and he was desperate to find a new way of living.

He didn't know what to do. He loved God and knew God loved him. He loved people, but he was afraid to let people love him.

He quickly revealed this very humble posture and brought some of his own inner circle into his PLL journey. He prepared these trusted friends, who loved and respected him, for the fact that he would

---

21 Matthew 9:37

be peeling off layers as he went on a quest to genuinely connect to others from his heart rather than his persona. It took courage to train himself in this new way of rest. By the end, he was able to lay down that heavy mask once and for all with anyone. He started to take off a layer of authority that was not necessary. Instead of always looking for opportunities to make a point or teach a lesson, he relaxed into genuine conversation in which he shared his own feelings about the conversation topic or how his conversation partner was impacting him. He still had a place of leadership, but he began organically influencing more often than directly instructing. He removed a degree of separation that had surrounded him. He had a new lightness about him that was delightfully confounding and highly attractive to people.

Sharon joined our Zoom call 10 minutes after the hour, disheveled and breathless. She was a nurse juggling a full time job and caretaking for an aging parent all alone. I do not know how she found any time to be with us, but she was desperate for a change. She was resentful of life. Still, she was tenderhearted somehow. Her siblings were not helping her with the duties of caring for her father, as he declined mentally and physically, and she was drowning. She loved the Lord. She wanted to honor her father. She understood the opportunity she had to love him, but she was confused. She couldn't see how honoring her Father in Heaven by taking care of her father on earth should be taking so much from her. She kept sacrificing her sanity and her physical health to make it work for just one more day.

She went on a journey with us and found the way of rest. She found a way to honor her father that was easier to bear. By the end of our course, her countenance was lighter, and she had the courage to declare boundaries with her family. She was willing to invest in outside help for her dad, although she was medically qualified to complete the care tasks. She courageously rearranged her life and moved from a place where guilt and duty took more than she had to give into a place of alignment where she could pour into her father out of her deep love for him while taking time to care for her own needs. She stopped living an "either/or" life.

Interestingly, everything in her life that was important to her was still addressed. She might even say more effectively so because she was cared for and loved as she cared for and loved her dad. It was still heavy, but her way of carrying it was better.

∞ Where Are You? ∞

What about you? Maybe your vista isn't as peaceful as our lakeside retreat. I borrow God's first words to mankind after the fall to begin our conversation today. He invited Adam and Eve to come out and allow themselves to be seen.[22] When they left His rest through their choice to rebel, this question was the first move in the chain of events that would lead to restoration. He already knew where Adam and Eve hid, and He knew what had caused them to hide, but He asked them to participate in being known. He sees you, but still He asks for your willing participation: "Where are you?"

It's exhausting to hide. He could have come upon our great, great (etc.) grandparents in fury, but instead He walked in the garden, as He did every evening, and called to them. Will you allow yourself to be seen today? This can be a terrifying prospect. Your experiences up to this point will dictate whether you feel delight or shame at the thought of being seen.

> *God asked them to participate in being known, and He asks you to participate in being known too.*

Another of our participants did not speak for the first six meetings. He served in the church dutifully but was exhausted and heartbroken underneath. His mother had died, and his father abandoned him in the wake of the loss. He didn't want to express it. He didn't know how to be seen. He didn't want to find his voice. It was just easier to hide. It's instinctive to hide. But he realized something important—hiding was making him exhausted.

The One calling your name has a love for you that covers a multitude

---

22 Genesis 3:9

of sins—the love that casts out all fear.[23] This is one of those opportunities to rewire our expectations and schemas. Come to Him and see how He will respond to you.

"Where are you?"

Sometimes the place we are in is a place of constant spinning. There is a lot of movement and sweat, but when you look up at your surroundings, you haven't moved. It's terrifying, and the terror drives more frantic activity. Like a car stuck in a muddy ditch, hitting the gas hard only digs the car further in. And exhaustion sets in.

I'm inviting you to stop spinning. You don't have to create constant motion for motion's sake. It takes courage to stop. Keisa stopped trying to hold her ministry together on her own. Sharon stopped being everything for everyone. I had to stop thinking I couldn't rely on my team to do more. One participant decided to stop avoiding. You may not quite know what to stop yet, but you have momentarily stopped to read this chapter. That's a start!

This is a chapter of unwinding. When a fan reverses direction, it doesn't do so instantly. Even though the direction has changed, all we can perceive at first is the fan slowing down. Then it stops. *Then* it slowly picks up speed in the reverse direction. We may have to do a lot of unwinding to live from rest.

Just this past month I was on the phone with a couple, the Hutchinsons, whose world was falling apart.

They hadn't been sleeping. They didn't know what to do. The wife's lifelong dream had crashed at her feet; they were facing potential bankruptcy, and they did not have a path forward. They turned and turned to find every direction walled in.

I simply reflected to them, "It sounds like there is death all around you."[24]

As we paused there with no attempts to put a good face on it or force a positive perspective, the Lord brought to mind Psalm 23:

---

23 1 Peter 4:8, Proverbs 10:12, John 3:16, Romans 4:7, 1 John 4:18
24 Keller, Timothy. *Counterfeit Gods : The Empty Promises of Money, Sex, and Power, and the Only Hope That Matters*. New York, Riverhead Books, 2011.

"Even though I walk through the valley of the shadow of death, I will fear no evil, for You are with me."

We encouraged one another with this reminder and the rest of the Psalm:

"You make me lie down in green pastures. You lead me beside quiet waters."

They came to realize while we were on the phone together that it was time to stop spinning. There was no place to go except right through the valley. And they would face it together with their Good Shepherd.

Sheep don't lie down unless they feel safe.[25] Sheep don't drink unless the Master works to provide good water.[26] He knows our frame; He is mindful that we are made out of dust.[27]

Even if there is death all around you, He is the author and sustainer of your life.[28] He will walk with you even through a figurative or literal valley of the shadow of death.

> *Give yourself a chance to be there without deciding if it is good or bad*

Right now we are reflecting, taking note of our current state and situation. Sometimes we immediately judge ourselves and bring down swift mental condemnation, or we offer false cotton candy positivity. But please, wherever you find yourself, give yourself a chance to be there without deciding whether it is good or bad. Just be. In the space you create with that pause, maybe you will have room to receive something from God.

Let's go ahead and create one of those quiet, reflective moments we were talking about just now.

---

25 Keller, Phillip. "Chapter 3: He Makes Me Lie Down in Green Pastures." *A Shepherd Looks at Psalm 23*, Zondervan, pp. 33–34.
26 Keller, Phillip. "Chapter 4: He Leads Me Beside Still Waters." *A Shepherd Looks at Psalm 23*, Zondervan, pp. 46–50.
27 Psalm 103:14
28 Colossians 1:16, Psalms 54:4

> ### Selah Moment
>
> If you are reading in a place where you can use your voice out loud and you are willing to pray, use your voice and tell God where you are. When you use your physical voice to call out to Him from where you are, there is no more hiding. When you hear your mouth form the words, you speak to your own soul as well as to the Lord. Reflect on where you are; say it out loud, say it to someone else, or write it down. Or maybe something in your environment symbolizes where you are. For example, maybe an empty, crusty pot in your sink would represent the feeling of being completely spent. The pot is meant to be full of soup to nourish others, but maybe you feel empty and unable to nourish yourself, much less others. You're too tired to even clean the dish.

∞ Go Slow to Go Fast ∞

I ask you to take your time because deep learning is a self-motivated discovery. Discovery is usually a slow, multistep process. Time is a form of grace. I often encourage our participants to go slow to go fast. I have to go slow with myself often, especially when I am stepping out of my comfort zone, and I am asking you now to give yourself permission to go slow, as well, as you digest this book.

I have met the God who delights to take His time with me. He spoke the entire universe into motion in 6 days but takes nine months to make our bodies and a lifetime to mold our souls into the image of Himself. Alan Deutschman did significant research on the choices of people who were presented with a situation in which they must change their lifestyle or die. He found that even when faced with the threat of death, people did not change when simply presented with facts and fear. But he found that they were willing to change within the context of relationship and reframing.[29] I cannot simply speak and expect my reader to listen and be better off. I want to empower you to go on your own adventure with the Lord (relationship). I will give you questions, prompts, resources, and frameworks (reframing), but they are all just starting points. You must do the work of putting the practical pieces together in your own life, and this kind of work is SLOW. Work may sound like the last thing you want to do right now, my weary reader, but it isn't work in the way you have been doing it so far. It is effort, but it isn't grit-your-teeth-and-push-through toil. It is the work of yielding, which will make more sense as we continue.

Just a couple of months ago while leading a men's PLL course with another coach, Bob, one of the participants, Daniel, wanted us to hurry up and get to the point.

I am inviting you into the work of yielding

He huffed, "I don't have time for this. I want the bottom line. Let's just figure out whatever we're supposed to be doing here."

I didn't immediately respond to his words. I just acknowledged his frustration and continued presenting the content and encouraging interactions. About 3-5 minutes later, I reflected his words back to him.

"So you said you don't have time for this?"

"I never said that!" he defended.

"Actually, those were your exact words." I quietly asserted. Everyone else in the group had heard him as well.

He was silent, dumbfounded.

I was curious on his behalf.

"What do you have time for? Do you have time for pat answers? Superficial solutions?"

He was quiet, realization dawning on his face.

I continued, "The work of transformation doesn't give you those things. It's icky; it involves a loss of control. There's an element of vulnerability that we don't normally experience in day-to-day life."

---

29 Deutschman, Alan. *Change or Die*, Harper Business, p. 109.

He made a conscious decision to enter the discomfort of going slow to go fast. Once he was able to let go of this point, he was one of the participants who got the most out of the process because he took the time that heart-change required.

Daniel Kahneman theorizes that we generally tend to have two thinking modes. There's an analytical, slow-thinking, digesting mode, and there are knee-jerk, fast, reactive judgements that we make.[30] While this is a simplistic explanation of the brain's function, for my purposes here, it helps to illustrate the transformative process. The time it takes for the two systems to be in sync is always longer than we expect. I often call this transformative connection "knowing in your knower."

When we are in a transformative state, the slow mode needs to have time to process and to challenge the way we've always thought. This is a physical process as much as it is a spiritual process; our neurology is forming new pathways much in the same way the brain learns new pathways for motor patterns in physical therapy.

In 2003, I was strapped into a harness between two parallel bars with several PT attendants standing around me. Late stage neurological Lyme Disease had paralyzed the right side of my body. It was time to try to learn how to walk again. With every attempt to move my foot, my back would arch or my arms would flail. The harness and the compassionate team encouraged me with each failed attempt. It took over a year, but I did eventually learn how to walk again. And my favorite athletic trainer, Tammy, came to know the Lord in that arduous journey we took together. Tammy understood that the process couldn't be rushed. She didn't judge me for the thousands of thrashing and flailings. She taught me that physical healing sometimes is very slow, and I taught her that spiritual transformation is also a slow process. We learned how to go slow to go fast, together.

Neurons follow the most commonly traveled path like water down a hill or deer on a path through the woods. The more often the path is traveled, the clearer and easier the path becomes. Lyme was like a hurricane ripping up all previous roads, but Tammy and I cleared the trees and marked the path again and again. We get to choose the path of our neurons for both motor patterns and thought patterns. We initiate

---

30 Kahneman, Daniel. *Thinking, Fast and Slow*. New York, Farrar, Straus and Giroux, 2011.

that steady, repetitive, alternative stimulus like a stream of water that can shape earth and stone in a new place over and over again until there is a groove that is deeper than the old one. Take a hammer to it, and you may crack the stone.

One participant was a self-professed road rager. He wore Jesus well until he got behind the wheel of a car. His aggressive words and maneuvers while driving put his wife on edge. The stress had very tangible physical ramifications due to her significant health issues. His eyes were opened to the impact he was having on her, and something tender was activated in him.

Over time, each boneheaded move by another driver prompted a gentler response of either prayer or recognizing that he himself had done the same thing before. Now, even in very stressful driving situations, he is not only able to control the car but also his actions, because he controls his thoughts. His love for his wife motivated him to take his foot off the gas of his reactions. He also found that, in addition to increasing his wife's peace of mind, his own mind and body were more at rest in the car and when he arrived at his destination.

At any point, he could have aborted the effort. The work of learning to rest for him was about restraint rather than fight. It did require effort, but the result was peace. Over time, he began to wear Jesus well in the car. The key is, this happened over time.

If we are willing to allow ourselves the time to be a work in progress, then that God-created, slow processing mode can inform the fast. When my knee jerk reactions don't reflect Christ, that's not a time for self-condemnation but a time to go slow to go fast. It's time to be curious with ourselves. Not "What's wrong with me or what's wrong with them?" but "How are you working here, Lord?" or "What do I need, Lord?" When we allow an unpolished, unfinished truthful reality of our situation to be fully exposed, there is an opportunity. This is a place in which we can experience either threat and wounding or protection and healing—it's more than a place of transparency; it's a place of vulnerability.

When my client admitted that his driving reactions were hurting his wife, that he felt bad, and that he wanted to change, he became vulnerable to a deeper desire to love his wife.

Transparent says: "Well, I'm in a ditch. But hey, whatever. It was the rain that made me slide into the ditch."

Vulnerable says: "I'm in a ditch. I don't want to be in a ditch. Will you help me?"

Both begin with a true admission of where I am. But the second involves another layer of honesty, longing and the possibility for alternate choices. Do you want things to be different? Do you want to be well?[31] Where do you want to be?

We can be bullish sometimes, even about our honesty. When we are still protecting ourselves, we won't allow the opportunity for further hurt, but that also means we won't allow healing either.

When I'm stuck, I'm in a mode of reacting, of doing things the way I've always known. What I've always known is comfortable. This is what we stop—we take a break from reacting. We choose the discomfort of slowing down.

The Lord says that He is the lifter of our countenance.[32] The lifting implies that something has caused our hearts to fall. Sometimes I'd rather stay in my sullen place, jaw locked, than let the tender hand of God lift my face. Head down. Nose to the grindstone, or checked out completely. Would you let Him lift you out of that pit?[33]

Through the ages He has sought the hearts of man: "Where are you?"

He creates an opportunity to turn toward Him rather than away from Him. In a state of vulnerability, we show up to our relationship with the Almighty empty-handed and expectant.

∞ Under a Broom Tree ∞

Maybe you feel able to respond to God's question with a strong voice, or maybe you feel a little shaky as you attempt to whisper, "Here I am."

---

31 John 5:6
32 Psalm 43:5, Psalm 3:3
33 Psalm 40:2

Maybe you are feeling a bit like Elijah as he sat under the broom tree after a long battle and wanted to die. His voice was feeble and weak. His soul was dejected and tired.

This story ministered to me deeply during my time of extreme fatigue with the growing ministry, as I described in our opening story. As I sank into that recliner, I could barely shoulder the responsibility of taking care of myself, much less a full time career and a national ministry. I was caving under the weight of it all.

I received a text from my dear friend, Billie: "The journey is too long for you."

That text connected all my tension, responsibility, fatigue, and desire back to Scripture. I did feel like Elijah. I was battle-weary from all of the clients, all the courses, all of the personal battles participants brought to fight together in PLL, all of the uncountable ER visits for my health, all of the pushing without a break. I needed refreshment from the Lord. I allowed my team to rally around me and carry the things that had become too heavy. There were about two months that I did very little, and my team kept the ministry afloat as I recuperated with the Lord.

The Broom Tree story, tucked away in 1 Kings,[34] tells how Elijah has just conquered the prophets of Baal. It was a major feat—a showdown of 450 prophets of Baal versus one prophet of Yahweh. He got to watch God answer him from Heaven with fire. And yet when Jezebel threatened him, he ran in terror. How could that happen? Where was he?

We see a brief image of his posture right before the story of his flight. He had climbed back up to the top of Mt. Carmel and bent down to the ground with his face between his knees. This is not the posture of a man who feels triumph. He did not exult on the mountain with his hands to the sky. He needed lifting.

I put my head between my knees when I have nothing left. I put my head between my knees when I am sick to my stomach or when I feel I may pass out. We do not get an explicit description of his emotions here, but bring yourself to the last time you had your head between your knees and remember. Maybe your posture of despair is a little different.

As I have faced my own frailties and weaknesses, my view of Elijah's response is compassionate. He was a servant of the Most High God

---

[34] 1 Kings 19:1-8

who was tired and needed to receive. This is the mindset into which Jezebel's messenger delivers her words: "May the gods deal with me, be it ever so severely, if by this time tomorrow, I do not make your life like that of one of them [the prophets whom Elijah had slain]."[35] Elijah knows God's power, but maybe he has also witnessed Jezebel's cruelty in situations where God did not intervene. We see in the previous chapter that Jezebel was "killing off" the Lord's prophets.[36] He knows how prophets die. So he runs.

Now let us see what only God can do. Elijah is war-torn and exhausted. In his vulnerable state, he prays, "I have had enough, Lord. Take my life; I am no better than my ancestors." The journey was too long. God knew that Elijah needed nourishment. The God of all comfort provided in Elijah's moment of despair.[37]

> *For just this little while, sit and let Him lift.*

So as you sit in the dirt next to that empty pot, strong servant of the most high God, one who worships in spirit and in truth but is tired and needs rest, just sit. Sit with Him. No more spinning of wheels. For just this little while, sit and let Him lift.

Now, look down at that empty pot and ask the Lord to fill it spiritually with what is required. What do you need to receive from Him in this moment? This moment—not tomorrow, not yesterday but right now. Is it His love? Is it His strength? Is it wisdom? What will God give you in this moment that you can't provide for yourself? What is He showing you? What is He telling you? God will do what God is going to do. This is work from Him beyond anything I will put in these pages; it's what the Lord will write in your heart. And those things He writes can never be taken away from you. Put the book down for a moment here and close your eyes. Take as long as you need.

I have many things I want to share with you over the course of our adventure together, but most importantly I want to empower you to

---

35 1 Kings 19:2
36 1 Kings 18:3
37 2 Corinthians 1:3-5

connect with the Lord.[38] He is the One who can heal, refresh, invigorate, and renew.[39] Maybe circle the word in the previous sentence that resonates strongest for you. There is one verse that has come to mind over and over for me as I have prayed about writing to you:

> "A bruised reed He will not break, and a smoldering wick He will not quench, until He brings justice to victory; and in His name the Gentiles will hope" Matthew 12:20

We do not have to be unbruised. We do not have to be burning brightly. We can come before Him with our smoking candle, unable to stand up quite straight, with our tired and our questions. His love is the warm hand that straightens the reed and shields the wick from the wind.

We have talked about being in a place of constant spinning, a place of rubble, and a place of weariness. All of these have something in common. We are stuck. Because I learn better from my mentors' vulnerabilities and trials, I invite you into mine. It is one of the many gifts I hope to give you on our journey together.

∞ Stuck ∞

For many years, I worshiped a "god" that was a construct of my imagination: safe, predictable, one that I could control. When I finally opened up the Word of God for myself, I met a stranger who somehow was the One who had been seeking me all my life. This was a holy God, a God of mystery, a God who refused to be controlled, a God who did not work with manmade formulas, and a God who had His own timeframe for all He did. He was no respecter of persons and showed no partiality to anyone.[40]

When I met this God at 28 years old, I was both frightened and

---

38 Hebrews 4:16, Hebrews 10:19-22, James 4:8
39 Psalm 103, Psalm 23:3, Jeremiah 31:25, Acts 3:19, Isaiah 40:31
40 Acts 10:34, Romans 2:11

comforted because I realized the imaginary god I had created could not carry me into heaven in his arms. That idea might help me feel in control here on earth, but the facade was about to be shaken. God says that all that can be shaken will be shaken until all that remains is that which is unshakable. And when we are stuck, something needs to be shaken! I was about to be shaken to my very core.

So here is the beginning of the story of the end of my self-reliance.

I gave birth to my second son, David, a few months after my 30th birthday. Shortly after he was born, I started having strange neurological symptoms that didn't make sense.

One of these strange instances happened at the grocery store. I was reaching for a jar of pasta sauce when I lost connection with my right arm. It dropped, useless, to my side, and the jar shattered on the ground.

I would not say I was stuck yet, but I was struggling. I was treated for meningitis; I was treated for migraine, but nothing seemed to help. I had all the tests and scans several specialists could think of, but they could not find anything abnormal. Eventually, an internal medicine doctor came to a diagnosis: depression.

This was the point I stopped sharing my experience with others, because I didn't want to feed the narrative that I was depressed. I went into hiding. I struggled silently for several years. No one knew. But the symptoms were increasing in intensity, variety, and frequency. I was really losing control of this thing. I felt a shadow over me, and I ran hard from it.

Every Friday in the fall of 2001, I delivered pizza with my friend Jerry at school for the kids' lunches. One Friday I saw her in the hall after missing a pizza delivery.

She looked surprised to see me and asked, "Where were you?" I looked at her disoriented, with no idea what she was asking about. I did not understand her question, and I didn't know how to respond. I felt very lost. She cocked her head and her eyes searched my face.

"Are you okay?"

"No… but I don't know what's wrong." I tried to move on. I was still keeping my secret, but it would become too much to hide before long.

On March 2, 2003, I collapsed, seizing, and then fell unconscious just inside my front door in my own vomit. Friends who stopped by on a whim found me and took me to the emergency room. Finally, I received a concrete bit of information: My brain had been swelling. All of these symptoms had been indicators of the rising tide of inflammation in my brain. Whatever this was, it was taking over, and nothing I was doing was slowing its siege.

Where was I? I was trapped in my body. I was still trying to hang onto my self-reliance, although it was being violently shaken from my hands. I was stuck.

Now before I tell you any more of this story, before I tell you the good, the ways God tenderly held me, the things He taught me, or the way the story turned out, I need to check in with you. Stuck has many faces. You may not be stuck in the particular way I was, but you might have nowhere left to turn. All you see are barricades, warning signs, and high cliffs. You have nothing – just empty hands. You may be so weary you are living just one hour at a time. Keep reading.

∞ Mighty Hand ∞

When I crashed that Sunday morning in March, I did not know at the time that the Lord had gone before me. My world completely fell apart and came undone at the seams. I could not ask for help; I couldn't ask anyone to pray for me. I was in so much pain, I couldn't even pray for myself. Has that ever happened to you? Have you been in so much pain of any kind that you could not pray? But we always have an advocate for us given to us by the Father in His Son Jesus. Holy Spirit intercedes for us with groanings too deep for words.[41] I was beyond words, but I was never without Someone to pray for me.

The timing of that day meant that the entire church was mobilized to pray for me, because Tom was playing bass for worship when he received the news. The friends

> *I was beyond words. But I was never without Someone to pray for me.*

---

41 Romans 8:26

who found me have no memory of me calling them, and I have no memory of calling them. Little glimpses of His sustaining during the storm were already becoming evident.

I quickly became sicker after this. But as my world shrunk and my self-reliance atrophied along with my muscles, I was never alone. The crucifixion took on new meaning. Jesus sat with me in my suffering, showed me His nail scars, and guided my heart to quiet waters even as my body truly felt like it was on fire.

He prepared my heart for this road as I watched dear older sisters in the faith walk out that faith every day in Florida. These simple treasures passed to me from just a couple years before became activated in ways that I could never have predicted at the time. Simple things like gratitude became safe places for my mind to rest when my body could find very little. I learned what it meant to "give thanks in all things."[42] I knew it was important to "guard your heart, for it is the wellspring of life."[43] I knew that gratitude would guard my heart. I want to share the verses with you that I clung to like the life preservers they were:

> *"Oh, give thanks to the Lord; call upon His name; make known His deeds among the peoples! Sing to Him, Sing praises to him; tell of all His wondrous works! Glory in His holy name; let the hearts of those who seek the Lord rejoice! Seek the Lord and his strength: seek His presence continually!"*[44]

I did not want to feed despondency. It made the pain worse. His presence became a refuge for me. So I kept figuring out how to turn to Him. His mighty hand transformed my hiding, which had kept me stuck, into humility and a posture of receiving from His hand. Before, I hid and ran, but soon I learned to rest even in the pain.

Romans 5 challenged me to view my current suffering differently. My nearly all-consuming pain was put in the context of:

> *"We rejoice in our sufferings, knowing that suffering produces*

---

[42] 1 Thessalonians 5:18
[43] Proverbs 4:23
[44] Psalm 105:1-4

endurance, and endurance produces character, and character produces hope, and hope does not put us to shame, because God's love has been poured into our hearts through the Holy Spirit who has been given to us."[45]

I sang as these Scriptures directed me to sing while I was able, and it did guard my heart. Today, I still sing as I go about my days. I didn't know at the time that singing had a physical effect on my body as well, through the stimulation of the vagus nerve, but it was fortifying to my soul. Singing is an exercise in healing, overcoming, and declaring God's goodness from rest.

I knew all these verses when I was well, but they took on a whole new timbre when I was sick. I had to choose each day – actually each moment of each day – whether or not I truly believed them. The illness forced the decision. I had to fix my eyes on Jesus; He was my only hope. I had to surrender to and rest in His sovereignty and timing. I had to yield to Him. The effect was tangible. If there was ever a moment that I looked to the waves surrounding me like Peter and tried to ask the "what ifs," the pain itself would grow more intense.[46]

When I started living beyond "today", this too became a form of toil, and God's grace was not there. My dear mentor, Elizabeth Mitchell helped me to understand "grace for today" many years into my illness as she was grieving the death of her 11 year old son.

I told her, "I could never go through what you went through!"

She simply replied, "You're right, you couldn't… Because God hasn't given you the grace to do it. If God allows something to pass through His hands, He will also give you the grace for it."

That gave me hope for today. Today has enough trouble of its own without "what if-ing" the past or the future.[47] No longer running from my situation but sitting with the Lord caused a subtle change from transparent prayers in which I spoke with Him about my fears but held onto my ability to control them, to vulnerable prayers that brought my fears under the reality that He holds all of those eventualities in

---

45 Romans 5:3-5
46 Matthew 14:30
47 Matthew 6:34

His hands and that He was with me, shaping me, in the present. I was in pain, but I was at rest.

My most vulnerable prayers over the years have been the most simple and the most desperate:

"Lord, the doctors have given up on me. I'm scared. Please comfort me."

"Lord, I'm finding myself creating my own destiny again, and I don't want to do that – what is the next best step for me to take with _____?"

"Lord, I'm so afraid my mom will die before she knows You. Please don't let my mom have the heart of Pharaoh. Turn her heart of stone into a heart of flesh."

"Lord, I'm hurting in our marriage; please deliver us from every evil in our marriage."

"Lord, I'm scared for my children; please protect them while they are staying with that person."

"Lord, I don't understand this passage, and it hurts to sit with it. Can You please help me through this?"

I humbled myself over and over under the mighty hand of God. If you've felt His hand, you know that it can be very heavy, even as it is very comforting. I was living *in* every moment of that season not running, not hiding, not resisting, not even questioning, just being in it. This mindset stopped the useless spinning, and it created quiet in my mind and heart. Although my body could find no respite, He was teaching me how to live from rest in my soul, which was truly the greater gift. The pain accelerated the decomposition of pride, expectation, and self reliance, creating rich spiritual soil that now nourishes my soul. Nearly everything He has given me about rest, all of the content of Promised Land Living, came from this time or has its roots in the relationship we formed through it.

Finally, I got the phone call, "Your result was positive for Lyme

> *Although my body could find no respite, He was teaching me how to live from rest in my soul, which was truly the greater gift.*

disease. Please schedule an appointment for next steps." After so many negative tests, this positive one brought some mixed emotions.

Two months later, I was able to have my first appointment with a doctor who specialized in Lyme. He let me know I was officially one of the sickest people on record with Lyme in the state. By autumn, I had a PICC line to do a year of 6 different IV antibiotics. These antibiotics wreaked havoc on my immune system and digestive system, but as anyone who has fought a serious illness with serious medication knows, it was also finally raining down destruction on the Lyme, so I was grateful.

The pain wasn't done, the paralysis wasn't done, the Lyme wasn't even done, and I still didn't know if I would ever walk again. But whatever the future held, the Lord was training me to rest under His mighty hand.

This is the place that I was finally able to hear His voice, once all my walls, all my self-reliance, all my hiding was stripped away. His tenderness with me was profound. That's where I want to go next with you. How might He speak to you where you are?

CHAPTER TWO

Still Small Voice

How do we draw near to God?

ONCE WE MOVED to Raleigh, I found another mentor who laid a solid Biblical foundation for me in her inductive Bible study. I stayed after class one evening as chairs were stacked and tables were folded away into closets. I shared a couple of things with her that I felt the Lord was saying to me. Her eyebrows furrowed the longer I spoke, and I summarized my story to end it sooner. She was clearly displeased.

"Cheryl… do not be too hasty to attribute things to God."

I left feeling confused. Yes, maturity and discernment take time. But her hesitation created distance in my relationship with God. There was some wisdom mixed into her controlling caution, but as I started to mature and develop my own relationship with the Lord, she struggled to adjust with me. My growth led to more intense dialogue between us as I found my own voice. Instead of coaching me or having real conversations with me, she subtly began to try to put me back "in my place." This was one such moment.

There are very few instances that I have received a very clear word for word message, but I receive nudges and encouragement from Him often, sometimes daily. And I get to witness His prompting in the hearts of clients and PLL participants, which is even more amazing to me. His voice brings rest, and it gently draws us deeper into rest. How did I get from that place with my Bible teacher to the place I am now where I can more easily recognize the work of God? How do I know it's Him?

∞ Is God With You? ∞

As we journey on together, you might notice my tendency to ask questions. I want to begin each new section with a question to orient you to our next cove on our canoe ride together and give you a chance to think about what you believe about each topic. I pray that this is an opportunity for you to unearth the truth that you already do know, connect it to fresh truth from the Scriptures as God reveals places of incompleteness in current understanding, sink it deeper into your soul, and allow it to set you free. Pause and let His voice cut through like a church bell on a cold foggy morning.

When we cannot hear Him, we find ourselves feeling much more alone than we actually are. This puts us in a space where we try to live the Christian life on our own. We take on control and weight that were never ours to carry. We try to grope for the narrow way on our own, we try to sanctify ourselves on our own, we try to gain wisdom on our own. That is absolutely exhausting.

There is a view of God described as "Deism" that describes God as a clockmaker who designed the universe with rules, wound it, and let it go.[48] A deist believes that God exists but does not interact with the current flow of things. That He is real, but He is "out there." But what if He is only out there because we hold Him at a distance?[49]

Before God ever came in the flesh as Emmanuel, He showed Himself as being a God who desired to live with man in the way He set up the Old Testament tabernacle.[50] This was so important to Him that He called it sin when the Israelites did not believe He was with them.[51] Our God describes Himself as being very near. Acts 17:28 has often been interpreted to mean nearer than our own breath. He takes up residence

---

48 Duncan, Dr Ligon. "What in the World Is This World Thinking? God the Clock-Maker." *Reformed Theological Seminary*, 9 June 2004. rts.edu/resources/what-in-the-world-is-this-world-thinking-god-the-clockmaker/.; "What Is Moralistic Therapeutic Deism (MTD)?" *GotQuestions.org*, www.gotquestions.org/Moralistic-Therapeutic-Deism.html.
49 James 4:8
50 Numbers 2
51 Exodus 17:7

inside of us and has promised never to leave.[52] The church is referred to throughout Scripture as the bride of Christ to illustrate the devotion and longing God has for us.[53] It is His longing to be anything but far. Immanuel reminds that God is with us, now, but we sometimes act as though we have to go looking for Him.

Josh Garrels wrote a song that mesmerizes me every time I listen to it. My best environment for listening is flying down an open road alone at 10 to 15 miles over the speed limit. My windows are partially down, and I am in what Josh describes as "beyond the blue."[54]

I used to need a lot of props to attempt to hear God's voice, like I used to need recipes to tell me what spices blend together when I cooked. Or maybe like how I needed my coaching books to help me to know what questions to ask someone. But over time, open roads and profound lyrics became unnecessary. I learned how to release myself into the beyond and listen instantaneously, no matter where I was or who I was with.

This opening into the beyond, beyond what our five senses and even our gut can comprehend, is something I can absolutely, unequivocally assure you that you are capable of accessing. God designed you to be able to hear His voice![55] And even more wonderfully, God wants you to hear His voice.

Without connection to Him, we remain stuck. I can't free you, and you cannot free me. It doesn't matter if I help you identify exactly how you're stuck, why you're stuck, or what flavor your particular stuck is. You cannot pull yourself out. You must partner with Him and invite Him to show you beyond the blue. Intimate connection to the Father through His Son Jesus with the guidance of the Holy Spirit is the cornerstone of everything to come. It is okay if you don't quite know how yet, or exactly what I mean by this. I know you have already tried everything you know how to do.

Do you believe you were designed to hear God's voice?

---

52 1 Corinthians 3:16, 1 Corinthians 13:6, John 14:7, Romans 8:10-20; "What Does God Mean When He Says, "I Will Never Leave You nor Forsake You" (Hebrews 13:5)?" *GotQuestions.org*, www.gotquestions.org/I-will-never-leave-you-nor-forsake-you.html.
53 Ephesians 5:22-33, Revelation 19:6-9
54 Garrels, Josh. *Beyond the Blue*. 2011.
55 John 10:27

This is an important question. The answer determines whether or not you will be able to receive from Him. If you do not believe you were designed to hear Him, you will brush off everything He sends your way as coincidence, weird, or a figment of your imagination.

This happened to me one day early on in my walk with God, pre-Lyme, as I was driving down Litchford Road on my way home from a friend's house. I feel the words "Call Gretchen." enter my mind. "Call Gretchen?? Cheryl, what are you talking about? I'm not going to call Gretchen, we haven't spoken in over a year. She's going to think I'm weird." So I brushed it off.

If you do not believe you were designed to hear Him, you will brush off everything He sends your way as coincidence, weird, or a figment of your imagination.

Later on, I did wind up running into Gretchen. I told her how I thought of calling her a few days before. She got very still, and the sadness she'd been ignoring filled her eyes.

"Oh wow. I really wish you had called. That's when I got some terrible news about my mom."

It's okay that I missed that one. It helped me learn what it sounds like and what it feels like. Sometimes we hear, we know it's His voice, and we respond. Other times we hear it, think it's odd, and we write it off. But if you do not believe His voice is a possibility, you will find another explanation for His prompting in your life every time.

This question I am asking is personal; it is about *you*. Not whether or not you think man in general has heard from God or can have a relationship with Him, but you in particular, as you hold this book in your hands or listen to it on audio.

Do you believe you were designed to hear God's voice? If you do not believe this, let's pause here to give you time to ponder this question. Come back to this book if you find yourself ready to continue.

∞ Does God Still Speak? ∞

I believe that answer is yes, God does still speak, but it is your answer that affects how you will interact with God. We will go through many Scriptures together to explore this question in the hopes of either piquing your curiosity or assuaging concerns that He doesn't speak anymore.

We get to know God through the 'Logos' word, which is His written Word of Scripture. It is the plumbline by which we rigorously measure all the things we might hear as we learn to discern His voice.[56] As we mature, we train to rightly divide His Word. My learning occurred through Precept ministries, where I trained diligently to understand the context of a passage first and then interpret within that context.

There is another level of maturity, however, in our communication with God. Maturity also requires a direct dependence on the Lord through listening for and responding directly to His voice as He "highlights" Scripture or nudges your heart as you move through the world. We will delve into the 'Rhema' word in these next few paragraphs. The combination of an inductive method of studying the Word (Logos) and a very personal interactive relationship with God (Rhema) provide us with protection from the humanity of both those who love us and may mistakenly misapply Scriptures on our behalf, and those who would intentionally manipulate and wound in the name of God.

Listen to sermons, seek wise counsel, and be teachable when those wiser offer you their words. And as you do so, check in with God for yourself; be a "good Berean."[57] "Study to show yourselves approved workmen who need not be ashamed, rightly dividing the Word of Truth."[58] Simultaneously, we want to grow in intimacy in following the voice of God as He speaks to us *directly*. I hope to establish for you that communication with God is both Logos *and* Rhema communication and not either/or.

---

56 Grandchamp, Greg. "What Is the Significance of a Plumb Line in the Bible?" *Bible Study Tools*, Salem Web Network, 25 May 2022, www.biblestudytools.com/bible-study/topical-studies/what-is-the-significance-of-a-plumb-line-in-the-bible.html.

57 Acts 17:11

58 2 Timothy 2:15

Cultivating your own ability to have a conversation with Him will create delight and security that no circumstance can deny or steal from you. As you continue to develop your relationship with your heavenly Father, you will find the intimate personalization of your walk with God developing both in depth and richness. It is crucial that the only go-between who mediates your relationship with the Father is Jesus Himself. This foundation will not be shaken when people inevitably disappoint.

Our brief exploration of this question of how and if God speaks begins in Genesis. You were created in the image of God.[59] That design includes the ability to hear His voice. This was demonstrated to us in the Garden of Eden, where a very intimate relationship between God and man took place. That ability to communicate did not change when Adam sinned. He was still able to hear God's voice after he partook of the forbidden fruit when God called to him, "Where are you?"[60]

For centuries after this, the Lord primarily spoke through prophets. These are people who are described as being carried along by the Holy Spirit.[61] Under the Old Testament covenant, the Holy Spirit did not indwell all of God's people at all times but fell upon certain people at certain times to empower them to act or speak in the interest of God and His people.[62]

One of these prophets was Samuel. At night as a young boy growing up in the temple, he mistook God's voice for Eli the priest's.[63] Multiple times, he came to Eli's bedside to answer the call. Eli eventually recognized that it was the Lord speaking to him. Eli had been trained and discipled to recognize the voice of the Lord. He sent Samuel back to his bed with instructions on how to respond the next time the Lord spoke: "Speak, Lord, your servant hears you."[64]

Moses spoke with God directly, face to face, "as one speaks with a

---

59 Genesis 1:27
60 Genesis 3:9
61 2 Peter 1:21
62 Exodus 35:31, Numbers 27:18, Judges 3:10, Judges 6:34, Judges 13:25, 1 Samuel 16:13, 2 Samuel 23:2, Ezekiel 2:2 (Not an exhaustive list.)
63 1 Samuel 3:1-20
64 1 Samuel 3:9-10

friend."⁶⁵ He called to Moses with His own voice.⁶⁶ All of the prophets spoke with God directly.

Remember Elijah? When he went up on the mountain to speak with God, God did not speak in the strong wind, earthquake, or fire, but in a still, small voice.⁶⁷ By the way, this story comes right after our Broom Tree story in Chapter One. The Lord's voice not only brought comfort but also a real solution to his weariness.

The mode of operation changes when we move into the New Testament. We can orient ourselves to the chain of authenticity by the author's words in the beginning of the book of Hebrews: "Long ago God spoke many times and in many ways to our ancestors through the prophets. And now in these final days, He has spoken to us through His Son."⁶⁸

We know that Jesus did not come to abolish the law and the prophets but to fulfill them.⁶⁹ He is now the fulfillment and the way to know God. He says, "I am the Way, and the Truth, and the Life; no one comes to the Father but by Me.";⁷⁰ "Whoever has seen me has seen the Father.";⁷¹ and "I and My Father are one."⁷²

God says twice about Jesus: "This is My beloved Son with whom I am well pleased." The first was during his baptism with John,⁷³ and the second was on the mountaintop during the transfiguration.⁷⁴ The second time, God adds a command: "Listen to Him."

Jesus, established as God's Son whom we are to accept as a reliable speaker for God as being one with God, said, "I tell you the truth: it is to your advantage that I go away, for if I do not go away, the Helper will not come to you. But if I go, I will send Him to you." ⁷⁵

Holy Spirit, also known as the Helper or Paraclete, is He who

---

65 Exodus 33:11
66 Exodus 19
67 1 Kings 19:11-13
68 Hebrews 1:1
69 Matt 5:17-20
70 John 14:6
71 John 14:9
72 John 10:30
73 Matthew 3:17
74 Matthew 17:5
75 John 16:7

indwells us, sealing us for the day of salvation.[76] His is the voice to which we attune our ears. The Holy Spirit is referenced in Jesus' great commission as the third member of the Trinity, "baptizing them in the name of the Father, the Son, and the Holy Spirit."[77] In the New Testament, the Holy Spirit is also described as the Counselor and Comforter.[78] We meet Him as a part of the Godhead in the beginning as "Ruach Elohim," the Spirit or breath of God that was hovering over the surface of the deep.[79] Holy Spirit's role is described in the Old Testament as "The Helper" with a different word, "ezer," in the context of the battles.[80] He is a strong defender, a preserver of life, a sword, and shield with ears open to the cry of the defenseless. His character is consistent throughout the Bible, although less familiar to humanity until His mighty move-in day in Acts 2.

In Acts 15, the Holy Spirit spoke in the hearts of Peter, Barnabas, and Paul. They so recognized His voice that they wrote the words, "It seemed good to the Holy Spirit and to us..."[81] In 1 Corinthians, Paul describes for us that the Spirit instructs him about God and instructs us, as well.[82]

God spoke to John, exiled on an island,[83] to Peter on the roof in the middle of town,[84] to Elijah on the mountain, and to Phillip on an empty road, and He can speak to you wherever you find yourself now. We hear the "rhema" word through Holy Spirit, who is the personalization of

---

76 1 Corinthians 1:21-22, Ephesians 1:13-14
77 Matthew 28:19
78 "Strong's Greek: 3875. παράκλητος (Paraklétos) -- Called to One's Aid." *Biblehub.com*, biblehub.com/greek/3875.htm. John 14:18
79 "Genesis 1:2 Parallel: And the Earth Was without Form and Void and Darkness Was upon the Face of the Deep. And the Spirit of God Moved upon the Face of the Waters." Biblehub.com, 2024, biblehub.com/strongs/genesis/1-2.htm.
80 Exodus 18:4; Deuteronomy 33:7, 26, 29; Psalms 20:2; Psalms 33:20; Psalms 70:5; Psalms 89:19, Psalms 115:9, 10, 11; Psalms 121:1-2, Psalms 124:8, Psalms 146:5; Hosea 13:9
    "Strong's Hebrew: 5828. עֵזֶר (Ezer) -- a Help, Helper." Biblehub.com, biblehub.com/hebrew/5828.htm.
81 Acts 15:28
82 1 Corinthians 2:10-16
83 Revelation 1:9
84 Acts 10:9-29

the truth revealed to us in Scripture.[85] Holy Spirit trains us to recognize and respond to Him as our guide.

Sometimes when we read the Bible, we can feel like the Ethiopian to whom Philip was sent, "How can I understand [Scripture] unless someone explains it to me?"[86] Philip became a picture of the rhema, responding to the questions of the Ethiopian, making it personal, writing it indelibly on the Ethiopian's heart. Holy Spirit in us helps us to receive the message of Scripture.[87] The Helper teaches us all things and brings to mind the truths we have already learned.[88]

Holy Spirit is sometimes hard for us to wrap our minds around. We can imagine a glorious Father or a Son of Man walking the earth, but what can we bring to mind when we think of the Holy Spirit?

"Ruach: the breath that moves through everything."[89] He is like the wind.[90] We cannot see Him, but we see the leaves move in the trees and the flurries of dust picked up from the ground. He animates us beyond our natural inclinations, empowering us and making us more like Himself. We don't know where He comes from or where He is going, but we hear the sound.[91] God's voice is described both like many rushing waters and a still small voice. I see His movement in the hearts of the people around me, so subtle I could almost mistake it for something less than divine. But I know I didn't create the movement, and I know that person was struggling, feeling very stuck. Time and again there is an unlocking moment as we enter the mystery of the Holy Spirit interacting with His people.

Is it possible that the eyes of our hearts recognize our Maker even though our physical eyes have yet to see Him?

---

85 Page, Roy. "GREEK WORD STUDIES ῥῆμα, "Rhema" Meaning "Word" Strong's 4487." *Logosapostolic.org*, 2025, www.logosapostolic.org/greek-word-studies/4487-rhema-word.htm.
86 Acts 8:30-33, brackets inserted to clarify the implied object pulled from the contextual scripture
87 2 Corinthians 2:1-16
88 John 14:26
89 Staff, Logos. ""Ruach": The Breath That Moves through Everything." *Word by Word*, 26 June 2019, www.logos.com/grow/the-breath-that-moves-through-everything-a-survey-of-ruach/.
90 John 3:8
91 John 3

My friend, Sloan, visibly locked up in his own mind, quickly alternated between crossed arms or clasped hands in front of his face for 45 minutes. He had raised tense shoulders, furrowed brows, and argumentative comments for our meeting that night. Where was Sloan? He was under a shadow. He was wrestling. If we put him in the original story of the garden, he was behind a bush, unwilling to be in the light of God's presence.

But by the end of the evening, he had leaned back; his arms were open. He was light, laughing, and free of the lie he'd wrestled with for decades. It would unlock his marriage, his relationships with his children, and the way he approached his work.

I didn't do it. In fact, my body shook with the effort of the restraint I sensed I needed from Holy Spirit as I allowed this man to go on his own journey with the Lord. I wanted to give him my opinions, my assessments, and my advice, but it was as though there was a gentle finger over my mouth, lifting only to inspire and allow one question that would reveal the path he could choose to take or to remain as he was. Everyone in that Zoom room witnessed the work of Holy Spirit as He created connections for Sloan, and the truth dawned on his countenance. I have the privilege of witnessing this over and over again each time I am a part of a course or a training. It is my humble privilege to be used by Him to create environments where holy animation of the soul is invited.

Sloan knew where to find the truth already in his mind, but his heart was having a hard time accessing it. When we took the time to be present with him as he struggled, to listen deeply enough to reflect what he knew back to him, he was able to quiet enough to hear God's voice. Delight followed.

When we still ourselves, the temporal barriers of time and dimension fall away with the movement of the Spirit. He will not always whisper. Someday we will be released from our earthly containment, so restrictive and groaning. Yet moments like Sloan's await you and me more often than we perceive.

Mr. Hutchinson, who went through the valley of the shadow alongside his wife in Chapter One, reported two things he discovered through their experience. The first was that he did indeed have a real relationship with God. The second was that he would not always hear God's voice. He found that those two realities could coexist, and he could be okay.

Mr. Hutchinson was discovering the intimacy of the gospel. The Rhema, as I refer to it here, is so deeply personal it is like a code word shared between two spies on a covert mission. You know, and He knows. What I have come to recognize as His voice is based on clear experiences of something other than my own voice later confirmed by direct outcomes beyond my control. These experiences are filtered through what I see in the Bible, the unchanging character of God, and the corroborating testimonies of others in the faith.

This journey into the deeply personal engagement with the Father is not without its own set of bumps and bruises as we learn to distinguish our desires and wish lists from His voice and instruction. I don't always trust that what I think I'm hearing from God is truly from Him, but I'm training to take my unctions, inspirations and gut feels before the Father for Him to shape and inform. That, too, draws me into that rich relationship with Papa. It takes time to recognize His voice when He speaks to you directly. A missed opportunity for deeper rest occurs when we forget to bring what we think we are hearing or seeing to Him. God desires to train our disciple's ear and the eyes of our heart to hear and see what He wants us to see and hear. We all start as young Samuels.

I recall a friend, a mature believer in Christ, whose mom was dying. She was convinced that she heard from God that her mom would experience physical healing and would rise from the hospital bed. Her mom passed. That became a crisis of faith moment for my friend. Did God lie to her? Knowing His character, she could unequivocally say, no, He did not lie to her. Did she not hear Him correctly? She sat with that and it scared her to think that her desire for her mom to live was so strong that she might have missed God's voice. But as she continued to work through it, she recognized the mercy of living with that hope for a time, helping her to advocate for her mom. During her grief journey, she was able to release her disappointment, not in God but in her lack of attunement to God, and she grew from that.

God is always working. God is inviting us to join in His work. Our spiritual eyes and ears take much training to enter this realm of hearing, speaking, praying, acting. We will not always interpret correctly. We will not always understand what He's doing even when we are participating in the work with Him. That is all part of our training that comes from our position of rest in his Son. The Lord tells us that if any of us lacks wisdom, we can ask Him. Not only will He give it but pour lavishly.[92] But often we don't. We're afraid to ask, and we don't know if we'll like what He'll tell us. Or we're afraid we'll be wrong or we'll look like a fool. Could you allow yourself to go on a journey like Sloan?

∞ How Does God Speak? ∞

As I continue on in this journey with you, I will be sharing many things. But I'm not trying to get you to see anything my way or to do things like I do. What I do want to do is connect you to the One who does reveal, does teach, and does heal. He is the One who invites you beyond. Beyond what you know, what you can control, and what you can predict. I have no concrete outcome in mind. I just want you to *be* as you read, and as you are willing, allow your heart to interact with the stories presented and the One who is seeking you.

What I'm inviting you into is a conversation directly between you and the Lord. And yes, it is possible that someone will come along to confirm what you heard or to help you understand that something was not from the Lord. But it will begin with developing your living, talking, breathing relationship with the Lord first.

The first time I really sought guidance from God was quite child-like. When Tom and I were baby Christians, a few years after my spit-up baptism, his time at IBM in Florida was coming to a close. We had always said we would go back home to Chicago to be closer to family, but now that the opportunity presented itself, neither of us really wanted to go. We realized we loved visiting, but we didn't actually want to live there anymore. This shared discovery presented a new problem: We didn't know where to go. We had two young kids, and we had to leave.

---

92 James 1:5

We were sitting together out on the lanai thinking about this together when Tom asked me if I wanted to pray. Being new to the faith, this was our first time praying together. We were brand-spanking-new Christians learning how on earth we walk our everyday life with God. We didn't even know how to pray together practically. We looked at each other. It was dark, so it wasn't quite as awkward as it could have been. He stuck out his arm, which was my cue to hold his hand. We looked at each other again. He bowed his head, so I bowed my head. Then he prayed a very simple prayer with childlike faith.

"God, we don't know where to go. Would you please show us where we need to move? We need Your help. Amen."

We pulled our hands away. We looked at each other. We looked out at the yard. We didn't say anything for a little while.

Then Tom said, "What about Raleigh, North Carolina?

"I could see myself living there." I responded. I had never been to Raleigh! I knew absolutely nothing about Raleigh! But I had a sense of calm as he mentioned the locale.

Two months later, Tom and I were living in our new home in Raleigh. We never looked back.

We first get to know God through His Word, and we learn to know the sound of His voice and the things that are "just the kind of thing He'd say," as sheep learn to know their shepherd's voice and a baby knows its mother's voice. The "hearing" of His voice is not necessarily audible, but there is a knowing—a knowing in your knower. There is a resonance. I knew Raleigh was a good place to go with a knowing that came from a part of me I didn't know was there yet – Holy Spirit within. The Scripture says that His Word is active, sharper than any two-edged sword. It's so sharp that it can divide between bone and marrow.[93]

Have you ever tried to cut the skin off the back of pork ribs? Think about how hard that is to do. His Word just cuts through all that. When you have that moment of resonating clarity, that cutting through, understand that is one quality of the voice of God, and you may be hearing Him. I am confident now as I look back that it was the voice of the Lord because of the way life confirmed His foresight in that guidance, and I can reference qualities about the experience that

---

93 Hebrews 4:12

help me to recognize His voice in the future. It truly did cut through everything—guilt about saying no to being closer to family, fear about going someplace unknown, anxiety about future income, and loneliness about leaving our greenhouse community in Florida. There was an energy with this gentle knowing in my heart, but not a nervous or anxious energy. It felt like a settledness, a calm in my belly, like a seed of truth about me and my life had just been planted deep within me.

This was not about me trying to avoid honoring my mother or father; I did not have that heart issue. Nor was this about running away from a problem. There were so many things it wasn't about that it could have been very easy to thoroughly confuse myself. Instead, I had to focus on God's character, which was that He provides a path forward and my sense of "knowing." That's all I had to go on. And in my early stages of faith, it was enough.

Baby Christians that we were, we didn't seek a lot of confirmation. We just knew and went; that is one of the blessings of early faith. As we keep walking, sometimes we make things complicated, but that is alright. It's all a part of growing and maturing. We don't desire to go back and recreate that newness, but we press through to a place where it becomes simple again. As an executive coach, I often share with clients something I learned from a fellow coach—a continuum of going from the shallow and simple through the complex and then into a deeper form of simplicity once again.

Naive Simplicity → Complexity → Exquisite Simplicity

Simplicity without complexity will not ultimately sustain us, because life is complicated. Our histories, questions, and situations have many facets. Even our knowledge can confuse us at times. But as we continue with Him, the broader strokes of understanding begin to emerge. We become familiar, our trust deepens, and things become simple again. Often, He confirms that the message is from Him through His written Word and with alignment with His character. Fleece tests are okay.[94] Doubt during the complex stage is real. But choosing not to act in this stage will lead to stuckness again. Action protects from stagnation.

---

94 Judges 6:36-40

Another descriptor I can give you is the way He guides us into the future. He will either give us pictures of the preferred future He has for us or just enough information for the next rock we need to step on, a lamp to our feet.[95] When you're hiking in the dark, your flashlight will only reveal so far ahead, even if you have a good idea of what the end will look like.

My son and his wife went on a whitewater rafting trip once where the Olympics had previously been held in Tennessee. The guide would shout instructions to each side of the boat about how to paddle. They reported it was less than five minutes before they were obeying the guide instantly and wholeheartedly because they truly felt as though their life depended on it. If he said to dig in on the left, they dug. If he said paddle harder, they strained with every bit of strength they had. If he said jump in the middle of the boat, they jumped.

God tries to get our attention; He seeks us.[96] But if I'm always so busy, paddling, paddling, paddling, and I am overwhelmed by all of my senses, that is a state where it is difficult to hear and to recognize the still, small voice.

Now there is nothing wrong with seeking God for confirmation. The river metaphor breaks down a little bit because there is time for that. God desires immediate obedience, but He does not rush anyone. A telemarketer will bully you into buying stuff and rush you into making a panicked decision about something you don't want or need. God is exactly the opposite. He is patient with us. I can't recall anyone who was able to discern God's voice and obey like that river guide the first time. But as you get to know His voice and you get to know His heart, there is an opportunity to grow into that. He knows the river, and He can see the rocks.

This is why earlier on in my walk, before my ears were more attuned, I needed a while on the open highway before my mind was quiet enough that it didn't drown out the still, small voice. Another great hearing mode for me is walking, especially if it involves nature. If I am not so fortunate to be able to get out, even the shower can be a quiet enough space. But with time, I have become able to hear Him even in the midst of my conversations with others.

---

95 Psalm 119:105
96 Luke 19:10, Ezekiel 34:11, John 6:44, Jeremiah 31:3

Still Small Voice

The ears of the heart hear things in a way that is most like a gut instinct or an intuition. In Jewish tradition, the soul was considered to live in the belly, lower than the western language of "heart" implies. Scripture describes living water flowing from our belly.[97] This is why when I am discipleship coaching, I ask my listener to put their hands on their bellies and to listen from there.

Be warned, our own voice with its anxieties and pressures can speak from there too. We often overthink and get in our own way when it comes to the voice of God. I'm often curious about what makes us overthink. I wonder if it has to do with the lie that I have come across in many relationships with Christians who subconsciously believed for a time that "everything has to be hard" when it comes to the Christian life. If there was a decision to make, they would assume that the process of hearing Him would be complicated and that God would automatically want them to choose the option they least wanted. It is hard to find the simplicity sometimes, but take heart, He will show it to you as you continue to seek Him.

There's this little Scripture tucked away in Isaiah that starts to help us understand. It says you will hear a voice behind you instructing you in the way you should go.[98] While our senses are bombarded with everything in front of us from the news; social media; the voices of others; the voices of the past; and fear like a ticker tape parade complete with loudspeakers, trumpets, and trombones, we need to be trained to quiet those voices in front of us and tune our ears to the still small voice behind us, just like Bruce Olson to the piping turkey.[99]

In his biographical account, *Bruchko*, Bruce Olson was ministering to the Indians in the jungle of Columbia.[100] As they walked through the trees, one of his companions turned to him and said, "You hear that?"

"Hear what?" He asked in confusion. There were so many sounds he couldn't make out the wind from the trees or the birds from the bugs.

"The piping turkey!"

"I can't hear it." He shook his head. But then he paused to listen, and

---

97 John 7:38-40
98 Isaiah 30:21
99 1 Kings 19:11
100 Olson, Bruce. *Bruchko*. Charisma Media, 18 July 2006.

pretty soon he was able to hear the low, reedy cry of the piping turkey as loud and clear and beautiful as if it was the only sound radiating from the jungle. In that moment he asked himself how many times God's voice had been like that piping turkey, and he just didn't take the time to tune out the noise to tune into His voice. This moment for him became a powerful touchstone through times of captivity and suffering to remember that God is still with him in the midst of the chaos and speaks even if he is unable to perceive it at the moment.

We tend to want everything fast and immediate. God doesn't work that way. It's not in the sparkling or the loud. It's so fleeting sometimes you have to catch it in your soul. It's a quiet rustling that briefly quickens your spiritual sense. Listening becomes a go slow to go fast moment.

> *God is still with us in midst of the chaos and speaks even if we are unable to perceive it at the moment.*

I remember reading a book many years ago called *God Guides* by Marianne Geegh.[101] She was in India doing missionary work and humbly recognized that she did not have all the answers for the people she served. But she knew that God did, so when a person was questioning, struggling, doubting, or lacking direction, she would do a few simple things. She would give them space to share their concern, she would assure them that she had understood, and then she would invite them into prayer with God. They would enter the beyond together.

These people were coming to her stuck, but they were willing to get out from behind their bush, out from under the shadow, and she was willing to bring them to the light instead of casting her own shadow on the situation.

They would sit there silently for as long as necessary until such time as one or the other of them heard something from the Lord. If Mary heard first, she would ask if they had heard anything. If they had not, she would ask if they would like to hear what she sensed going on in her spirit—for permission is very important. God would consistently

---

[101] Geegh, Mary. *God Guides*. Holland, Mich., M. Geegh, [19.]

enter the situation when a person came to Him. She invited them more to His presence than to a solution.

Over and over again in that short little prayer guide, I learned so much about what it meant to invite God into our concerns and to posture ourselves into a space to be able to hear and respond. My need for speed gradually began to regulate to the voice of God. Stop, download, wait, listen, and observe. And when He speaks: act. Typically there is an opportunity to walk into His words almost immediately, whether that directive is something as simple as a specific action that responds to His instruction or a deep mindset shift.

I am convinced by the Scriptures shared above that every single person is made in the image of God and has been designed with the ability to hear from God directly. As you read the following stories, pay attention to what comes to mind for you. Maybe there will be a memory that comes into focus, or a current situation, or a deep knowing that wells.

All of these situations in my life or friends in the ministry involve a crossroads, a crisis, an error, a sense in the gut, or a persistent nudging. No matter how near or far we live or what else we have in common, we all share this one most important thing—our relationship with God. Seeing the love they have for the One I love and His love for them knits our hearts together, and it makes us family. Let's go to the beyond.

∞ Mike ∞

One of my team members and her husband were contemplating moving. He received a less-than-ideal job offer in a different state, and he was seeking the Lord's wisdom on how to respond. Should he take the job?

We were on the phone processing the decision together and he said, "I don't think I can do this, it's not in a great area, it's not great pay, we can't find a place to live, and our current area is a perfect place for the kids. But at the same time, I haven't been able to say no to it."

My ears perked up at that. I responded, "Did you hear what you just said?"

"What did I say?"

"Something is telling you you can't say no. Is it possible you've already said yes, but you haven't grown into your yes?"

Mike sensed he was being invited beyond the blue—the place where God's prompt meets us in our uncertainty and we find we can't say no, but we haven't quite gotten to a yes. The view is not what we expected. The questions come in by the hundreds as the potential consequences for us and those around us cause us to pause. The door opened for my friend, and he had to stop there for a moment and sit in the questions and the profound vulnerability.

He invited me into his vulnerable place, and like Mary Geegh learned to do and recorded in God Guides,[102] I sat with him in it as he took in the view of what was beyond. In the end, the "couldn't say no" turned into a solid yes.

They are making less money, but God provided. His family received money from a donor to make the move, and he was invited to preach at their new church twice soon after their arrival. That invitation fulfilled a long-standing desire left previously unfulfilled in other appointments and was not promised in the job description. An old friend got them into a house through an unseen connection. They didn't know about any of these things when they made the decision to leap, but there was that small nudge in his heart. When we obey, we don't always have all the information, but He makes the way known to us as we step forward.

∞ Anna ∞

Anna, from Ukraine, joined the call a little bashful, blinking and looking down often, but smiling in the quick flashes she allowed her face towards the camera. She was very young, barely in her twenties.

---

[102] Geegh, Mary. *God Guides*. Holland, Mich., M. Geegh, [19.]

She was a strong believer involved with an international discipleship ministry, and she loved the Lord. But she was riddled with anxiety. It held her back from fully participating in both daily life and ministry, and she fought hard to break those chains as she walked through PLL. The more she exercised the 7 Step Shift® (I'll walk you through the framework in Chapter 7) into the truth, the freer she became. The anxiety didn't disappear, but it moved from the driver's seat to the passenger seat.

During the last few weeks of the group, Russia invaded Ukraine. Her eyes were wide as she shared her plans to flee the country, but then something changed. She heard from the Lord that she was not to become a refugee but instead to become a city of refuge. How did she hear it? The Discipleship Coach had mentioned in passing that we become cities of refuge as we walk in the truth of Jesus, no matter where we are or go. That passing statement to a group of missionaries lodged deep within her soul (we are talking serious bowel level here). She chose to stay in the country and work in a local church to provide refugee relief. This young woman, whose anxiety could be crippling even in peacetime, chose to turn towards the conflict with her face set like flint in wartime. The voice of the anxiety was now replaced by a different voice—His voice of authority.

The shelter served 200-400 new people every day. She worked from the moment she got up to late at night, providing food, beds, and meeting whatever other needs they could. She reported that she found refuge in God and carried that with her into the work. She shared the gospel and started discipling people in this shelter with the same gifts given to her, including the 7 Step Shift.® She loved seeing His character expressed in this church's safety for the refugees. "He is that shelter for us when we just run to Him. We see that we are not alone."

One young man who had passed through the shelter on the way to another country shared the gospel with his mother. Another took the gospel to her whole family, another took the gospel with her to Scotland, and another to the Netherlands. Hundreds of refugees were coming through each day and scattered across the globe the next, many of them taking Jesus with them. The ripple effect of this one courageous choice of obedience cannot be measured by earthly means. Yardsticks and tape measures move over!

∞ What Better Place to Be? ∞

I was starting to experience some progress with the treatment for Lyme when my local doctor decided he would no longer support the experimental use of IV glutathione treatments. This was the only medication my care team had found to prevent my going into a coma-like state. This news was terrifying. I had truly come to the end of what medicine could do for me.

My husband had heard about a place called The Healing Room. I didn't know much about it, and I didn't know if it would be any different than any other prayer, but we were desperate. We decided to go together.

You need to know I have experienced the failure of prosperity gospel rhetoric that promised me everything I wanted if only I had enough faith. It shattered on the reality of pain every time my body would fail, no matter what I did, how I believed, or how I prayed. But Jesus remained even more real and more steady. Sometimes it takes more faith to remain in the waiting. I knew nothing in my strength or control could tame this until God decided the time was complete, and I was able to rest in that. He showed me that Jesus Himself learned obedience through suffering,[103] so how could I be exempt from it?

The mystery of the cross is something with which to wrestle. Closely, all night, like Jacob. Jesus is our victorious King at the cost of the agony of soul and body. We cannot turn our face away or hold it at a distance. When you suffer, look at Him! Look at the flayed ribs heaving for breath and the blood running down the wood. He who did not excuse Himself from our messy lives but stepped in, suffering with us and for us. We share in His suffering; He is with us in ours.

Sometimes we become disappointed with Jesus because we had an expectation that Jesus would deliver us or those we love from every uncomfortable thing. When Jesus turned to the man on the cross next to Him, He did not say, "Aw, I'm so sorry this happened to you." Instead he received him in his suffering and promised him glory.

---

[103] Hebrews 5:8

You may feel like you're being hung out to dry right now, but Jesus is hanging right there with you. He is not going anywhere. I held up my desire for healing and deliverance again and again to Him, but it wasn't even my main request anymore.

I drove to The Healing Room with my heart in this place. My own strength was completely unmade with full confidence in His. I prayed out loud.

"Well, Lord, I'm really between a rock and a hard place now."

Immediately, as clearly as I have ever experienced Him, He answered, "What better place for you to be, Cheryl?

And that's all He said. So then I had to think about what I said: a rock and a hard place. What became clear, as He brought remembrance, was that Moses was between the rock and a hard place when God's glory passed by. Moses saw God's glory! What I came to receive in the car, in about a two minute period, was the confidence that He was either going to take me home in His mercy and I would be in His glory or that He was going to heal me and I was going to live and be able to give glory to God. But either way, I would not be living in a comatose state for the rest of my life. I went into The Healing Room with that very clear understanding. I had peace before I even started that process.

What better place for you to be?

In The Healing Room, Tom and I sat before a group of brothers and sisters in Christ who read me a series of verses specifically about physical healing. They asked me if I believed those verses were for me. I had to pause. It was a vulnerable moment. Of course I believed the Scriptures, but it was painful to hold the reality of illness in tension with those verses. After a few moments of trust and doubt duking it out in my soul, I decided to allow myself to be immersed in the truth of the Scriptures.

I closed my eyes for half a second, took a breath, dove into the moment, opened my eyes, looked the reader right in the eyes, and declared, "Yes, I do believe these verses are for me." He nodded and moved towards me to lay hands on me and pray. The rest of the people in the room followed suit, several of them putting their hands on my head. This gesture hurt terribly, but something mysterious happened in The Healing Room as they prayed.

As we left The Healing Room, Tom asked me if I felt any different. I inventoried my body and recognized an "energy" that was quietly moving through my body. Not like caffeine, more like youthfulness. As I climbed into the car, I looked down at the left foot gas pedal rigged to let me drive. My right leg felt normal. I removed the left foot pedal. Had healing begun?

It wasn't immediately obvious. But He lifted the Lyme from me that day, and I stopped spiraling downwards. My body did not descend back into that coma-like state 10 days later as it had when I had tried to come off the medication previously. One month later, in October of 2005, we went to the North Carolina State Fair as a family. I saw the rock wall from a distance and longed to climb it like a little girl. Tom was a little hesitant about my climbing, but he agreed. They waited in line with me, the anticipation building as we inched closer.

It was my turn. I climbed into a harness reminiscent of the one used two years earlier in PT. After a brief "shiver and shake" at the memory, I approached the wall. One rock at a time, my hands and feet held me. One inch at a time, the rope retracted into its place above me as my progress gave it slack. As I got higher, the hope and excitement rose in my throat. By the time I reached the top and rang the bell, I was sure that God had healed me and I was done with Lyme. Tears pouring down my cheeks, I turned to look down at my family. Tom had his hands in the air like I had scored a touchdown, and the kids were jumping up and down cheering in celebration with me.

If you came for a complete theology on physical healing or even a seasoned perspective, you will not find one here. I am still learning, and I am still healing. And there is so much more healing He has done in my soul beyond the physical healing, and, in fact, sometimes as a result of physical suffering. I still would have more walking to do through autoimmune disease in the aftermath of the violent Lyme treatments. I still struggle with my body now 20 years later. My body demands varying amounts of prednisone and presents like I have lupus, but I continue to be sustained by Him through it all. Life still hurts. I am a part of creation that groans for the return of the Lord.[104] Please see the passage in Romans 8 cited below for encouragement about that point. I sum up my journey in this way: outwardly I am wasting away, yet inwardly I am being renewed day by day.[105]

It's easy for me to forget what I just told you. Shortly after my healing, I took red sticky tabs used to mark pages in a book and I bookmarked every page of my Bible that had a verse on it that I had to embrace, personally, in that Healing Room experience. Those red tabs serve as my scarlet thread of remembrance. The thread weaves God's Word together for me and reminds me to not discount the totality of God's counsel. The red tabs remind me to stay hungry and curious. The visual prompt encourages me to keep pressing into the One Who knows me fully. Clinging tightly to those verses alone can be painful, but clinging to Him is not. Together they declare that this is a personal walk I'm taking with Him, not an analytical one, nor a theological one, nor one of duty or discipline first. Those red tabs declare that God's relationship with humanity is now and will always be personal to me. Christianity is an immersion faith that is to swallow me alive and make me whole, not a philosophical thought to be dissected and pulled apart by a finite creature who then would lose all sense of reverence and awe with futile exercises in knowledge. I know that He is so, so good.

About 10 years ago, I was surprised to experience a deeper form of healing that came from surrender. Tucked away on the bottom of my office bookshelf was a book outlining 50 bike trails in Raleigh. I so wanted to explore these trails with my two adventurous boys. It sat there, silently, daily reminding me of what was never to be. The book was laughing at me, but God was wooing me. Finally, one day I got down on my knees in an act of worship and removed that book and the dream from my bookshelf and out of my heart. This created space for me to live into what God was doing and not what I wanted life to look like. I could put that desire into His good hands so that I could

---

104 Romans 8:18-28
105 2 Corinthians 4:16-18 (NIV)

stop carrying the heavy weight of unmet longings. Even now the tears fall and the heart yearns as I recall that moment. It was hard. There was loss. God is good, and there is great hope. Those two states of being can co-exist in our relationship with God. There is rest there. Rest in the longing. Rest from the hanging onto something that may never be. Rest from the clinging to that which is far too heavy to carry anymore. Would you let your own longings surface for you *with God?*

We live in tents that rip and tatter; we get sick and age, but one day we will be in our permanent dwellings. Between now and then, He wants to heal our hearts in our deepest secret places, those wounds that you hide from others, maybe even from yourself.

Will you let Him speak to you there in your valley?

Over the next few pages, I hope to train you in a posture of open and humble listening, primarily with the Lord but also with those around you. It may feel awkward or vulnerable at first, but I hope you will take the risk with me. His table has been set while war is all around. He beckons us to dine with Him. He's waiting to pour out wisdom until your cup overflows with His life which will sustain you through your handbreadth life.[106]

---

106 Psalm 39:5

CHAPTER THREE

Listening

"Discernment is a quality of attentiveness to God that develops over time into the ability to sense God's heart and purpose in any given moment. It is a way of being. Seeking the movement of God's Spirit so we can abandon ourselves to it."

RUTH HALEY BARTON

THE PHONE RANG. I recognized the number. It was my sister-in-law, Eileen, affectionately nicknamed "Winks." We had a politely strained relationship. I had never truly been accepted as part of the family, although I'd been married to Tom for many years. Just two years prior to this phone call, I had cleaned up dishes from our stay at their home. Winks thought I was accusing her of not keeping a neat house for guests, and I was concerned with not being a good houseguest based on my own rearing. The two systems clashed once again, and we did not speak to one another for over a year. To say things were fragile between us was being generous.

In the past, I had always "over talked" and filled in the awkward silences in our conversations. I felt like I did my part to mend invisible fences for the sake of Tom during our attempts to stay connected. However, as I went to answer this time, I heard that quiet rustling in my soul: "Do not try to make small talk, Cheryl. Let the conversation be what it will be." I was curious about what I was sensing and decided to follow the lead. Whether it was just me being tired of standing in the gap or God standing in the gap for both of us, I would respond to the nudge.

"Hi Cheryl, it's Winks."

"Hi Winks, good to hear your voice."

Silence

"Well, I guess there really wasn't any reason to call except to say hello."

"Thanks for the call, Winks. It's always good to hear from you."

As I hung up, I wondered what that was all about. My heart was thumping a little harder, but my mind, interestingly enough, was not racing. I let it go and went on with my day.

That evening I received an email from Winks. She mentioned that the conversation seemed stilted, and she wanted to make sure everything was okay.

And then I recognized it! God was moving between the two of us! The God of reconciliation was setting a new pattern for us that we could enter into together. I paused and then responded via email with the following:

Thanks for asking, Winks. Everything is okay for me, but I would love for everything to be okay between us. I long for a real relationship with you. I've learned that everything I say and do is construed from the assumption that I am trying to control. Because of that, I have very little room to move or be genuine in our relationship. But know that it is something I long for with you.

I prayed and pushed send. It was hard to leave my computer. Thankfully, it wasn't even an hour later that I received a reply:

You've given me something to think about, Cheryl. Something good. I think you are right that I have boxed you in. I would like to work on our relationship as well. Would you be open to that?

And just like that, 20 years of reciprocal icy judgments and pain melted into a puddle for Winks and me to go romping and splashing in with bright yellow rain boots. To this day, we have a very deep love for one another. She does not believe in God the way I do, but she tolerates my prayers, my reflections on what He is doing in my life, and once in a while she even asks a question or two. She knows I'm not controlling, changing, or judging her. Our conversations are easy. There is eagerness to be together. Only God can do that! It's amazing to look back on that moment and realize that if I hadn't listened, we might still be stuck. She is, in many ways, one of my closest friends now. By the way, when I called to tell her I wanted to include our story in this book and read it to her, Winks affirmed that I am one of her closest friends as well, with tears in her voice.

I learned a lot about the concepts of closed and open listening through my relationship with Winks. For many years, we used what I call a "closed" listening approach in our discourses. We talked around each other. We talked behind each other. We talked through each other. We talked at each other; however, we were not talking with each other. Our schemas, family dynamics, loyalties and insecurities were what we heard and what we listened to, blocking our ability to be in a real relationship with one another. Until God showed me how to unstop my ears and listen in a new way.

Jesus often began his sermons with "He who has ears to hear, let him hear."[107] Lord, may I have ears to hear You. As the Winks story tenderly and soberly illustrates, hearing the Lord first determines how I will listen to those around me. Learning to listen is the next development of exploration together. We know God speaks. We know He has designed us to hear His voice. Now we add the complexity of hearing His voice in the context of our relationships.

I've learned that the gospel is quiet. It doesn't scream; it woos. Its appearance is not overtly attractive. Its power lies in its single most humble action: the relinquishing of all rights of divine royalty and succumbing to a gruesome death. It doesn't shun the worst of offenders, yet simultaneously is holy. It fulfills long-awaited promises in ways that confound. Its purity is breathtaking. Its demands are simple and arguably most understandable to a child. It is unwavering in the message of hope, immovable in its intention to bring peace, and unyielding to any modification. We tune our ears to this story that refuses to die over the millennia.

Quite the conundrum faces us as we walk through the moments of our days, and suddenly we perceive something. We hear "it." We hear it in our bellies. We hear it beyond that which is quickly comprehended or recognized. We hear it behind us while the world shouts its profanity at us and our own voices in our heads confuse us.

---

107 Matthew 11:15, Matthew 13:9, Mark 4:23

What are we to do? I don't want to stop and listen. I'm on a timeline; I have appointments; I have an agenda. Life is happening, and now this quiet nudge shows up? But this nudge is our compass. Let's revisit this idea of listening together. There is no point in going on a journey with the Holy Spirit guide if my ears are not attuned to the surprisingly hushed sound of His voice.

Looking deeper at closed listening—you can hear, meaning you perceive a hushed movement (sound). However, unless you pause long enough to discern the moment, you go on with life as usual. You will not be changed by the living waters of truth that Holy Spirit wanted to stir in your little body of water. Transformation in us begins with listening.

Transformation in us begins with listening.

God made a path for Winks and I that didn't exist. Below you will be introduced to six closed listening styles extracted from the Scriptures. In summary, all six people groups or individuals had encounters with God yet missed Him. Winks and I missed each other. I was missing God (or more honestly, not engaging with Him in my struggle) and therefore unable to change my way of relating in my horizontal relationships. As we explore these different styles, see if you might see yourself in one or more of these styles. I know I see several of these in myself but especially King Herod.

∞ Closed Listening ∞

Begin by jotting down the name of one or two people with whom you interact frequently and the conversations are at best strained. When we take participants through this exercise, most often it is a spouse, a child, or a parent that is selected. As you read through these six closed listening styles, ask yourself which style you tend to use with the person you selected and how it might feel to be on the receiving end.

Let's start with our first closed listening style:

Know It All: This style of listening is portrayed in Scripture by the Sadducees—it's 'sad you see' because they thought they knew it all already! They didn't have a need to learn anything new. There was an air of superiority among them. Biblically speaking, these people missed the resurrection because they were closed to Truth that went beyond what they could explain with logic.[108] They were unteachable. They believed they had nothing more to learn and missed the chance to know Jesus. All closed listening styles carry a similar theme: the inability to focus on relational connection. For this style, the focus is on logic and reason.

In a conversation, the Know It All thinks they've helped by providing logical and reasoned explanations, tons of data and facts, avoiding the possibility of validating emotions or intuited concerns by another. The expectation is that they are helping by providing information they deem necessary to solve problems. Luke 8:10—they were hearing but not understanding. This can cause exasperation in the other person. They feel "missed", leading to defensiveness and the need to prove that their concerns are valid, or it can cause them to shut down, feeling misunderstood or overloaded.

Is there anyone who comes to mind when you think about the ways you listen to others? Is there anyone you overload with information? Is there anyone you cannot learn anything from?

How do you think this listening style affects them?

Steamroller: King Herod is a prime example of the "Steamroller" style in the Bible. Herod believed he needed to keep everything under control. He didn't want any uprisings or insurrections. He felt pressure above from Caesar and below from the people. He was a commander in chief of sorts, and he was used to taking charge. This type of listener is the one who has to take charge of the conversation so it's controlled the way they think it should go—that way there are no conflicts or surprises! They don't care about the perspective or concern of the other – they only care about control. They give orders, trying to force someone to settle down. When I was in this listening style, my husband liked to call me "Large and In Charge!" This style can often bring injury to a tender heart.

---

108 Matthew 22:29-32

The unfortunate recipient of this style of listening often feels run over. Their attempts at bringing in different perspectives are not just challenged, they are completely shut down. There is no room for "useless" conversation that could disrupt Steamroller's demand for a predictable outcome, leaving the speaker literally speechless or so angry that a real battle ensues. Who do you see yourself using this listening style with? How do you think this listening style affects them?

Self-Righteous: The Pharisees typify self-righteousness in the Word. Pharisee comes from the Hebrew word prushim or "detached one." The Pharisees detached themselves for the sake of a life of purity. Have you ever talked to someone who seems to be ready to pounce with a mandate for how you should be thinking? Your heart is not what matters at that moment. What matters to them is that they ensure you are aligned with what they believe is right.

The Pharisees expressed devotion to God, but because they became so limited and so extreme, they actually became quite distant from God and the common people. Their agenda overshadowed everything and closed off any opportunity to know the Truth and to know God's people.

This type of listening style is closed to deeper heart matters. The emphasis is on appearances and what is said on the surface, rather than what is going on underneath-the heart of the issue. This person filters things through their limited and focused agenda, and if what the person is saying doesn't fit with that, it is immediately thrown out. There is no willingness to sit with ideas or hold them in tension to see how the conversation might evolve, and there is very little compassion. There is zero curiosity engaged in this style of listening. They listen only to determine if what you say aligns with what they believe is right. If the Sadducees are ruled by logic and reason and the Steamroller is ruled by control, the Pharisaical closed listening style is ruled by rightness rather than right relationship.

You might think of this kind of listening as agenda-driven. These people use the word "should" a lot. How does it feel when someone drops a lot of "shoulds" on you? Do you know anyone who listens like this? Do you see qualities in yourself that resemble a Pharisee? How do you think this style is impacting your relationships?

Naysayer: Throughout Scripture, the children of Israel were Naysayers. How many times did the Israelites see God work, but when the next problem came along they usually responded with, "It will never work," or "We'll never fix this." This type of listening is classified by a generally pessimistic and negative view of anything—how quickly negativism can close off growth in dialogue and relationship! You see the worst, anticipate the worst, live like the worst is inevitable.

Many years ago I had a prayer partner who was very much an "Eeyore."[109] It literally wore down my patience so thin that I had to put space between the two of us. No matter the discussion, she would find something to complain about. Attempts to "lift" the conversation were met with an accusation that I was being insensitive about whatever situation we were discussing. In the end, I had to gently remove myself from the relationship. I loved her, still do, but she was absolutely closed to experiencing joy in our relationship.

When in the naysayer listening style, a person becomes less concerned about a vital healthy relationship and more concerned about being validated in their misery. Commiseration motivates dialogue but does not permit for more positive aspects of a conversation to take root.

Do you know anyone who listens like this? Who do you see yourself using this listening style with? How do you think this listening style affects them?

Judge: In the New Testament, the Sanhedrin became famous for their judgmental listening. Who were the Sanhedrin? They were the supreme religious body in Israel. There were 71 leaders among the Great Sanhedrin who gathered in the Temple, although smaller councils met in various locations throughout Israel to judge matters.

Have you ever felt wrongly judged before? You sit across a coffee shop table and share something with a friend, but as soon as you say something slightly off-center or unexpected, their eyes change, and you know they

---

109 Milne, A A, and Walt Disney Enterprises. *Disney's Winnie the Pooh*. United States, Mouse Works, 1996.

don't hear anything else you say. They're just waiting for the chance to tell you that they do not approve or how you should act about the situation.

I would classify this type of listening as judgmental, not judicial. The listener thinks they know what they are hearing without taking the time to confirm their assessments. A judicial listener would take the time to confirm their theories and take the time to understand the perspective and heart of the listener and then make judicious assessments. But even then, in the decision to share or not, a judicial listener would exercise restraint, recognize their own shortcomings, the Lord's role as final judge, and respond humbly and with grace. The judgmental listener is sometimes frightened or threatened by the suggestion that the speaker does not completely align with them in values. This listener may even try to pressure the other person into alignment.

There is a subtle differentiation from the Pharisaical closed listening style which is ruled by rightness rather than right relationship. The judgmental style is not concerned about rightness – it is motivated to judge, end of story. No matter what you say, it will be assumed to be wrong until proven differently by the judge. Pharisees want *things* to be right. Judges want *you* to be wrong. In that moment of closed listening, neither is interested in entering a real relationship conversation.

Often the judgmental listener judges in a certain manner just to have things fit into their scope, to substantiate their theories, or to suit their frame of reference for the purpose of making things go their way. Remember the Sanhedrin? They wanted Jesus to be arrested and condemned before He even arrived before them, so they crafted a hearing that was only partially based on truth and resulted in false judgment—that He was blaspheming!

How sad when we listen to someone, wrongly judge the intent of their words, and by doing so miss an opportunity to know the truth about them! The judge is concerned with proving you are wrong. It makes life simple and controllable but also very lonely and isolating.

Do you know anyone who listens like this? Can you think of times you play the judge in others' lives? Or, have you had someone else play the judge toward you? What is the effect of this listening style?

Handwasher: The last listening style we'll explore is called the "Handwasher" style. Do you remember the Roman governor Pontius Pilate from the Scriptures? What did he do when confronted with Jesus and the charges that were brought against Him? He tried to please the people and make light of problems. He was unwilling to attach any personal investment into the matter of Jesus and his future. He even went as far as 'washing his hands' of the entire situation! This type of listening is characterized by artificial or shallow consolation. It is listening that has no skin in the game—that offers pat answers or canned responses, just to try to get the person to go away or to avoid unpleasant emotions. How discouraging it must feel to share matters of the heart but get a bandaid slapped in their general direction with no real connection with the listener.

Pilate had power but acted passively. He gave it away. How often do we act passively, not permitting the power of God to be enabled in us? Do you know anyone who listens like this? Which relationships in your life do you find yourself washing your hands of? How do you think this listening style affects them?

The above closed listening styles could be summarized by the words of Jesus when He quotes Isaiah: You will indeed hear but never understand, and you will indeed see but never perceive. For this people's heart has grown dull, and with their ears they can barely hear, and their eyes they have closed, lest they should see with their eyes and hear with their ears and understand with their heart and turn, and I would heal them."[110]

When we engage in dialogue yet are closed to the relationship with the person in front of us, it causes injury to the body of Christ. As you consider how these listening styles affect the person you are listening to, consider also how that is impacting your relationship with them. I could tell you story after story of mediating conversations between two people that if either had been willing to be open to something bigger than themselves, the relationship would have had an opportunity to flourish and both could experience healing. My personal grief is very real as I experience this first hand or witness it happening to those around me.

Let's do a final reflection on closed listening, creating a go slow to go fast moment right here:

---

[110] Matthew 13:13-15, Isaiah 6:9

> ### Selah Moment
>
> 1. Which closed listening style do you tend to use the most with the person you jotted down?
> 2. What are you telling yourself about that person when you are using that listening style?
> 3. What are you telling yourself about God when you are using that listening style?
> 4. What are you telling yourself about yourself when you are using that listening style?
> 5. What are you telling yourself about the situation when you are using that listening style?
> 6. What is the impact on the relationship when using this closed listening style?
>
> Your responses to these questions will help prepare you for "shifting" into an open listening stance. Everything we do at Promised Land Living is about shifting from the death grip caused by lies we believe into the open spaces God is preparing for us to live in. Becoming aware of how we listen is the starting point for the remainder of our journey together.

Now that you are aware of a possible closed listening style, you are entering a lifelong journey of listening differently! May I be the first to tell you there is no perfection or arrival as we are always in draft form until our perishable puts on the imperishable. If we are not at rest, death and decay will chase and taunt us. When we are at rest, we become more fully conscious of how we are partakers of the divine nature now. The juxtaposition of a time-bound body with a heart set on eternity creates a battle ground for our attention. A hurried life cannot hear. When time-bound thinking is put in subjection to our willing participation in our divine nature in Christ, we know rest. Being at rest creates an environment that allows us to hear God and one another.

When my mind says hurry up, my ears close. When my heart is open, it asks, 'What is the opportunity here, God?'

It takes practice to slow down long enough to hear the Lord and other people. This is another "go slow to go fast" process. Remember the image of the water-carved groove in the stone?[111] Each time we shift our thinking, we choose which direction we want to wear our path into our minds instead of taking the path of least resistance (which is what neurons will do unless otherwise instructed). Perhaps just start with laying aside one of the styles in one relationship. I sat in the "Steamroller" seat again just the other day with my husband. That is the rut of closed listening I myself am most often guilty of falling into. But my family has taught me how to quickly course-correct in my relationships with them. It happens less and less on all sides as we grow. How easy it is to act in the flesh with the people that are closest to us, even though we desire to love them the most!

Shifting from closed listening to open listening helps us prioritize the life-giving voice of God and breathes new life into our relationships.

The practice of prioritizing His voice, the source of truth, will be pivotal for learning to walk in the way of rest. Look back at the Selah box above and notice how I have asked you to pay attention to what you are telling yourself. The things we tell ourselves about ourselves, others, and God can come from a million different places, and those things may not always be true. Often this is the place that life-draining lies can get between the truth we know about God in our minds and the lack of joy and rest that we experience in our hearts. This not only happens in interpersonal conversations, but we are constantly talking to ourselves about everything we experience.

I have created a tool called the 7 Step Shift® that helps us realign with God's voice . We will unwrap the seven individual steps and other uses for this tool as we continue on together in Chapter 7, but for now let's practice a simpler version of the shift together in preparation for a future conversation.

---

[111] Becker, Peter. "Scientists Find out Why Dripping Water Hollows out Stone." *Stone-Ideas.com*, 2022, www.stone-ideas.com/92858/why-dripping-water-hollows-out-stone/.

7 Step Shift ®

 **CLARITY**
Become aware that something isn't right by noting what is happening in our body (we call these symptoms).

 **CONVICTION**
Invite God into the situation to show us how He wants us to think about it, confessing any lie we are believing.

 **COURAGE**
Ask God for one small step to take into the truth He has revealed to us, courageously taking that step.

© 2024 PROMISED LAND LIVING · WWW.PROMISEDLANDLIVING.COM

Feel free to refer back to this page as we explore practical ways we can invite God into our daily interactions with others. The Selah moment above helps us gain clarity, the prayers will help us receive conviction, and His presence gives us the courage to walk in the truth in our lives outside of these pages. Here we go!

∞ Open Listening ∞

I'd like to invite you to remember a time that you felt deeply seen and heard. What did that do for you? How did it feel? Take that memory with you into the next sequence.

Let's practice open listening together. Theory doesn't change us. Theology doesn't change us. Knowledge doesn't change us. Even understanding alone doesn't change us. Understanding can bridge to the heart, but it doesn't reach the heart. I thought for many years that if I could just get someone to understand, they would change. But that isn't true. So what changes us?

There must be a desire of the heart that makes us willing to choose to cooperate with God's truth even when it makes no sense to our logical or emotional ways of thinking. Have you ever wanted to be one way but you act another? While we want one thing, the desire for something else is stronger. At the heart of transformation is the desire of the heart. This can lead to understanding as a part of transformation, but there must be that desire that drives willingness to engage in relationship and reframing. We will do a lot more with this in a few chapters, but we need to start somewhere!

Transformation occurs when we bump up against our ingrained and practiced patterns and decide that they no longer serve us. This may be fueled by our desire to be a true image-bearer of Jesus. Sometimes though, the motivation is not fueled so much by matters of faith but matters of desperation, pain, or attempting that last-ditch effort. God can use all sorts of things to help us transform. He is very creative! I'm inviting you into this creative space with God to see what only He can do in your relationship as you practice showing up differently.

Let's start with your own motivation for practicing open listening. What would be your reason for trying this shift into open listening? Perhaps jot that down now.

Imagine you are across the table from that "difficult" person in your life. The relationship is strained, you keep missing each other, or maybe you don't have much of a relationship at all, even if it is someone close to you.

Let's see if we can press through to something new. Are you willing to extend the gift of listening?

1. Invite God into the situation.
   As you sit there, begin with acknowledging that God is with you as He always is.
   Lord, I thank You that You are with me, and You will never leave me.
   This helps us to enter the situation with a sense of safety, so that we can think clearly.

2. Practice seeing the other person.
   Look the other person in the eye, and take a moment to be curious about where they may be coming from today, what it feels like to be them. Listen for His voice instead of listening for answers as you observe. What do I mean by that? We can start with things we know are true.
   I know you love this person, Lord.
   Sometimes when I have been in these moments He has prompted me with, "Instead of telling them what you think, why don't you ask them what they think?"

Another time God corrected me. "You think you understand, but I need you to listen."

3. Guard the truth about who you are and who they are in the context of who God is.

    Notice how I put the word "difficult" above in quotes. They are triggering to you in some way, and that is your responsibility to work through. Not everyone is worthy of our trust or honor, but everyone is created in the image of God and worthy of at least that dignity. The enemy is the one who wants to shame us. He is the accuser, not Jesus.[112] We make the accuser's job easier; we even do it for him when we shame ourselves or the people around us. God doesn't even want us to call one another a fool or stupid.[113] It is like Him to straighten what is bent, strengthen the weak knees, and build one another up so we do not go out of joint.[114] We need to exhort one another, lifting up, dignifying, honoring the image of God they bear.[115] As we open our hearts to recognize and acknowledge the other person's dignity, our ears begin to open as well. The things they say begin to sound a little less ridiculous, and we find that we are more willing to take time to think about things from their perspective (this is not about agreeing with them; rather, it's about truly hearing them). As we interact, I continue to invite the Lord into our conversation.

    What are you doing here, Lord? What do you want me to see?

4. Find something to celebrate.

    Look back at that person again, beloved of God. There is always something to celebrate in another person, even if only the opportunity is that while they live, there is a chance for redemption in their life. *Thank You that there is still time for redemption in this person's life.* Or *Thank You that they are willing to have a conversation with me.* There are many other possible iterations of this small, thankful prayer.

---

112 Revelation 12:10
113 Matthew 5:22
114 Isaiah 35:3, Isaiah 42:3
115 1 Thessalonians 5:11

Even when we are doing a lot of listening, there is still our side of the conversation to consider. Recently, I have been pondering that passage that says we are to speak with spiritual hymns and songs of praise to one another. Twice in the New Testament (Ephesians and Colossians), Paul instructs us to address one another in psalms and hymns and spiritual songs. Check out the order of his instruction in Colossians 3:16.

1. Let the Word of Christ dwell richly.
2. Teach and admonish one another in all wisdom.
3. Sing psalms and hymns and spiritual songs with thankfulness in your hearts to God.

If I'm going to talk to you, I want it to come from the place where Christ is dwelling richly in me. If I'm going to share with you, I want it to be from His wisdom. And if I can't find a reason to give thanks, if I don't have His song of praise and joy exuding from me, I've got no business telling you anything. When I feel that response rising swift and ready, I take a quick check. Most of the time it's so fast it's more like a glance heavenward and a simultaneous stop or go in my gut, but sometimes I need to take my time and form the words in my heart.

Is this a time to speak or to keep my mouth shut, Lord?

I don't always call it right; I put my foot in my mouth at times, but at the very least I try to keep Jesus' example before me. Jesus dignified everyone. Jesus saw everyone. Jesus listened to everyone. Jesus addressed anyone who was in His path, even the "brood of vipers," reminding them that each of us will be held accountable for every careless word.[116]

I need to be in the Word. I need to chew the cud, as they say. I need to graze in the field of His everlasting Word and slowly digest, over time, all the spiritually rich nutrients that come from that grazing. This is both for my benefit and for your benefit. If I don't have that, I cannot really listen to you, because I haven't learned to listen to God. Yes, I'll hear you. And sadly, yes, I'll miss you. And we both leave the conversation lonelier and more frustrated than when we began it.

Dignifying each other includes speaking the truth. Respect isn't just making someone feel good and stroking their ego. When you respect

---

[116] Matthew 12:34-37

someone, you are willing to be honest with them. Always speak the truth in love,[117] keeping in mind the grace surrounding us and sustaining us. We must keep the truth of who we are and who they are in the context of who God is.

As we adjust our view from "difficult" or whatever other label you may have on this person to a view of them as God's beloved, and as we learn to allow God to say whatever He will say, it naturally begins to open our attitude to hear their heart. There is room for something beautiful there. We can begin to experience true curiosity about them.

∞ Curiosity ∞

I've thrown about a page of hypotheticals at you. Return to it as you practice open listening with others, and your experiences will begin to contextualize some of those concepts. But Cheryl, how do I do this? Where do I even start? The answer is curiosity.

My relationship with my mother was rocky, and later I'll color in more of the story for you. For now, I will jump the timeline a little bit. The moment that changed the way I related to her from wounded child to adult relator was a moment much like many others we had had together. She was yelling at me. She had sought me out, cornered me in the bathroom, and seemingly out of nowhere exploded all over me about a tender moment I'd just had with my grandmother. She was attacking my character, intentions, and anything else that came to mind, all seasoned heavily with curses, really putting me in my place. I was an adult at this point. I'd had both of my children, and for the first time I didn't feel the need to react directly to her. I started to really see her.

She was so good with the kids while they were little and didn't have too many opinions of their own. She was so tender, so gentle. It felt like a little bit of whiplash to watch her relate to them and then experience her rage in private. This time I was able to look behind what she was throwing at me to identify why she was throwing it at me. I was curious about what brought this out in her. I found myself wondering, "What

---

[117] Ephesians 4:15

is she really afraid of?" The more I listened to her in that context, the more I realized that she was truly terrified of something. Instead of anger, instead of defensiveness, compassion for her flooded me.

In general, when people are loud, oftentimes they are very afraid of something. The loudness is an attempt to gain some kind of control. The next time someone is loud with you, maybe ask yourself what might be going on for them behind their bluster.

Curiosity is the opposite of judgment. When I was having frequent friction with a friend who continued to miss my heart in a way that caused pain for both of us, I had one request for her: "Will you please choose to be curious with me?" Curiosity derails the conflict cycle. It hamstrings assumptions and deflates anger. Scripture tells us that "love believes the best," but sometimes we don't even know how to do that.[118] Curiosity opens the door to that possibility.

Jesus trains us to be curious again. Who touched me? Who do you say that I am? Do you want to be healed? He was curious for the person across from Him who perhaps was no longer curious. Everyone assumed things about the powerless, handicapped person, especially in a society that relied much more on the body's functioning for livelihood. But Jesus asked lots of questions. "Do you want to be well?" is one He asked often. I believe His tone here was heartrendingly gentle.

An accusatory tone may sound like "Do you even want to be well?" with the implication that the sufferer had not done everything they could and that the affliction was perhaps their fault. Which, by the way, was a ubiquitous belief of the time: that illness and handicaps were direct results of sin.[119] But Jesus does not share this view per John 9. His heart towards people He encountered regularly moved Him with compassion, moved Him deeply in His gut.[120] He longed to gather Jerusalem like a mother hen gathers her chicks under her

Jesus trains us to be curious again.

---

118 1 Corinthians 13:7
119 John 9:2-3
120 Ortlund, Dane. *Gentle and Lowly: The Heart of Christ for Sinners and Sufferers.* 2020. Crossway , p. 26.; Matthew 14:14, Matthew 15:32, Mark 6:34, Luke 7:13; "Strong's Greek: 4697. σπλαγχνίζομαι (Splagchnizomai) -- to Be Moved in the Inward Parts, I.e. To Feel Compassion." *Biblehub.com*, biblehub.com/greek/4697.htm.

wing. He says of Himself "I am *gentle* and lowly in heart" (emphasis added).[121] The eyes behind this question were surely the warmest and most welcoming eyes you can imagine.

This question gives room for the receiver to be desperate before Jesus, to feel their desire and pour it out to Him. Or it provides the opportunity to be honest with themselves and see that they really don't want to be well. Sometimes there are hurts we just aren't ready to let go of, or habits we don't really want to break. There is personal responsibility here, too, for what will happen next, but no blame. He is curious, but He will not force anything on us. This question also asks for consent before He does anything. Oh, how kind He is! Even though He already knows our desires, He wants to hear it from us. Maybe He wants us to hear ourselves, and He wants permission to touch us. "Do you want to be well?"

> ### Selah Moment
>
> We love because He first loved us, so before I ask you to try to be truly curious with someone else, would you allow yourself to experience His gentle curiosity about you? I asked you to let Him see where you are in Chapter One. Will you now let Him see where you are hurting?

He won't touch it unless you want Him to. Are you holding onto any hurts right now that you are willing to hold up before Him? Like my 3-year-old granddaughter runs to me: "I hurt myself," and holds up her boo-boo for a kiss. Some scars are harder to show. We cover them with bandages and later strategically with clothes and titles; they aren't pretty. Sometimes they still hurt.

It is safe to show Jesus our scars, because Jesus' wounds show us that He has suffered, and they are also the very means of our healing.[122] He

---

121 Matt 11:29
122 Hebrews 4:15

is a High Priest who is able to sympathize[123] with our weaknesses. This sympathy is more than just pity; it is feeling it with us. After all, we are a part of His body. Jesus still had scars even on his resurrected body. Put yourself in Thomas' sandals on that day.[124] How do you think it felt to see and touch Jesus? Those scars coaxed Thomas over the finish line of belief. They are a constant reminder of the fact that He entered our humanity and willingly chose to suffer so that He could heal you–it was worth it to Him. If we forget this, we forget that we can trust His curiosity for us.

And He may even ask you a wonderful question: "Do you want to be healed?" Please do not turn away from the Healer in your suffering. Or, as we will discuss below, in your shame. Remember that while He remains curious with you on your behalf, He remains gentle.

---

123 "Strong's Greek: 4834. συμπαθέω (Sumpatheó) -- to Sympathize, to Have Compassion, to Suffer With." *Biblehub.com*, 2025, biblehub.com/greek/4834.htm.
124 John 20:24-29

CHAPTER FOUR

Interlude

LET'S TAKE A break from paddling, pull up on this bank, and enjoy this little waterfall we've found. The movement of the water is more than a trickle, but not so loud that we can't hear one another. Maybe grab yourself a snack. Many years ago, I coached a color guard for a small marching band. I was always telling my color guard girls they needed food for their brains! They often looked like they were getting away with something when we'd break for a snack. I know I did it much more often than other coaches. Anyway, I want to sit on this rock here for a moment with you because the rest of this book might seem like a blur if I don't do these two things:

1. Remind you of your journey with Jesus up to this point, or
2. Invite you into a journey with Jesus as we continue

I want to take a moment here and ask if maybe you are hearing God for the very first time right now? Some of my readers are already followers of Jesus, and some of you may not be. This interlude is important for each of you, as Chapter 5 will build on this moment. It's a moment of suspending all work, duty, toil, and even the effort of reading this book. It's the purest invitation I can offer to you—an invitation to remember and an invitation to receive.

Perhaps I should start with my own story of how Jesus found me. My earliest memories of God are from the pew of a Catholic church. I was a bony little thing, a little too tall for my age, and I didn't want to attract attention. The overarching theme of all these memories was hunger. We weren't allowed to eat before communion, so I never had breakfast on Sundays. We would stand up, sit down, kneel, and then stand up again. Each time we stood from a kneeling position, I would get dizzier. Sometimes I tried to hang onto the pew in front of me while we stood to keep from falling over as I became more lightheaded, but a single glance from my tall, solemn mother towering above me and I would snatch them off.

I remember seeing a figurine of Jesus above the priest's head. It was hard to look at him on the cross. I hated that He had to suffer so much for me, His head hanging to His right in a despairing posture.

I would pass out from low blood sugar at church often, causing my mother endless embarrassment and fury. Eventually, she got special permission from the priest to allow me to eat before communion. This was Christianity for me for a long time. Fear, shame, and self-denial to the point of self-harm for the letter of the law. I didn't know if I was more afraid of my priest, Mom, or God, but I was going to stay on the straight and narrow. Straight and narrow like a razor blade.

I would later attend the Lake Geneva youth camp. Sitting around the campfire, the camp counselor was sharing how Jesus loved me. That was the first time anyone had ever told me that I was worth loving. I "accepted Jesus into my heart" that night, as we call it in the church these days. I still remember the flames dancing around in that fire as I felt this lightness causing me to dance inside. I felt very self-conscious about what I was experiencing, and so I kept my stonewall game face on. Although I suddenly felt safe with Jesus, that didn't mean I felt safe with anyone else. That night I learned that Jesus loved me. But I didn't understand who He was loving.

I didn't realize at the time that there had been an exchange, an exchange of my filthy rags for his glorious, righteous, white garments. I still felt dirty, but I felt loved. I didn't understand everything yet.

I didn't understand my need to die to myself or the call to die to sin. I didn't see myself as a sinner, a victim of abuse, covered in shame, totally rooted in original sin and pride. I had yet to come to understand what needed to die—that was okay, it wasn't time yet.

> *I learned that Jesus loved me. But I didn't understand who He was loving.*

Fast forward to my front porch at twenty-eight years old.

My spiritual mentor, Elizabeth, shared the gospel with me, and I patted her on her arm and said, "Oh, I already know Jesus! I prayed to receive Jesus in 2nd grade at a bonfire. I know, I know, I know."

She left with a dubious look in her eyes. That look made me angry.

If I was truly in Christ, that exchange would not have made me angry. I would've experienced the love of Jesus Christ: *Thank you, Lord, that Elizabeth is sacrificing time to come share the gospel with me. Thank you, Father, that You have already brought me into a loving relationship with You.*

But instead I was indignant and offended. And truly underneath, I was mortified. What if I truly wasn't saved? What if God was having her knock on my door because He was knocking on my heart? No way would I be vulnerable with her—people weren't safe. So I continued attending Bible study with all the right answers to all the questions.

Then one night, our Bible study leader's wife asked if I'd read "Loving God" by Chuck Colson.

I responded, "Now, Kris, I don't need to read any other books about God. I just need the Bible; everything I need to know is there."

I didn't know what I didn't know, and it scared me. I was protecting my heart. But by the end of the night, I decided to take the book home with me and read it.

As I began the book, I had a dream. I was in Germany protecting Jewish children from going to the concentration camps. I had a very small flat home with an open floor plan. I felt very proud of myself because I was doing the right thing in protecting these children. Having been hurt as a child and called to protect children, I was fulfilling my mission. Suddenly there was a knock at the door. As I walked to the door, I could hear the boots of soldiers coming up the steps of my home, and there was nowhere for the children to truly hide in the small space. They cowered underneath the buffet table. I opened the door a crack. The soldier looked at me and then over my shoulder. I knew he saw the children under that table.

His eyes cut back to me. "Are you hiding Jewish children in this home?"

I paused for a long moment, and I woke up with a cold, sick feeling in my belly. For weeks, I talked with God about this. Why didn't I say anything? Why didn't I respond to that question? I know. I woke up too soon; I didn't have a chance. The answer was obvious: there was no reason for me to say anything. I had no peace, though; none of these theories sat well with me. I felt deeply troubled in my soul.

About a month into my private disturbance, I came to a section of Chuck Colson's book where Jesus has died on the cross, and the repentant sinner on the cross next to Him is waiting to die. Chuck paints this picture of soldiers standing underneath him deciding when to break his legs because it's almost sundown. He thinks, *How could they be talking about breaking my legs as if they're talking about what they are going to have for dinner??* Something grips his soul, *How could they not, for if I were them and they were me I would be doing the same thing.*[125]

At that moment, I fell to the floor and sobbed.

I knew why I didn't answer that soldier in my dream. Because if it was about trying to save those children's lives or trying to save mine, I would've tried to save mine. And in that moment, the Lord showed me the depth of my sin. He gave me this gift of understanding who He died for—a sinner, a wretched sinner who had nothing but the filthy rags she wore. All of my illusions of altruism and noble protectiveness, all of my right answers—all rags. All of my life was tainted with sin. To borrow the metaphor Ortlund uses in *Gentle and Lowly*, if sin were the color blue, I did not occasionally say or do something blue; all that I say, do, and think, even the best, had some taint of blue.[126] I now understood who Jesus was really loving when I met Him as a second grader by the campfire, and in that moment I withheld nothing from Him. I gave all of it to Him: my filthy rags, my pride, my hurt—all of it. I came up off of that floor clothed in the righteousness of Jesus Christ. He bought my life. He brought me to life.

I felt so free! I was completely seen, completely paid for, and completely loved. It really was finished.[127] All my struggling, all my doubt, all my useless attempts at goodness, and all my mistakes. I really understood who Jesus was. I understood His true love for me. I understood the

---

125 Colson, Charles W. *Loving God.* Zondervan, 1983.
126 Dane Calvin Ortlund. *Gentle and Lowly : The Heart of Christ for Sinners and Sufferers.* Wheaton, Illinois, Crossway, 2020, p. 47.
127 John 19:30

true nature of sin and that I was free from all of that! For the first time, everything came together. I was so deeply and completely forgiven, I was able to forgive others in my life.

The next thing I did after standing up was to pick up the phone to call my mother.

Through tears of joy, I exclaimed, "Mom! I forgive you for everything! Jesus has forgiven me of everything, so I can forgive you."

She did not believe she had done anything needing forgiveness, and she was still very skeptical about my explorations of anything outside of Catholicism, so she angrily responded, "I don't know what the **** you're talking about, Cheryl," and hung up on me.

I laughed when she hung up. I understood that she didn't know because five minutes earlier I didn't know! I laughed with joy at the release. I laughed with joy at the opportunity to immediately offer what I had just received. I felt weightless. Delight.

> *It didn't matter to me that she couldn't receive my forgiveness—it mattered that I gave it.*

It didn't matter to me that she couldn't receive my forgiveness—it mattered that I gave it.

This is the model Jesus showed me! He forgave. Period. The question that was left for me and for every human being is: Will I receive that forgiveness? When I receive it, I experience redemption—a big word that means I am now free of all guilt. When I receive it, I am bought by Jesus. Bought out of the marketplace of sin, darkness, and death.

I let Jesus buy me! And I hoped that one day Mom would let Jesus buy her. But my gift of forgiveness to her was simply an expression of the gift Jesus gave me. No strings attached.

What is happening for you as you hear my story? Perhaps this can be a moment of shifting into an open listening stance: To be curious on your own behalf and to tune into that quiet rustling in your own soul. Perhaps you are starting to experience the God who pursues.

If you have not met Him, allow me the profound honor of introducing you to Him. He has always known you and desires that you may know Him. As you "see" His face, you may find that He is familiar to you because He has been involved behind the scenes in your life since the very beginning. You bear His image; He has made you to be like Him.

He who made you, Love Himself, the Creator of the Universe, knows you inside and out. He knows the number of hairs on your head, and He loves you deeply.[128] He is more powerful than an ocean in a hurricane,[129] and He has tenderly caught every tear you have cried.[130] His thoughts about you outnumber the grains of sand on the beach.[131] He gives attention to clothing every flower, and takes notice when the smallest bird falls to the ground.[132] He says you are so much more precious to Him than those things, and He takes careful loving notice of every detail of your life.[133]

Perhaps this attention is uncomfortable to you, maybe there were those in your life whose attention always meant judgment, shame, punishment, or danger. God does not seek to find fault in His careful attention. It is more like how I saw my daughter-in-love run her fingers around the hairline of her newborn daughter, her eyes mapping every vein of the temple, adoring the eyelashes, and finding the tiny cupid's bow of an upper lip. Or how my son's eyes didn't leave his bride the first time we saw them together after their honeymoon. God delights in you even more than this. Scripture describes Him as singing over you with joy.[134]

The shame you may feel knowing you are unworthy of this love is alright. This love is still here for you. He took care of this part, too. He is holy, completely unstained and perfect, the highest Good that exists. We are not good, and we know this when we are honest with ourselves.

This difference separates us from love, and separation from God is death to the soul. We can feel it in part now while we live in our bodies, but after physical death that separation becomes permanent in what Scripture calls Hell. He is grieved by that separation, and He made a way to be with you. He loves you so much that He gave His only Son

---

128 Luke 12:7
129 Psalm 93:4
130 Psalm 56:8, Isaiah 53:4
131 Psalm 139:18
132 Luke 12:22-31
133 Matthew 10:29-31
134 Zephaniah 3:17

to die in your place and, with His power, raised Him from the dead on the third day.[135] Scripture tells us that it was for the joy set before Him that He endured the torture of crucifixion.[136] The joy set before Him was the joy of removing the separation between Himself and us. It was the joy of seeing you coming from a long way off and being able to run to greet you with a bear hug that picks you up and leaves a few of His tears on your shoulder.

He will not hold Himself back from you. He who did not withhold His own Son will not hold back from you.[137] He has done everything to show us how much He loves us and how far He is willing to go. How will you respond to Him? In this moment, you, like Peter, stand in the boat of your daily life, going about your business as he went about his day of fishing.

Jesus approaches, extends His hand to you, and says, "Follow Me."[138]

If you take Jesus' hand you are saying, "I want to be known by the One Who knows all things." You are saying yes to His path of both death and resurrection. Many have taken this path before you. You join the ranks of a multitude who now cheer you on from Heaven and from our various places on earth.[139] We who say yes to the eternal and turn our backs on the temporal become signposts that read: He is the way, the truth, and the life! Not me, not man, not religion, but Jesus. You are saying yes to the great exchange of your filthy rags for His righteous white robes.[140] You are saying no to your former life. You are saying no to being in charge. Following Him means you will now have a relationship with the One Who knitted you in your mother's womb.[141] We spend so much time on DNA studies and genealogy websites, filling in the blanks of our history. There is an innate longing in us to be known, fully. His is a delightful, sometimes terrifying, compelling and irresistible invitation to those who determine that nothing else matters as much as being enveloped by and living from Love Himself.

---

135 Romans 5:8, John 3:16, Mark 16
136 Hebrews 12:2
137 Romans 8:32
138 Matthew 4:19
139 Hebrews 12:1
140 Romans 13:14, Isaiah 64:6 Psalm 132:9
141 Psalm 139:13-14

You become unsnatchable![142] God performed the great separation for you. He separated you from your sin, separated as far as the east is from the west.[143] You are free to receive His love without concern for your former, rotting, spiritual stench; it is gone. The aroma of Christ is what the Father now smells; the righteousness of His Son is what He now sees.[144] And may I be the first, perhaps, to tell you that He delights in you getting to know Him as your Father. He is a Father who knows you, and calls you His child, who will leave the ninety-nine to go find you,[145] and will run to you when you turn towards Him.[146] He never stops waiting for you, loving you or being concerned for your transformation.[147] He desires to give you good gifts and already knows your thoughts and concerns before you have even known how to articulate them.[148] And on top of all that, He gives you part of Himself, His Spirit, to guide you, protect you, correct you and work through you.[149] During your dark storms of life He longs to gather you under His wings.[150] He will find you in the deepest pit and lift you out. He is the one that will turn your sorrow into laughter,[151] and is familiar with all of your griefs.[152] His love for you transcends ability to fully understand. This is your Daddy.[153] You are His child.

This is a moment of receiving I hope I am creating for you – to expand your ability to receive the infinite love of your Father. I understand that for some, that may have triggered you. I have encountered many father wounds among both the men and women we have ministered to. Bring Jesus into that part of your heart too. Allow God to infuse you with Himself, filling the cracks and gaps, creating wholeness you didn't even know could exist, stronger than any epoxy glue.

---

142 John 10:28
143 Psalm 103:12
144 2 Corinthians 5:21
145 Matthew 18:12-14
146 James 4:8, Luke 15:20
147 Isaiah 30:18, 2 Peter 3:9, Psalm 86:15
148 Matthew 7:9-11, Psalm 139:4
149 1 John 4:13,
150 Psalm 91:4, Matthew 23:37
151 Psalm 30:11
152 Isaiah 53:3-4
153 Romans 8:15

Over time you will experience that His promises are true, and He promises He will not abandon you. He tabernacles with you now and forever. Nothing can snatch you away from His tender, pursuing, everlasting love.[154] Nothing. You get to spend the rest of your days learning what it means to walk in the newness that He gives you in that love.

Are you ready for the journey of a lifetime? There will be times that it is hard, and there will be times of sheer delight. But one thing I can tell you is that the love that you have experienced today will go with you. Wherever He takes you, He will be with you.[155]

It's time to learn how to walk in that love. For those who have known Him for a long time and for those who chose to enter His arms in this very moment, it is time. Walking in that love creates rest. Let's rise from here and continue our journey.

---

154 Romans 8:38-39, Jeremiah 31:3
155 Matthew 28:20, Hebrews 13:5

CHAPTER FIVE

Abiding in the Vine

How do we rest?

I HOPE THAT while remembering your first moments with Jesus and His love for you, you experienced a little quiet and warmth in your soul. In the beginning, it's easy to experience strong emotions, including exuberant joy and deep peace as our sin is lifted for the first time. However, this initial euphoria wears off and then what? Abide. Resting in the finished work of Jesus sustains our relationship through the quieter moments and the rougher waters of life into deeper joys.

How do we rest? The short answer is "confession." That word may not feel like rest to you. It didn't to me either, for a long time.

∞ Good Confession ∞

One afternoon, during an all-day summer color guard practice, we took a snack break. We sat in a circle on the cool, smooth gym floor. It smelled like deodorant and the plastic gym mats curled up in the corner behind us. After everyone had eaten, I opened my Bible on my lap. I could see the spiritual hunger on the girls' faces. If there was ever a day I didn't give a devotional, more than one of them would ask me why I didn't, so I kept bringing my red tabbed Bible along with my flags, Gatorade, and sunscreen. They all slowly ended their conversations and waited expectantly.

I looked around and asked the girls to give me a word that came to mind for them when they heard the word "confession." It was quiet for a moment as their faces turned down, and they searched for words.

"Punishment." One of my bolder girls broke the silence.

"Hiding."

"Secret."

"Shame."

"Guilty." More and more voices joined with more of the same responses. The girls who didn't answer nodded along with the rest, several variations of pained or withdrawn facial expressions among them. I paused for a moment to make sure everyone had had a chance to speak their mind. I looked at each of them, listening to the heart cry beneath the words. I prayed for a moment and asked Him to loose this burden on them.

"Oh girls...," I began with compassion in my heart, hoping they could sense it. I remember when I, too, would have responded that way. I grew up with what my sister and I covertly called the "guilty Catholic conscience." No matter where I turned, I felt guilt, shame, and condemnation. Later in life, my Bible teacher described it as rather than having just a tender conscience, I had a hypersensitive conscience. It was a brutal way to live. This poorly regulated conscience made me continuously terrified that I would screw up. At the same time, I believed I couldn't admit I was wrong because there was no place safe for me to do so. It was quite the trap.

This was my opportunity to help re-regulate these tender consciences so that they would be trained to run *to* the Father rather than run *from* Him in their many future hours of need.

I continued, "What you are describing is what happens before repentance and confession, when we are hiding. He does not stand aloof and huffing with arms crossed. When we confess, He is overjoyed! He pleads with us to come to Him and share our weaknesses, our infirmities, our places of sneaking and stealing and lying and jealousy. All of it! He can handle it all. And He knows it all already. He delights to see us coming, and He runs to us like the father ran to the prodigal son.[156] He loves when we take delight in Him.[157] We feel the

---

156 Luke 15:20
157 Psalm 37:4, John 4:14

pain of our own hiding and sin and think this is God. This guilt and pain you feel is not from God, this is the consequence and the pain of the hiding."

I looked down to my Bible and began to read:

There is therefore no condemnation for those who are in Christ Jesus. (Romans 8:1)

If we confess our sins, he is faithful and just and will forgive us our sins. (1 John 1:9)

God forgives the guilt of our sins. (Psalm 32:5)

Once we repent, the Lord brings times of refreshment! (Acts 3:19)

I looked up periodically to see if it was landing for them. Can't go too long, or it could get preachy. I saw earnest expressions, drinking in the Scripture, and the hope that it brought. Together, we were parsing out the difference between condemnation and conviction. The two were getting conflated and confused in their minds. The relief was palpable as the words of God were like a balm to their bruised and raw consciences, not unlike my guilty Catholic conscience.[158]

In my years of discipleship and being discipled, I have found that this moment with the girls reflects the angst that so many have in their faith journey, and it affects members of all denominations. It's a moment of possible stall out and confusion. We ask, "What happened to me? I came to know Jesus, so why does He seem like a stranger to me? Why am I still sinning? Why do I find myself in darkness? Do I even know Him at all?" And when we can't figure out the answer to these questions, we settle into the stall. We become stuck.

Two weeks before writing this chapter, I was in Philadelphia to speak to a group of believers who were passionate for the Lord. There were pastors, city leaders, business leaders, and even tribal leaders from other countries joining us for a single purpose of intense prayer and edification for the sake of spiritual revival in Philly. I had checked my PowerPoint 100 times. I went over my opening statements again and again. But I didn't feel settled. I prayed. I recognized that I needed the courage to let God be the one to minister to the people directly. So I let go of the reins.

I looked out at the room. I saw eagerness in their eyes. They were hungry. Hungry for what, I wondered? "Lord, meet them. Feed them."

---

158 John 8:32

I stepped out from behind the podium; I stopped trying to be "the speaker." I took out my meager two loaves worth of grace and mercy and trusted that somehow God would multiply and distribute to all who had need however much was required.

And then something happened. A holy hush. I had never experienced it before. The room was perfectly still. But it was not a silence of boredom or checking out. I didn't know what it was, so I asked. A woman chimed in—she was in awe. Others nodded. Something was awakening in them. Something that had become sleepy, perhaps even dormant was stirring.

Next, I told them the story of Rosa Parks. When she was asked why she didn't give up her seat on the bus, she replied that she was tired of tolerating the way things were.[159] I asked them, "What are you tired of tolerating?"

I shared the process of the 7 Step Shift® with them, which I will share with you soon, and then the audience paired up with one another. I encouraged them to take 1 minute each to share and confess to one another, and then instructed them to take 2 minutes to pray for one another. At the end of the process, they declared the truth to each other about God as relevant to each situation. The volume of the room slowly rose throughout the exercise, excitement swelling.

As I left the front stage, I asked these brothers and sisters if we could please remind one another of Shabbat Shalom. Someone started singing the song "Shabbat Shalom", and more voices joined him. Before I could make it down the aisle, the entire room was on its no longer tired feet, dancing, praising, singing, crying, hugging. God multiplied, met, fed, and strengthened that group of believers. I shared nothing with them except the gospel Himself.

Oh God... I'm asking the same prayer now, Lord, for the reader. Lord, meet him. Lord, feed her. Multiply my meager offering and be magnified in their hearts. Expand their little vessels to receive what You have for them. Whatever they need, I trust You will meet them on this page. The purity of Your gospel cuts through anything. Anything. We are so gunked up. But You are so good, so pure.

The following is what I shared with them. Here we go.

---

[159] ""The Only Tired I Was, Was Tired of Giving In." | OUPblog." *OUPblog*, 22 Apr. 2013, blog.oup.com/2010/12/rosa-parks/.

∞ Remember. Return. Rejoice. ∞

At age 28, I became unfettered from all of my personal quests, concerns, hurts, betrayals, losses, and secret sins. All of it just washed away. I was light. Carefree. Like a little girl dancing with butterflies in an open field. His burden was what He promised—light. His yoke felt easy. My movement through life was simple. I was clean.

All too soon that moment gave way to duties, frustrations, tiredness, and broken promises. My fresh start became a mess. I didn't read my Bible enough. I didn't pray for people I said I would pray for. You get the idea. Freedom turned into to-do lists and even a sense of obligation.[160] I was getting lots of instruction on how to act like a Christian. I felt like I was losing myself to the demands of the faith. I was going to Bible studies, I was serving, I was reading my Bible, I was giving, I was trying really hard not to sin. As you look at my growing list, what are you feeling in yourself? When I asked the group in Philly that question, this is what I heard: Frustrated, tired, irritated, useless, hopeless, weary.

What would be your words?

I felt all of those. And I tried harder for a while, but then I quit. I knew something was off, but I couldn't figure out what it was. Where was my joy? Where was my relief? Where was my peace?

Then it hit me. I was hiding behind good behavior. I was making up for my feelings of lack and my history of failures through my good works. After all, didn't Jesus say he had set before us good works in advance that we would complete?[161] Didn't He say to not grow weary in doing good?[162] Didn't He say to carry the cloak of the enemy that extra mile,[163] forgive 70x7 times,[164] and so much more? Didn't He say all those things?

He did.

But you see, the relationship was swallowed up by duty rather

---

160 Galatians 5:1 "Stand firm then and do not allow yourselves to be burdened again by a yoke of slavery."
161 Ephesians 2:10
162 Galatians 6:9
163 Matthew 5:41
164 Matthew 18:22

than service flowing out of the relationship. Somewhere, somehow, I reversed this and returned to a works-based mentality. If we live there for a long time, this can become what feels like drifting away from the faith in our exhaustion.

This was revealed to me when I read Galatians—they were being called foolish for having started in the Spirit and then returning to the Law. That got my attention. That sounded like me. Cross the T's. Dot the I's. Yep, that sounded like law to me.

So I stopped everything I was doing. Stopped teaching, stopped trying to read the Bible for x amount of minutes every day, and stopped worrying about all of my prevailing sinful behaviors of jealousy, coveting, etc. I stopped all focus on those things. I shifted.

I remembered.

I turned my eyes to Jesus, who was, is, and always will be the author and the perfecter of my faith.[165] And in that moment of stopping, I began to abide. I didn't know about the word "abide" yet. But I knew that's what I needed to do. I confessed that all my works are like those filthy rags. I confessed that it was He who saved me, and nothing has changed since that moment. He saved me when I was in the middle of sinning, of screwing up, of shirking responsibilities. I didn't know the depth of my need for Him then, and I still don't know the depth of my need for Him now. That's part of the beauty. For every new understanding, I get to embrace the gift I have already received at a deeper level. It becomes more priceless to me as time goes on, as I live more years, and as I recognize my stumblings more often.

Paul, not directly but indirectly, talks about this in his own journey. He first introduces himself as the least of the apostles.[166] Then the least of the saints,[167] and finally, by the end of his life, he calls himself the chief of sinners.[168] But never, never does he stop calling himself a child of God.[169]

I was trying to be perfect instead of walking in His perfection. I was

---

165 Hebrews 12:2
166 1 Corinthians 15:9-11
167 Ephesians 3:8
168 1 Timothy 1:15-16
169 Romans 8:15-17

trying to prove I was worthy of this gift. What a trap! Paul understood this trap and called the Galatians, whom he loved dearly, foolish for stepping into the trap of running a race, carrying a load that God never intended for us. I had joined the ranks of foolish thinking.

Abide. Such a mysterious word to me for so many years. I didn't realize the simplicity of abiding. And the importance of it. I got tripped up in my red cape of self-reliance and my bias for action. "What do I *do* to abide? How do I know when I'm doing it?" The concept of *being with* was foreign to me. Abiding would remain a mystery for me while my understanding of God's love for me remained veiled.

I remember my mom asking me to just sit with her towards the end of her life. No way was I gonna do that! I would take care of her appointments, research the cancer, navigate the paperwork, cook, clean the house, or coordinate visits, but don't you dare ask me to just sit with you. That was too scary to consider and should be avoided at all costs.

So there I was, taking the way I interacted with those in authority over me into my relationship with Christ, who was now my Commander in Chief. And my job? Serve! Duty! Action! But sit with Him?

And yet there was Jesus, patting the blue couch just like my mom did, and asking me "Come sit with Me." And for many years I said, "No way."

But when I stopped, I really stopped. I said, "Okay, Jesus, I'm going to sit with You." The honest truth was I couldn't do that *until* I stopped. All of my activities, as beautiful as they were, done with complete sincerity up to that point, were attached to a need that I couldn't quite name. It was too deep for me to reach.

This moment of stopping was the first time I practiced the mystery of abiding. But I still didn't quite understand what He was leading me to do. Stopping and sitting with Him was a good restart, but I needed a new compass for reentering the commotion of daily life. I wanted to follow the way of His streams in the desert.[170]

And then it hit me.

Abide simply means I remain in the rest Jesus gave me. I am in Him,

---

170 Isaiah 43:19

and He is in me.[171] That's it. It means that Jesus did what I couldn't.[172] It means that now that it's done, I can't undo it.[173]

As we get deeper into resting in the truth of that finished work, our expression of it will become more varied and nuanced. This can look like bringing your mind again and again to still waters to drink in thoughts about what He has done, the finished work. It could be meditating on how He has made you, what you are becoming, His promises, how deep His love is for you, and how nothing could separate you from that love. But most of all, it is acknowledging that He is *with* us at all times, in all moments, and *being* present with Him. He is Emmanuel, and He is with us in our quiet times but also in our cars, our walks, our phone calls, our diaper changing, our working, our key/phone hunts, our doing dishes, our cooking, our meetings, our celebrating, our grieving. Our assurance comes from our abiding, not from our doing.

> *Our assurance comes from our abiding not from our doing.*

Paul and Silas sat in a jail cell with their feet in shackles, buried under injustices, sore and hurting from a brutal beating, but they chose to sing. When the earth's shaking came, their chains fell off, and the door sprang open; they did not even think to leave. For them it was more about who was there; they used their freedom to talk to everyone there about Jesus. How could they possibly have this mindset? They were completely at rest in Jesus even though their bodies had none.

Abiding is simply a constant, perpetual declaration that He is with me. He is worthy of all praise, honor, glory, adoration, and awe. And in the face of every doubt, feeling, or circumstance that may speak to the contrary, He does love me, He lives within me, and I seek to surrender more into His love and His glorious work both in and through me. I continue to decrease, and He continues to increase.[174] The rest is His completed work. He has sat down at the right hand of the Father, and

---

171 John 17:21-23
172 2 Corinthians 5:21, John 14:6, Romans 5:9, Matthew 5:17
173 John 10:28-29
174 John 3:30

there is no more work to do.[175] No more sacrifices. No more bloodshed. No more striving. No more working for your peace. We resist trying to earn anything—love, acceptance, assurance. Instead, when we rest we perpetually live in a receiving posture. We can live in fight or flight with our fists balled up, ready to defend and demand, or we can walk through life with our hands open to what He, the Giver of good and perfect gifts, will give us.

Do you doubt that you're worthy? Declare His worthiness. Abide.

You screwed up? Go to the throne of grace in your time of need. Abide.

Have you become aware of a new sin pattern or reengage in an old sin pattern? Confess immediately and ask for your affection for Jesus to grow stronger. Abide.

Do you feel lost? Forsaken? Betrayed? Remember that Jesus will never forsake you or leave you. Abide.

And once you recall that truth, you live FROM that truth. You live IN that truth. That truth is living. That truth wants to shape your every thought, your every movement, your every everything.

Train (Paideia as referenced earlier about discipline) to have the finished work of Christ, which you received, consume your life. Every discourse, every disappointment, every deed.

And as we abide, we become fruit bearers. We are more patient, more loving, more kind, more self-controlled.[176] The flesh that has ruled our lives and trampled others' lives is quieted. It's not in charge anymore. This happens because the soul is experiencing a steadfast security, nestled in the heart of Jesus Christ because it is determined to abide. It's no longer in survival mode. It lives to abide.

This concept of abiding is central to living the life that God promises. Not church attendance. Not singing, serving, or suffering. None of it. Anybody can go to church, but not all will be changed. Anyone can serve, but not all will reflect Christ. Everyone will suffer, but not everyone will open themselves to how God can work even through our suffering. It isn't the doing of any of those things but rather Who you do it with. The difference between a life "on fire for God" and a

---

175 Hebrews 10:12
176 Galatians 5:22-23

lukewarm faith is abiding. You cannot work yourself into being on fire with the strength of your own passion; you will burn out.

And how crazy is it to think that abiding means to stay put—no matter what. We choose to be immovable in the finished work of Jesus.[177] We have nothing to prove to anyone. Nothing. We declare this continuously to ourselves. Instead, we have one job—to continually receive the love of Christ into our souls. That love shapes us into His image and empowers us to serve others around us from that image-bearing position.

Below is the ministry's Contending versus Cooperating model, which very succinctly depicts what I am describing.

Working for Rest or Working from Rest

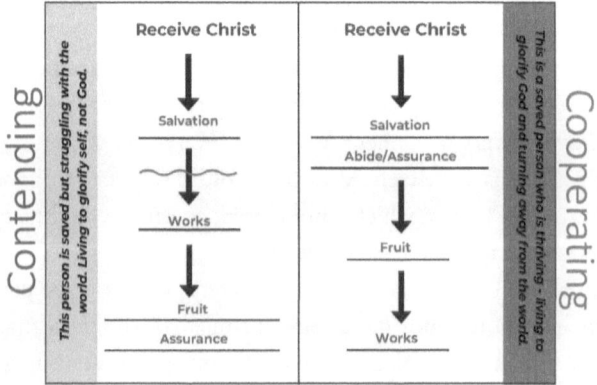

Somehow we wind up on the left column. Like the beloved, foolish Galatians, we forget that the work is already done. We have our salvation secured in Jesus, but we forget, and so we start trying to work to secure our salvation by our own strength—after all, faith without works is dead, right?[178] Then we hope that our works create some fruit—you know, the fruit that will not burn at the time of our judgment. And if we don't see it happening the way we think it should, we raise our hand to re-profess our faith because maybe it didn't "take" the first time. Maybe I'm not really saved. Maybe my screw-up was too big for God.

---

177 1 Corinthians 15:58, Ephesians 4:14, 2 Corinthians 11:3, 1 John 2:24
178 James 2:26

Or maybe I'm just being a beloved, foolish, little Galatian and need to remember that the work was already done by Jesus and that is enough.

Once we remember, "Oh yeah, this is not what living for Christ is supposed to look and feel like," we return. Return to what? We return to our rest in Christ's finished work. Rest that He restored our relationship to the heavenly Father. Rest that is permanent, eternal. Rest that originates from Jesus. Rest that gives us permission to wait upon the Lord to have our strength renewed.[179] Rest that declares that no matter how long, how hard, or how much we must endure, we have hope that is eternal.[180]

And as I abide, I experience powerful, stamina-making assurance. I can withstand and turn away from the temptations, the verbal assaults, the excruciating pain, the interminable wait for a diagnosis—all of it. I can live through it because I am living in Christ. I remain immovable in my position. Steadfast.

We call the left column *contending*. On that side, we are saying that what God did was not enough. That somehow we have to add to the finished work of Christ. We call the right-hand column *cooperating* because this position is where we are declaring that God said it is finished, we believe it, and we will stand firm in it.

At any moment we might find that we are forgetting and beginning to think we've got to add to God's finished work. In a momentary lapse of spiritual lucidity, we begin to tell ourselves that God is not enough and that we have to be more. As soon as we become aware that our peace is evaporating, and we are instead experiencing any of those things described earlier (our symptoms), it becomes an opportunity to shift over to the right-hand column.

The more mature we are, the faster we recognize when we are contending and the faster we want to return to cooperating. That is the goal. We do not condemn ourselves by asking why we are so weak? Why did we got off track? Why we blah blah blah? Run to Him. Don't give the sin of unbelief even a second thought. It deserves no energy.

---

179 Isaiah 40:31
180 Romans 8:18

∞ Again and Again and Again ∞

We will inevitably return to a way of toil, but every time we also get the opportunity to return to our rest again and again and again. Whether with striving vs. rest, a sin struggle, or a personal tendency, it can be discouraging to revisit something we already learned. Plaguing thoughts like "I thought I was past this" or "I haven't grown or changed at all" may fill our minds. Some version of dejection, failure, disappointment, or shame enters and tramples our well-being. It can cause that wick to flicker again. I am hoping this next tool serves to encourage you. The question is not "Why am I here again?" but instead "Am I recognizing it faster? Do I want to lean into Christ in these moments, or do I want to avoid Him?"

To help folks identify whether they are stuck or not, we created something we call the snail framework. God does not keep us stuck in spiritual eddies.[181] His movement is forward advancement and growth. Many times it seems like we are dealing with the same thing over and over again, but it is more like a spiral staircase than a never-ending loop.

Enter: the snail. It seems sometimes that we revisit the same thing over and over again.[182] And that can make us feel stuck. I want to distinguish between the stuck where we don't have any movement and the perceived stuck where we're revisiting something that we thought we had overcome before.

I have drawn here a spiral or something like a snail shell with the letter C in the center. I have also added these dots along the way within the spiral of the snail shell with an arrow to demonstrate the direction of movement. That dot represents anything that you are working on in your faith. It could be not judging someone or not telling white lies or having control over your anger; fill in with anything.

What is one of the things in your walk with Jesus that just keeps tripping you up? You've made progress, you maybe even think it's fully behind you, and then you seem to stumble and fall. Maybe even write it in the margin here.

---

181 Philippians 1:6, Isaiah 34:19, 2 Peter 3:18
182 Proverbs 24:16, Romans 7:15-25

This can make us feel very stuck. But ask yourself the following questions to help you differentiate whether or not you're truly stuck or just battling "Is it happening less frequently? Do you recognize it more quickly? Do you desire to get out of that behavior faster? If the answer to those questions is yes, you are not stuck; you are moving towards that center of Christlikeness.[183] So while you may revisit that same thing, you revisit it at a deeper level. You are being transformed into His likeness!

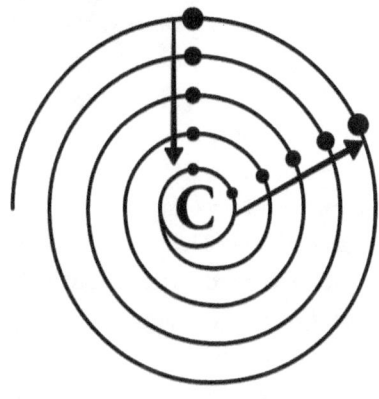

But if, as you continue revisiting something, you deny it, dwell in it longer, and resist moving beyond it, then you're not moving towards Christlikeness – you are stuck.

A righteous man will stumble. And he will get up. And he will get up again. And he will get up again, and again, and again.[184] My desire for you, my desire for myself, is that when I stumble I will turn to Him, I will confess, and I will get up and keep walking.[185]

If I live on one of those outer layers with something, and I believe that's as deep as I can go with that concept, there is no more opportunity for growth or healing, no more opportunity for anything. So every time this comes up, maybe it's anger at a mother or father, maybe it's a trigger from an injustice that was done to you or your family that still is held somewhere deep in the recesses of your heart, or maybe it's something about your temperament that you believe is unchangeable but is causing damage. Perhaps there's some repetitive behavior that's genuinely hurting those whom you love, but you feel you cannot stop. These are places where we remain on the outside of that snail shell. We can tell we are stuck because there's no movement towards Christlikeness in this area—we are stalled out.

---

183 Ezekiel 36:26, Hebrews 3:15
184 Proverbs 24:16
185 Hebrews 4:16

I am sure I have many, many areas in my life where I'm still stuck that I am not aware of. And that doesn't scare me. It doesn't drive me to spin my wheels. I don't need to go looking under every rock in every corner of my heart all the time; I can let the constant vigilance go. This, too, is rest. Because in God's good time and perfect way, He will reveal what I need to know. We can trust Him with our sanctification journey. When He does reveal those things, I get the opportunity to respond to them. I reflect on what's going on in my life, I receive what He's giving to me, and I respond to that with my life.

The fullness of joy comes in the intimacy of our relationship with our Lord and Savior. To be able to pause and watch the leaves dance in the breeze, the sunlight flicker on the water, the birds catch a small thermal, and the squirrel feasting on his freshest acorns. And to say, no matter the storms about, no matter the enemies that threaten to pounce, no matter any or all of the worldly cares or concerns, we experience what Karl Barth describes as defiant joy.[186] How is that possible? Because it flows from a heart that is abiding and sees from eyes that are fixed on Jesus.

∞ Blessed Assurance ∞

The last stage on the left-side of the Contending versus Cooperating model is assurance. I mentioned it briefly as I encouraged you to abide. I want to take a moment here to address a symptom that soul after soul has confessed in the privacy of living rooms and quiet coffee shop corners:

> They do not have true assurance of salvation.

If you are living with this fear, this lack of security, it is no wonder you are tired. The amount of energy you must be expending on fighting, intentionally ignoring, or solving this must be exhausting. How can you possibly rest even for a second if you don't know that your

---

186 Barth, Karl. *The Epistle to the Philippians*. SCM Press, 16 Oct. 2012.

days will end in rest? An eternal mindset is one of the key elements of living from rest, but with this struggle, it is almost impossible to have an eternal mindset. Every time you think about eternity, there is a distinct *un*rest, so you actively try not to think about it.

This is one of the surest signs you are living in the contending column. Unfortunately, we have trained young believers to live there. Think about it: if you got saved in the context of the church, what did you hear next?

You have to find a good church, you have to read your Bible every day, you have to have devotional time every day, oh, and make it happen in the morning because that's when Jesus got away to the Father, you have to get in a small group, you have to get plugged in to serve, you have to share your testimony (nevermind learning how to write your testimony!), you have to attend Evangelism Explosion class so you can learn how to share your faith. Have to, have to, have to... Right?

No!

That's what church instruction told you to do. That's what well-meaning people told you to do. That's what a performance mindset told you to do. That's exactly what pride in the flesh would want you to do so you can check boxes and feel really good about yourself. That's what the Galatians were doing. "I have to go out and make things happen. If I can check enough boxes this week, I can call that fruit. If my kids are perfect and I say all the right things to my spouse, then I am going to have assurance that I'm really saved."

This is a life-stealing lie.

We turn to our mentors in fear, and they send us to book of 1 John, or the James passage "I will show you my faith by my works." It's true that faith without works is dead, but those works are only outward signs of an inward reality. The faith and the works are not the same; the faith spurs the works. Not guilt, not fear. Those works are not where our peace is found.

These are the kinds of burdens laid upon us by man-made religion. When men try to reach God on their own or use God's name to seize control and power, they create paths of self-righteousness that detour us from peace and rest. We can become enslaved by someone else's teaching or a spirit of darkness. God had to come to us. And this is why I don't want you to put your complete trust in my words or in any pastor or in anyone besides our High Priest Jesus. That's why I want to create all of these Selah prayer asides for you; that's why I want to empower you to listen to His voice. There are not many roads to God, only one narrow road, but there are so many roads with signposts claiming His name that can often leave us completely bound hand and foot with anxiety and striving trying to figure out which is truly the narrow road. The confusion can be terrifying. We can draw comfort from God's own words in Hebrews – that in these last days, He has spoken through His Son and we are to listen to Him.[187] You and I are to abide by Jesus' finished work. Nothing more and nothing less. Doctrinal concerns, theological differences, religious conflicts will remain until we no longer see dimly.[188] When the confusion strikes, return to the core of your faith: Jesus. It is there we find rest, once again.

We've worked really hard. It makes us tired. We've manufactured plastic fruit of some kind, and then we finally get to feel like we are really saved. Maybe. Like the shiny fake apples that used to sit in my mom's basket on our dining room table, this kind of fruit has no nutritional value for anyone—not for us nor the recipient of the work.

And then what happens when you inevitably sin or stop producing? Or even if you revert in a more dramatic way like Mary Magdalene in the controversial scene in *The Chosen* in which she gets triggered and leaves Jesus's side, returning to her old patterns?[189] See footnotes for the link. This is a fictional expansion of the story which is not in Scripture but represents a very real scenario for many people struggling to follow Jesus. She tells herself dozens of lies that keep her from returning to Jesus: "He already saved me once [He won't forgive me again]. I do have faith in Him, just not in me. I can't look up. I can't live up to it. I can't face Him." But Jesus welcomed her back and forgave her. Like

---

187 Hebrews 1:1-4
188 1 Corinthians 13:12
189 Come and See Foundation, Season 2, Episode 6 (Unlawful) Jesus saves Mary again: https://www.youtube.com/watch?app=desktop&v=yMMzDIiBy4g; Mary's original salvation moment: https://youtu.be/2R_odI1FWgk

Mary, you can look up at Him because you don't have to live up to anything. You are redeemed now and forever.

There is a living, delicious fruit that comes out of a walk with a God who loves you with an everlasting love, who can never stop loving you. We do start to make choices to spend more time with the Lord, to serve, to exhibit the fruit of the Spirit, but it does not come from us alone. Sometimes it's immediate; sometimes it takes time. The hiccups, setbacks, and burps in this process are not an indication of a lack of salvation but simply evidence that the good work is not yet complete (which is true for every believer who still walks this earth, by the way). We participate, but we can't do it without Him. When I became a believer, the first thing to go was my dirty mouth. I suddenly went from cursing every other word to flinching when I heard others take His name in vain. But I didn't grit my teeth and make it stop out of a "should" or to prove anything.

What happens for you when you hear an altar call from the pulpit? If you are one of those who feel compelled to raise your hand, if you feel fear of Hell, you are a part of the group I am talking to right now. I can't assuage your fear; I don't know if you are in Christ or not. But I can tell you that you are contending with God. Move to the right column, whether for the first time or the 50th. I long for you to experience the relief of resting in the finished work of Jesus.

When Jesus gave up His Spirit on the cross, He cried out with a loud voice and said, "It is finished." Finished! Period. Done. Hallelujah!! When we lean into this heavy yoke of working for our assurance, we ask, "But is it really finished?"[190]

We call the cross not enough and try to add to it. Jesus is seated at the right hand of God; His work is finished, and there is nothing we can add to it.[191] He gives us His complete righteousness; He took on the punishment for our peace, and our work is to allow more and

> *When we lean into this heavy yoke of working for our assurance, we ask, "But is it really finished?"*

---

190 John 19:30
191 Mark 16:19, Romans 8:34, Hebrews 12:2

more of Him to manifest in us.[192] There are two ways striving is used in Scripture: "strive against sin" and "stop striving against Me."[193]

Sometimes in order to start something, we begin with stopping something else, to make room for the new start. If we want to stop toiling, let's remove thoughts and language that say what He did wasn't good enough, that you're not worthy of what He did so you can't accept it. I wonder what is possible for you and me when we simply remove that kind of language/thinking from our vocabulary.

Some of you may not have one watershed moment that you can look back on when you crossed from death to life. Look at my story. Was I saved at Lake Geneva? Was I saved on my kitchen floor after I had my dream? Was I saved sometime after that when I fully yielded my self-reliance to Him or surrendered unrecognized parts of my heart? It doesn't matter. It does not matter.

We confuse the theology of "once saved always saved" with the ongoing sanctification process. We forget that we are in a perpetual state of being made whole. He is holding us in that state. It is an ongoing work. Scripture talks about us looking forward to the day of our salvation,[194] implying a future day of completion. God's words position us in rest as we learn to confidently stand on His promise that He who began this good work in us – *in you* – will be faithful to complete it. Let's "yes" and "amen" the following two passages together. I am reading it out loud as I write this – imagine my voice joining yours:

"And I am sure of this, that He who began a good work in you *will* bring it to completion at the day of Jesus Christ." Philippians 1:6

"All that the Father gives me *will* come to me, and whoever comes to me I will *never* [no, not ever] cast out." John 6:37[195]

My assurance is not in my salvation moment, it is in my abiding. It is all in Jesus; it's up to Him to know the moment. I trust that as I follow and put all my hope in Him, He will not walk me down the narrow road just to leave me outside Heaven's door. He is the one who

---

192 Isaiah 53:5, 2 Corinthians 4:10
193 Hebrews 12:4, Psalm 46:10, Acts 26:14
194 Hebrews 9:28
195 Brackets added from translation of original language. Suggested reading: "Gentle and Lowly" by Dane Ortlund Chapter 6 for more explanation and beautiful teaching on this verse.

Abiding in the Vine 101

will carry me in. I live following Jesus and putting my trust in Him daily. That is what salvation is: daily trusting Jesus. I will paraphrase Pastor JD Greear's words here: I wasn't saved 30 years ago on my floor or 50 years ago next to a fire; I was saved 2000 years ago on a hill called Golgotha. You do not need to know the day you took the first step towards following Jesus; what matters is that you are following Him today. Take the next step and follow Him. And the next step and follow Him.

Take it off, the patchwork conglomeration of works and memories or numbing distractions that assuage the fear, and put on the righteousness of Christ. Let the quilt of fire insurance faith fall from your hands like Linus' security blanket when he dropped it before his famous recitation in the Charlie Brown Christmas episode. Instead, put your hand on Jesus' head like a sinner would put their hand on the head of the sacrificial lamb at the altar in the Old Testament before its slaughter for sacrifice.[196] Wear His righteousness only.[197] Trust Him now; put your full weight on Him now, not only for your justification at the moment of salvation but for every moment that comes after.

If you have any kind of personal history of a relationship with God, know that we may only approach Him under the blood of Jesus. He has been drawing us to Him. He intercedes for us constantly on the basis of His shed blood. He is the One who began a good work in us and will bring it to completion.[198] He is the author and finisher of our faith.[199]

I keep saying His name, I keep saying "Him" because *He* calls us out, dear one. Our faith rests in the person and character of Jesus, not a ritual or a certain prayer, but Him Himself. How kind He is that He came. How wonderful that He cared for us enough to draw us out, that He is strong enough to keep us and wise enough to guide us into all righteousness. Keep following; keep trusting. Stop striving; abide in His love. As much as I want to, I can't fix this doubt for you, but He can. If the fear still clings, if this way of thinking is so familiar it feels set

---

[196] Leviticus 1:4, Leviticus 4:33, Greear, J D. *Stop Asking Jesus into Your Heart How to Know for Sure You Are Saved.* Nashville, Tennessee, B & H Publishing Group, 2018.
[197] Romans 13:14
[198] Phillipians 1:6
[199] Hebrews 12:2

in stone, ask Him to do what you cannot. Ask Him to be strong where you are weak.[200] Ask Him to lift it off of you and cast it into the sea.

∞ Into the Sea ∞

This is a prayer I modeled for a young woman I discipled who had been in the faith for a long time but could not find peace. We had returned to this point multiple times over the years. I listened, asked questions, and walked alongside her through it. We prayed together that He would lift the doubt from her. She had prayed the sinner's prayer more times than she could count, she had markers in her Bible about security of salvation, and she could preach a sermon on assurance from all of the encouragement and wise counsel she had received, but she could not shift out of this fear. It kept everything else she knew about faith at a degree of separation. Joy and peace were things she longed for and knew could be hers in Christ, but she could never allow herself to rest in them for very long. The fear would return.

During another conversation about this, I finally asked her, "What is left for you to surrender?"

At first she thought the answer was willingness to endure a variety of scenarios involving imaginary suffering.

With the benefit of knowing her well, I started shaking my head. "Honey, He's not asking you to do any of those things right now. What could you surrender about your life today?"

She was quiet for a moment, thinking through the way she lived her life. I prayed as we paused. *What are You doing here, Lord?* Then I had an idea.

"What about your rebellious spirit?"

She laughed, and I started laughing, too, at the smile she couldn't wipe off her face.

"You're even proud of it!" I reflected.

But then things got more serious as she considered the implications of those words. He revealed to her that there was still a rebel flag planted

---

200 2 Corinthians 12:9

in one of the back rooms of her heart. There was a quiet determination that although He was Lord in name and it was His house, she would be the decider. Her plan was to obey Him, but with the almost unspoken caveat that if there was ever something she really didn't like, she reserved the right to change her mind. She was going to follow, but she was going to follow Him her way. God was insistently poking at that closed fist, using even this spiritually disabling fear for good, although the enemy intended it for evil.[201]

She told me how she was swimming in the ocean a day or so after we met when a song[202] came to mind based on Isaiah 43, which was one of the first verses that had resonated with her as a child. She pulled away to be by herself and went on a walk. As she began walking, she heard low thunder over her right shoulder. She felt as though it was His own dear voice, a personal reference to previous prayer times. She began their conversation by surrendering the rebellious spirit and all her plans and fears. Her peace finally came, unbinding her soul and allowing new breath. The salt smelled just a little saltier, and the waves crashing in joyful expression of their power seemed like they danced for her. Delight.

The rest of the walk was spent sharing memories of the ways He had drawn her and their relationship together. With each step, she became more convinced that He had begun a good work in her and He was sanctifying her. She finally believed that He was with her. The thundercloud never shaded her path, and the way before her was so bright in the sun that the distance became lost in a warm haze of reflection of waves and sand. She felt as though she was seeing the way that her walk with Him would never end; she could finally allow herself to believe she would end her days with Him because she finally knew He was with her there. He cast the fear into the sea.

"I am with you always."

Her position in Christ is now, after many years, solid and secure. Was she saved before? Who is to know the moment she was born into eternity but God Himself? But she does know she rests in Him now. I hope that something in this chapter has helped you to feel more rooted

---

201 Genesis 50:20
202 Assad, Audrey. *Nothing to Fear*. Porter's Gate, 2019.

and grounded in the love that is yours in your own position in Christ.[203] That something helped you "know in your knower" or sink truth from your head deep into your heart. Our next stop will be to take a good, loving look at what your Jesus-responsibility is towards others. This will not flow from your position in church, your family, your community, your workplace. There is only one position that matters—and that is your position in Christ. All activity and attitudes in any of your roles now flow out of that position in Christ.

But before we do that, I'm sensing a need to breathe here.

Would you be willing to go back through this chapter and underline the one thing, just one thing, that will help you to remember to abide and train to become immovable in Christ?[204]

> ### Selah Moment
>
> Now, would you be willing to practice confession before the Father and confess where you have moved away from that position and how you are ready to move back into your proper position of abiding in the finished work?

---

203 Ephesians 3:17
204 1 Corinthians 15:58

CHAPTER SIX

Responsibility and Relationships

What are you responsible for in your relationships?

IF I TOLD you you were responsible *for* the relationships around you, how would you respond to that?

How about this:

If I told you that you were responsible *to* the relationships around you, how would you respond to that?

Intrigued?

I'm excited to talk about this topic with you. This chapter focuses substantially on the horizontal relationships as an outgrowth of what is happening in our vertical relationship with the Lord, which Scriptures call "one anothering." Before we can "one another" well, it is helpful to reset our relationship to the word "responsibility."

The story of the rich young ruler recalibrated me in my relationships. To recap the story, this young man comes to Jesus and asks what good thing he must do to have eternal life. After clarifying that only God is good and discussing the commandments, Jesus instructs him to sell all that he has and follow Him. The man goes away sad; he does not follow Jesus.

I want you to pay attention to what does not happen after he makes his choice. There is something conspicuously absent between verses 22 and 23 in Matthew chapter 19. There is no further interaction with the ruler. Jesus doesn't correct the man's thinking. He doesn't run after him. He doesn't guilt him into a forced admission. He doesn't threaten him. Instead, He respects the rich young ruler enough to just… let him go.

Jesus actually demonstrated three things with the ruler: First, He told the truth. He didn't sugarcoat it. Second, He felt love and great compassion for the man. Remember, Jesus knew better than anyone else what the consequence of this man's choice would be and was arguably the most motivated to save him from that outcome. Third, even so, He respected the man's decision to leave. Love respects the free will of the other person. Love does not manipulate or try to control.[205]

The relieving conclusion I drew is that we are supposed to show up with integrity and love to an interaction, but we let the other person sort things out for themselves. This release expanded my ability to minister to so many more people and protected me from burnout more than once. Some call this the "pace of grace" by which we walk in step with God's timing, direction, and rhythm.

Jesus' model of relating in the rich young ruler account is very different from how we tend to relate to one another. Normally, because we want to feel safe, we act a certain way to ensure a certain outcome. When I say outcome in the context of relationships, I mean our own desired end result or fulfillment of a situation. If I grasp to control outcomes, it subtly becomes about protecting myself rather than loving you. If I cling to some kind of closure that makes sense to me, you no longer make me feel safe because I cannot control you. If I let you sort things out for yourself, I am left not knowing what you will decide or do.

Jesus was willing to feel the pain of the rich young ruler's rejection to ensure the free will of the man was honored. I spent some time thinking about how I might describe how man's free will fits under God's sovereign will, but I don't think I can say it any better than Tozer did in *The Knowledge of the Holy*:

> *"God sovereignly decreed that man should be free to exercise moral choice, and man from the beginning has fulfilled that decree by making his choice between good and evil. When he chooses to do evil, he does not thereby countervail the sovereign will of God but fulfills it, inasmuch as the eternal decree decided not which choice the man should make but that he should be free to make it."* – A. W. Tozer[206]

---

205 1 Corinthians 3:15
206 Tozer, A W. *The Knowledge of the Holy : The Attributes of God : Their Meaning in the Christian Life*. San Francisco, Ca., Harpersanfrancisco, 1992.

When we honor the free will of our brothers and sisters, we honor the Lord as well. Let's look into a couple of ways this can unfold.

∞ Empowering Relationships ∞

When the kids were young, Tom and I led a small group at our church. We were eager to serve and love well. One of our group members wound up in jail shortly after bringing his wife, Maria, and newborn here from Guatemala. Maria did not speak English. She had no money and no place to stay, so she and her baby lived with us for months while the situation resolved. Pastor Doug stopped me in the hall one day and counseled me to be careful I didn't wear myself out with the situation. The thought had never occurred to me to regulate my involvement in ministry. My life was no longer my own, right? "Count it all as lost."[207] Live the sacrifice of Jesus. Anything we had was now the Lord's. "No one had need because all gave generously."[208] These verses reflected qualities I loved about the body of Christ and wanted to embody in the way I interacted with people. And yet, there was more to this serving than just pouring myself out to meet every need.

I had not yet come to understand this concept of stewardship which, simply put, is wise distribution of gifts, talents, and resources.[209] Wise distribution. Sounds so simple, yet, as with so many areas of my walk with Christ, it continues to develop and mature over the decades through experimentation and lots of trial and error. So often, like with Maria, I shifted from being responsible to her to taking responsibility for her as if it was up to me to make sure she had money, was safe, had medical support, etc.

Let's take parenting, for example. I am absolutely responsible *for* my kids when they are infants, babies, toddlers, and children, but something begins to shift as their minds, emotions, and wills begin to manifest through foods they eat, playground equipment they play

---

207 Philippians 3:8-10
208 Acts 4
209 Acts 6:1-6, 1 Peter 4:10

on, friends they choose, colleges they apply for… Before you know it, they are adults, responsible for themselves, even though they never stop being our kids. My friends with adult children and I often laugh about how one of our most difficult jobs at this stage in life is to keep our mouths shut. As their free will and the ability to wield it grows, my role gradually changes too.

Do you have visiting threshold limits for various friends and family members? You might have people you can hang out with for hours, maybe a day or two, but how about a week or two or three? What makes it hard to be with them longer? There may be many reasons this can happen, but I think one of those things is that we start seeing stuff. We might see how they raise their children differently. Or maybe we see the tension in the marriages of our kids or friends. We could see patterns of relating or living we don't agree with. We might see that they don't care about us the way we want, and we start feeling frustrated by the lack of perceived reciprocation. The list is endless for what we may begin to see and experience. We start seeing their stuff instead of seeing them. Welp, time to go! Nice visit.

If we never get over that threshold limit, if we aren't willing to engage with the mess and discomfort, we also never go deeper in that relationship. Our relationship will remain at that level of comfort. But how do we engage in a way that doesn't meddle yet still pushes through to a deeper engagement with those we care about?

If we start speaking into their stuff unannounced, uninvited, and without a deeper desire to know them, we really just want to know they will be okay by our standards. We nudge, ask questions that have our answer already buried in them, we tell our stories that hint at a better way of thinking about something, and so many more obtuse ways of interacting. This is meddling. And there is no sense of rest in it. We hook ourselves to a future outcome in their life that we must reel in ourselves. We can do this with anyone, but I am most tempted to do it with my kids. We have entered the realm of trying to control not one but two matters of life that are absolutely outside of our ability to control: 1. Outcomes, and 2. The free will of another person! We may cloak our efforts in a soft blanket of concern and convince ourselves that this is really about influence and not control, but I would beg to differ.

Meddling says "I'm not okay unless their outcome goes the way I want." Meddling is exhausting and guarantees failure. The moment we are tempted to meddle becomes an opportunity for us to shift back into living from our rest, to acknowledge that I am not in charge of outcomes for another person (other adults, not children). Our desperation leads us to "fixing." No one likes to be fixed. I don't like it; you don't like it; my kids don't like it; your friends don't like it; your Great Aunt Mildred doesn't like it; nobody likes it. When we attempt to fix, we unintentionally activate a battle of the wills with that person. We start stepping on their self-determination. How can we get into the messy without meddling on the one hand or abdicating all responsibility on the other?

We speak to their dignity. We see the potential and challenge them to live into that potential. I just observed this in one of my executive coaching calls last week.

By the way, I call all of my coaching clients Jack and Jill when sharing stories because I don't actually coach anyone named Jack or Jill. We begin the story with a very ticked off Jill. She is angry that her employer, Jack, keeps spending resources keeping people employed who are not pulling their weight, in her estimation. She also hates that Jack is always evangelizing to her, always trying to "fix her."

I translated his actions for them. "Jill, he is not trying to fix you. In his awkward and too forceful way, because Jack you are too forceful, he is calling you into a greater life that you haven't tapped into yet because he sees your potential."

Then when she and I were alone, I continued, "I didn't want to say this in front of Jack. But you know how you're so aggravated with him because he keeps so-and-so too long? Jack has kept *you* on for too long. He has put up with your sour grapes, pushback, and flack "too long" because he cares about you. When I started working with you, he told me 'I need you to go into these conversations believing she is going to work out, believing she can grow.' I didn't believe it at the time, but Jack did."

Jill was weeping at this point. She was so moved that he had this forbearance with her, and that she had such a safety in their professional relationship. Relationships are messy. Jack did not execute perfectly; we won't always do it right. But even a single step away from fixing and battling can create so much more room for love and movement in relationship.

While it will look different for each situation and for each relationship or group's unique dynamics, a respectful conversation will usually include some form of the following:

- Seeking permission
- Intentional restraint from drawing conclusions or acting on internal theories
- Genuine invitation to dialogue
- Demonstrated respect of the other person's boundaries
- Demonstrated respect for your own boundaries

Instead of either becoming avoidant or bulldozing your way into another's life unannounced and unwelcomed, you will become a safer person with whom to interact. Why? Because you are taking responsibility *for yourself* rather than for the other person. When we set boundaries we become safer for others to engage with us.

∞ Dependency ∞

The more dependent upon God I become, the more instruction I receive from Him on how to be healthy in relation to the people around me. The more independently I operate from Him, the more I risk creating an unhealthy dependency on relationships around me. When I'm operating with increased dependency on Him, my sins become less fulfilling and desirable, I gain clarity around my identity and my purpose, and I am less disrupted by dysfunction in relationships around me.

I drew a graph here for you to help visualize the journey of maturity as we move into greater dependence on God and to healthy interdependence with others. A codependent relationship is one like we were describing above: "I am not okay unless you are okay." An interdependent relationship acknowledges our need for one another, but there is differentiation. There is a clear line where I end and another person begins. With interdependency there is empathy and connection without demand or manipulation.

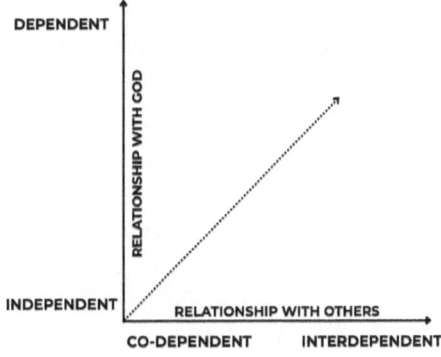

When I'm operating independently of Him, it's easier for me to engage in sins, distort the truth about my value, and judge those around me in very critical ways. In reality, our graph usually has a much squigglier line than the graphic, but it does still trend to the upper right corner as we grow. Increased dependency on God does not mean I'm immediately less codependent with you. What God dependency does do, however, is help me see these places where I live in a manner that tells me I'm not ok unless you're ok. It awakens in me an opportunity to function in a more healthy manner with my horizontal relationships. This might manifest in many different ways, but here are several behavioral changes you might begin to see:

1. I become more courageous in advocating for myself.
2. I become more compassionate in my responses to you.
3. I am able to recognize places where I need to put boundaries in place, to foster an opportunity for improved and rewarding relationships with those around me.

In no way does God-dependency lead to getting walked all over, being taken advantage of, or losing your ability to say no; quite the opposite! Instead, the "clinging to Christ" posture becomes an empowering agent, informing how we engage with those around us beginning with learning how to love ourselves in a healthy way and then translating that learning into loving others in a healthier way. This transition will disrupt the status quo of relationships. As I mentioned before, when one person changes in a relationship, the relationship changes 100% of the time. You invite others into being healthy with you. They may not want that. And while it will be sad if they choose not to be healthy, you'll be okay because you are becoming more God-dependent on the vertical and moving towards interdependence on the horizontal. You'll be okay, even if they are not.

I recall a lovely young lady who was sickened by the thought that if she didn't pray enough her brother might not "make it." The weight of responsibility she felt was tremendous. It took months for her to realize that while she was called to pray for her brother, she was not responsible for his outcomes. She was not responsible for his life (outcome), she was not responsible for his decisions (outcome), and she was not responsible for his salvation (outcome).

Ironically, her prayers were not demonstrating dependency on God. Instead, they were actually an attempt to control the situation, because she loved her brother so much. The process of detaching from the end result was laborious for her. However, as she began to confess a higher trust in her heavenly Father, this led to an ability to release her concerns about the outcome for her brother into His hands. And she found greater rest.

I'm happy to report, some ten years later, that her brother, in fact, is doing very well. And my little friend knows that her prayers were important, but ultimately it was in God's hands. She rejoices and celebrates. I called this beautiful soul to read the story to her. She remembered and reflected further: "There was a lot of giving over and taking back. God and I had lots of wrestling matches. It felt like there wasn't anything I could do, but worry was something I could do when I felt helpless. But over time, I would release my worry by confessing to God that He was in control."

∞ Distinctions ∞

Sometimes we need to define both what something is and what it isn't.

You are not responsible for:

- The emotions of others
- The thoughts of others
- The beliefs of others
- The actions of others
- How people respond to your boundaries
- Controlling outcomes

You are responsible for:

- Your own emotions
- Your own thoughts
- Your own beliefs
- Your actions
- Your communication
- Your boundaries
- Your integrity
- How you love others
- How you show up to relationships

Perhaps take a brief pause here and circle any items that bring clarity to a current situation for you.

Using fear to convince someone of something, using guilt to motivate someone, trying to fix someone—these approaches are taking too much responsibility in a relationship. Refusing to delegate (it's only done right if I do it), washing your hands of everything, or constant blame passing—these are all examples of too much or too little responsibility being taken. Intentionally concealing information or little "white" lies to control a situation or manipulate someone's opinion, even if you believe the ends justify the means, is controlling an outcome and taking too much responsibility.

We can get very enmeshed in unhealthy ways, tangling heart and puppet strings until sometimes it can feel like the only solution is to start cutting. But as you learn more of who you are in Christ and what your own free will feels like, it will get easier to release the people around you to their own free will as well. When I'm operating in His easy and light yoke, I become responsible *to* you, not for you. Honoring free will dignifies the soul.

Sometimes it's hard to tell where the lines are, but the Holy Spirit lends us discernment. The vertical relationship informs the horizontal relationship. If you don't know where the lines are in your relationships, ask Him. Talk to Him about that soul you love so much or are so fearful about. This is the relief of this mode of relating; we look to Him to help us know how to show up to our relationships.

> *When I'm operating in His easy and light yoke, I become responsible to you, not for you. Honoring free will dignifies the soul.*

Let's talk about another example. I was in a situation where I was giving a lot in a relationship, and it was becoming too much for me. There were a couple of ways I could've responded. I could've continued to give, hoping the other person noticed I was growing weary and released me, or hoping that the other person would start needing less. Either way, I would have continued until resentment and anger built up in me. I had set up a dynamic; there was no reason for anything to change unless I changed it. This could have led to an outburst and hurt feelings on both sides and maybe what felt like a more balanced relationship. But that also could have led to a loss of closeness, for then the other person would've started giving out of shame or trying to prove herself.

Instead I communicated that I was weary, that I was entering a new season in my life, and I could no longer keep going the way that I had been. Then I invited a conversation about what the dynamic could look like in the future. This created an opportunity for her to choose to love me freely. She also could have chosen not to do anything about my needs, but that would have been okay because I had set a new boundary about what I was going to do, and then she could do whatever she would with that.

She had no idea I was getting tired; it was my responsibility to communicate my needs. It is not the other person's job to anticipate my needs or read my mind. It is nice when someone knows you well enough to personalize their love for you sometimes, but it is not a foregone expectation. She also was safe to continue accepting love from me when I was able to give it. This safety comes from the trust that if something is wrong, we will communicate about it. I have lived in that hypervigilant, walking-on-eggshells state where I had to pick up on subtle cues or shifts in moods to navigate and avoid blowups, and I refuse to do it anymore in my relationships. I couldn't give as much as I had before, and it was my responsibility to decide how much I was willing to give.

We do not decide how much comes our way; we only decide how much we are willing and able to give. Someone who is trying to meter how much they receive will wind up either needy and entitled, because no one can give enough, or closed off and detached from the love that is being given to them because it's "too much."

But what does this have to do with rest? Anaya described her journey with PLL through a picture of a woman who is sitting on a hill overlooking the ocean. She described her relationship with the ocean and how it can heal. She said Jesus was washing away so much debris that had accumulated in her soul over the years from the lies she had been believing, but the most impactful moment for her was when one of the coaches gently told her, "That's not yours to do anymore," and the weight dropped from her hands.

That phrase now comes to mind often for her as she encounters more situations like that one. She was surprised that she was so content to release it, but she says she can move on now. She's so much lighter and more relaxed in just being His daughter. She is no longer trying to obtain validation from the relationships in her life through over-serving and creating dependency. She feels like a completely different person.

∞ The Messy Middle ∞

This is a vulnerable one for me to write, but as I write to you about responsibility and rest, I keep coming back to the situation that has instructed me the most over the past several years. One of my heavy loads has been in my marriage. Tom and I are in an intense process of learning how to be healthy at the time of this writing. Tom has been verbally and emotionally abusive for decades, and I hid and enabled it up until 2020. That is not to say that we have not had good times or that we do not love each other; we do. But the underlying dynamic has become increasingly intolerable as I have become healthier as a person and my eyes have been opened to how much damage I was allowing to both my heart and body. I am still learning in this situation, but I will share my experience of taking responsibility for myself with you here.

The exercise of "drawing the lines" for myself has been a dizzying struggle. While our marriage may take significant time to become healthy, I have come to a deeper understanding of the responsibility I do and do not have in our relationship. That understanding has empowered me to stop hiding, stop enabling, set boundaries, and begin healing.

Part of that life we built included a role in which I was the scapegoat (responsibility taker) for anything that went wrong in the marriage or home, in part because that had been my role in my childhood home. Taking this role was my best understanding of love at the time. I made excuses for Tom, I made myself out to be the reason he was angry or burdened, and I painted a very pretty picture as long as you didn't look too closely. We had an unspoken agreement to hide Tom's treatment of me from our sons. In an attempt to protect the boys from knowing the hard truth and to protect Tom from any negative light, I took on most of the responsibility in the marriage.

Admitting we were not healthy was the very beginning of the restoration process, but it was terrifying because it required changing how I viewed the narrative of my entire life. If I played the good, supportive wife who looked nice on the outside, I had a form of safety. But deep down, I knew I was hiding something for him. Those who were close enough to pick up hints were insistent that what I was calling "love" was not normal. It was hard to keep lying to myself and the world. I was getting very tired. Trying to protect a familial narrative that I'm familiar with is not resting.

It has taken me years to come out of that pattern of hiding. From first acknowledging the abuse to myself, to trying to change his behavior with any means at my disposal, to confrontations, to learning good boundaries, to retreating back into hiding, to working on my own responses, to seeking community, to counseling, to separation periods, to mountaintop and deep valley moments, this has been a long and exhausting journey with no clear resolution, but I will tell you I am not leaving that man. If he were to leave me, that would be his choice, but I will not leave him.

The decision to stay is on my side of the line; it is my choice (and by the way I'm not prescribing that it has to be yours). Our old pattern was interrupted when I began to realize that there were things within my control, and there were things that were not within my control. Tom's behavior was not one of those things I could control, try as I might. And it also wasn't mine to own. Your ability to articulate what is within and outside your control is a sign of growing and maturing around responsibility and finding deeper rest in God's love for you in the midst of life's tough stuff.

One of the early painful lessons I learned was that I was actually in the way of God's work in Tom's life. As I tried to navigate interactions with this person who was consistently injuring me, I was trying to create scenarios in which I was guaranteed a change in him. At the time, I was surprised to find that God met my requests that He discipline my husband with the response of about seven different passages in Scripture telling me the ways I needed to seek Tom's forgiveness. Tom was not off the hook for his stuff, but taking responsibility for my part actually allowed me to release Tom to the justice and ongoing work of God. I got to snuggle deeper into the arms of God and rest from the angst of wondering how I could manage the situation next.

I had our lines drawn in all the wrong places. I tried to take responsibility for Tom's actions and emotions, but I didn't own my own needs. I wasn't using my voice to stand up for myself, communicate my pain, or set boundaries; instead, I tried to replace God's voice in his life.

This was more than simple miscommunication. I was afraid to share my needs because I had learned over many years that they would be weaponized against me. But as I stepped into bravery with the Lord, I stopped trying to control Tom's behaviors and manage his growth. I changed, and the relationship changed. Tom had room to do (or not do) his own growing.

I have learned the hard way that responsibility necessitates making requests and choosing to reinforce boundaries when a person chooses not to honor them. We set boundaries understanding they may be breached, giving us a way forward that ensures the health and vitality of our soul. Boundaries act as loving, non-punitive protection for our relationships. If you would like some instruction on boundaries, the cited blog by Dr. Henry Cloud is a great starting point for exploration.[210]

As we navigate the twists and turns of the daily struggle that will continue to evolve and develop, I am happy to be able to share a relatively recent victory. A couple months ago, I was praying for our marriage during yet another rough patch. I started to ask my sister if she would have her husband call mine because I thought it would make a difference for Tom—a small way I might indirectly affect the situation again, right? But then I decided not to do that, and I rescinded my request with my sister. I needed to find rest again before I started taking matters into my own hands for the 1000th time.

Rest often comes through prayer for me. Prayer implies surrender. Prayer declares trust. Prayer invites God into our affairs so we are not alone. Prayer shifts me out of trying to control and into a place of release. And most of my prayers are very simple. That, too, is rest for me. I pondered the Lord's prayer where He asks us to pray "deliver us from evil." I began praying a very simple prayer: Lord, please deliver our marriage from every evil. The next evening, Tom told me he had a really honest phone call with Keith, my sister's husband. I was confused, so I followed up with Lauren.

---

[210] "Boundaries Let the Good in and Keep the Bad Out." *Boundaries Books*, 5 Dec. 2023, www.boundariesbooks.com/blogs/boundaries-blog/boundaries-let-the-good-in-and-keep-the-bad-out.

"Hey Sis – Tom let me know that Keith called him. How did that go down?"

"Right?! Keith came into the room. Out of the blue, he told me he felt compelled to call Tom, and he called him on his own."

"You mean you never mentioned our conversation, Sis?"

"Nope, this was all initiated by Keith, or maybe by the Holy Spirit!"

I ended the phone call in awe. I was touched that the Lord had done that for me. I was honest with my needs with Him first, in the secret place. It is safe to share our needs with the Father. There is no judgement. There is empathy, understanding, and dignity under the shadow and profound love of His wing. And this time He provided an answer that I could see with my eyes. I don't always receive that kind of response, but He does always provide a safe resting place. And from there, I could consider inviting other people to share my burden with me, typically those who are closest. For a long time I had lived under the lie that I couldn't be a burden to anyone.

I coped with the marriage issues by removing the opportunity for my husband to continue using my needs against me, but it also prevented any opportunity for him to step into his role as a husband. Concealing my burdens also robbed me of the opportunity to identify my needs for myself, articulate them, protect them when necessary, and receive comfort from others.

The next morning, I went to Tom and said, "I feel like we are falling back into our old pattern." He knew what this meant.

He responded to me, "I want to feel safe for you right now. I want you to feel like you can be vulnerable with me. Would you be willing to share something you are going through right now?"

I took a deep breath, released any expectations for how it would go, and made the decision that I would let Tom in.

"Because of this last autoimmune flare the last four months, the yo-yo effect of fluctuating medication, the frequency of the headaches, the inchworm effect of the calendar with the accumulating makeups, all of the conversations and follow-ups with doctors, I feel like life is just happening to me. I feel like I am alone on this little raft with a splintered fraction of an oar with one job: watch for the next wave. When it comes, paddle as hard and fast as I can into the wave to make sure my raft doesn't capsize. Every time I catch my breath from the last wave, another rises to blot out the sky and I have to make the decision to take up my paddle again or capsize."

Tom chose to use reflective listening. He continued in the new pattern and responded tenderly, "That sounds very lonely."

Even though it wasn't particularly lonely, I could see that he was trying to enter into this space with me. I continued the conversation. "It actually isn't lonely; I still feel very loved. I am just exhausted. I can't rest."

He was not defensive when I clarified his attempt to reflect what was going on for me. Instead, he looked into my eyes and responded. "I want to be the whale that comes up under your raft and carries you to the shore. I can't change your raft or your oar, but I can take you to the shore."

I think that might be the first time I have cried happy tears about something Tom has said to me. This kind of response is rare from him. But that hope is there for us. I carry this moment in my heart as a reminder that this is what can happen with mutual honesty and vulnerability. We rest in Christ, we invite rest into our relationships, and we let the other person choose how they want to respond to our invitation of rest.

The setbacks that make that memory feel like just a nice dream can be deeply disappointing, but we can have rest even in the middle of the confusing and the disappointing. When I own my stuff, I lift my husband up to holiness, I forgive again, I love, I carry the cloak an extra mile and another and another and another, but I still do not receive the outcome I am seeking, it is hard. My attachment to the Lord has been on an accelerated journey that often requires "block and tackling" of my hidden expectations or hope for my relationship with Tom. Sometimes we pray and pray, but we sit looking at the unexplained "no" or "not yet." This is the place we have to rely on God Himself beyond our understanding of the situation and even beyond our understanding of the truth. He sees the full picture, and He is still good. This is the place where I cling to my good Father's mighty hand. Just as I clung to His mighty hand through the physical pain of Lyme and continuing autoimmune struggles, I cling to it through the heat and pressure of this situation.

In the midst of this crucible, there are many things outside of my control. Tom's actions are outside of my control. My family's navigation of our situation is outside of my control. The reactions of others to our story is outside of my control. I write to you now from the "middle." You might be in the middle, too. Middle of building a community or transitioning out of one. Middle of a betrayal or extreme grief at recently losing a child. Middles are where we learn rest in new ways. While I don't know the way our story will unfold, I know the end. I know that because we belong to Jesus, there will be redemption and the working of all things for good whether I see it during my time on earth or not. Middles help us cling to truths that defy the bitterness and confusion of felt experience. Learning to rest in the middles lifts us out of chronos time and the interminable wait for relief. I know that I am a beloved cherished child of God even when I am rejected.

Why do I share this story here in the midst of a chapter about responsibility? Why would I share an unfinished, painful, messy illustration that exposes me and my most inner circle family business to public scrutiny? I share it because you are likely wading through something messy and unfinished yourself, and I think we need more believers who are willing to be real about our raw and vulnerable places. I'm not going to hide anymore. The concepts of free will and responsibility are empowering in these intensely painful places. The Lord gives power to the weak and strength to the powerless.[211] When you are underneath a situation like this, it can feel like getting wiped out by a wave: spinning underwater, lungs burning, water up your nose, shells in your bathing suit, and no sense of which way is up. But when your feet find the sand, you can propel your way towards the light at the surface. Recognizing the choices in front of us is like finding the sand; it allows us to put the strength we have in a productive direction and stops us from wasting it and floundering.

Perspective changes when we access God's design of free will and no longer live feeling forced into things – whether it's flying a plane to the mission field or staying in a marriage. Jesus went willingly to the

---

211 Isaiah 40:29-31

cross. The Lord encourages us to learn how to carry the cloak of our enemy an extra mile, willingly. Love doesn't demand. Love wills. His love draws me into His rest. His rest draws me into His love. And this divinely fueled cycle of love and rest both invigorates and instructs my will simultaneously. I have hope and rest here in the middle. I want to share that with you. The hope that you can live even while things are unresolved. The hope that you don't have to say, "I'll be able to be happy when ____. I'll feel better when ____." Your pain and struggle doesn't disqualify you from abiding in the Promised Land. We live in the already and the not yet. Jesus has already conquered sin and death and all its relatives, and we look forward with unshakeable confidence to the full manifestation of that redemption.

Relationships are messy. The concepts of responsibility and healthy connection can very quickly become muddy when we start to apply them to our real life relationships. But the truth remains that no matter how much duress we are under, with anyone – we have a choice. We do well to identify the choices that we do have so we can become responsible for ourselves. That is rest. That is empowering.

For you, maybe it's not your spouse. Maybe it's a drug-addicted adult child, a sibling who can't handle money well, or a parent who refuses to respect your boundaries. You believe that if they would "get their act together," your life could be better. The solution when we forget and neglect free will is to take responsibility for the other person. We want a better life, which we think can only happen if the other person shapes up. And we deem ourselves just the person to make sure that happens. We disempower, cause resentment, and create battles.

What do I mean by disempower? As long as we are cajoling or coddling or influencing, we disempower them because we take the responsibility off of them. We are still trying to control the outcome. Most likely because that outcome affects us in some way. But if we can release them to their own choice and stop being afraid of what their decisions will mean for us, then that person gets to feel the full weight of their decision.

This is not easy. I have a dear friend whose oldest son committed suicide. Her middle son is now a drug addict. The types of drugs available to kids now do not lead to bottoming out. They lead to death. He is an adult. What is she to do? The first and most important thing my friend does (and she does this very well) is walk in total, absolute, unapologetic dependency on the Lord. What does this dependency look like, practically?

She knows his life is not hers to save. She understands free will. She realizes she cannot control her son. She trusts God with the outcome, whether he lives or dies. She prays God's promises over him. Specifically, she prays Psalms 118:17 (NIV), "He will not die but live and tell what the Lord has done."

Wende is living a *responsible to* life toward her son.

Now I could jump in here and tell you all the things she has done to support him in his journey. I could give you the details of how she put him in two different detox situations, the content of the many difficult conversations with him, the endless prayer sessions with friends, or the outcome of the agonizing decision as to whether or not she and her husband should let him move in with them. That's what we crave to know. But the reality is if you are facing this situation, God's guidance for you will likely be a little different than His guidance for Wende because your situation is unique to you. We look for the prescription. That will give us control. Instead, I encourage you to look to the Great Physician and let Him be in control. As you do this, He will guide you on what you are to take responsibility for and what you can release.

There are a couple of Bible verses that illustrate this further. In Galatians 6, Paul first instructs that we bear one another's burdens, but then in nearly the same pen stroke, he says, "Each will have to bear his own load."[212] What is the difference? The word for load is the same word used for a soldier's backpack.[213] Every soldier must carry their own supplies, their own pack, but if a soldier is struggling under an added burden, such as carrying a wounded buddy, then, of course, his brothers should rally around to help.

In 2 Thessalonians, Paul instructed the church, "If anyone is not willing to work, let him not eat."[214] An example of "load" is the everyday difficulty of disciplining oneself to work, but an example of "burden" would be the

---

212 Galatians 6:2-5
213 Guckenberger, Corrie. "Burden vs. Load: Living in the Tension as a Coach - via Generosity." *Via Generosity*, 21 May 2019, supportraisingsolutions.org/burden-vs-load-living-in-the-tension-as-a-coach/.
214 2 Thessalonians 3:10

plight of a community member who is too sick to work for a time. This is also a lovely example of healthy boundary setting. The choice remains for the community member to work or not, and the boundary setter has clearly communicated what will happen if the boundary is not respected.

As difficult as things have been in our marriage, I am grateful that I have a husband who is willing to grow, learn how to respect boundaries, honor covenant, and learn how to love me in a new way. We are both on a journey towards greater health, and we are choosing to remain in our relationship while we go through this. I invited Tom to share his thoughts about the journey we are on, offering his perspective on our journey, and how difficult it has been for him. Here is what he wrote:

> *As the manuscript came together, Cheryl asked me from time to time if I was okay with certain intensely personal things being included, some of it quite painful parts of our almost 40-year marriage. The curated vignettes in these pages are helpful illustrations, and they signal to the reader that Cheryl's lived experience gives her the street cred required to speak on such matters. Our marriage continues to be a work in progress, heading generally in a positive direction but not without hitting the occasional speed bump (or deer…). Thankfully, as the saying goes, "a setback is a setup for a comeback."*
>
> *The Bible is replete with imperfect characters. They are just like us and their "junk" lets us know we are not alone. It can motivate our growth and sanctification, if we let it. All of our junk, mine and yours, can do the same, if we let it. Putting yourself out there is not easy, but redeeming one's story can minister greatly to others, and on the other side there is great freedom!*
>
> *Thankfully, God is continually about the business of setting captives free and bringing beauty from ashes for His glory. He is faithful in doing His part. As we do our part, discovering how we fit into His plan and doing our inner work, we will find the rest described in these pages.*
>
> *Cheryl put her entire being into this book. This was not easy. I just read the latest version of Chapter 6 (one of those painful parts) and it makes me love her even more! My bride draws upon the deep waters of her heart shaped by a lifetime of joys, sorrows and everything*

in between. It is a roadmap through Promised Land Living, her ministry of 20 years. It is also a manifesto of her life's journey. She loves Jesus, and she loves people, and she wants people to know Him

And now, let each of us put our paddles in the water and press on, for the journey continues.

Tom Scanlan

Selah Moment

Let Jesus show you where you are trying to control more than He is asking you to hold in your hands. Conversely, perhaps there is a place that you have been abdicating responsibility where you need to take it up. Maybe even draw yourself a map of your "jurisdiction," if you are a visual person. You may find yourself empowered to do things that can create change for you even if the other person doesn't change, and you may find relief from staggeringly heavy things that were never meant to be a part of your load. I am reminded of the serenity prayer:

> *"God grant me the serenity to accept the things I cannot change,*
> *Courage to change the things I can,*
> *And wisdom to know the difference."*[215]

∞ P.S. Go to Bed ∞

As we talk about our responsibilities and the choices we are empowered to make, I think about my adult kids and how often I still tell them to "go to bed." It's much different than the days when I would call them to brush their teeth and put on their jammies, laughing or gritting my teeth through the pre-bed zoomies. I loved hearing their

---

[215] Attributed to Reinhold Niebuhr, Lutheran theologian (1892–1971)
Niebuhr, Reinhold . *Serenity Prayer.* 1971.

reflections from the day and snuggling their little fuzzy heads close even if they'd only let me do it for a second.

Now, when I see seasons of pushing hard at work, battling insomnia or other stresses that lead to staying up late and getting up early indefinitely, I hope that they will make choices that prioritize sleep whenever possible. Not for my sake or peace of mind but for their own. When I went for too long without enough sleep during a time of caring for a family member with paranoid dementia, it caused a crash that sent me to the hospital for two weeks and had long-term negative effects for my autoimmune health. Lack of good boundaries and unhealthy family dynamics at the time played a part. Learning from experience informs me I don't want health crashes or even the smallest version of that for my family.

Heart diseases such as strokes and heart attacks are linked to sleep dysfunction.[216] It's also linked to inflammatory diseases,[217] depression, decreased cognitive functioning, increased incidence of accidents, etc.[218] Even just a little sleep deprivation, such as sleeping 6-7 hours instead of 7-8, doubles the risk of a car accident.[219] I have seen all too often, not just in myself but in clients as well, how quickly and quietly a lack of sleep can cause or exacerbate chaos in our lives and health. I have helped many executives find new sleep patterns as a part of our professional coaching relationship, because no one part of our life exists in a vacuum.

There are some facts for you, maybe a little fear, but that isn't going to do much for you, is it? Let's bring it into the context of your

---

[216] National Heart, Lung, and Blood Institute. "What Are Sleep Deprivation and Deficiency?" National Heart, Lung, and Blood Institute, 24 Mar. 2022, www.nhlbi.nih.gov/health/sleep-deprivation.

[217] "How Sleep Deprivation Can Cause Inflammation." *Harvard Health*, 29 Apr. 2024, www.health.harvard.edu/healthbeat/how-sleep-deprivation-can-cause-inflammation., Alex Barnes, Réme Mountifield, Justin Baker, Paul Spizzo, Peter Bampton, Jane M Andrews, Robert J Fraser, Sutapa Mukherjee, A systematic review and meta-analysis of the prevalence of poor sleep in inflammatory bowel disease, *SLEEP Advances*, Volume 3, Issue 1, 2022, zpac025, https://doi.org/10.1093/sleepadvances/zpac025

[218] See footnote 122 (or x-2)

[219] Pacheco, Danielle. "Driving While Drowsy Can Be as Dangerous as Driving While Drunk." *Sleep Foundation*, 24 June 2022, www.sleepfoundation.org/drowsy-driving/drowsy-driving-vs-drunk-driving.

relationship with the Lord and see if there is any reframing that can happen there.

I am spending most of this book talking about our spiritual rest, but I feel the need to take this time here to talk about our bodies, as well. Our spirit lives in our body, and the two are intricately interconnected. Neurotransmitters and hormones have a two-way relationship with our emotions and experiences of life; each drives the other. There are many demands on our time and on our bodies. There are some seasons in which sleep is very elusive, like the newborn stage for new parents. Sleep will not solve the spiritual unrest by itself, but it is still crucial nonetheless. God made our bodies; He is mindful that we are made of dust.[220] He has things to say about our sleep. He says that it is in vain that we rise up early and stay up late, eating the bread of anxious toil, for He gives sleep to His beloved.[221] Did you catch that last bit? He gives sleep to His beloved. You are His beloved, and He knows you need it.

Please don't try to be tough about it. Don't beat your chest and slam down another energy drink. I don't want my children to treat their bodies that way, and I don't want you to either. Lack of sleep can be an outward symptom of an inward reality that we expect too much of our limited humanity. Humans can truly be astounding, stunning creatures in the things we overcome, but doing so on no sleep is unsustainable. It will catch up to you. I hate to be the one to tell you this, but someone has to. From the woman who wore her red cape too long: You are not invincible. You are a human who lives in a body that will age and get sick much faster if you don't give it rest. Would you expect a car that requires diesel to run on a quarter tank of unleaded regular? No one is surprised when things start malfunctioning when a car is out of gas or full of the wrong kind.

I understand there are extenuating circumstances; I understand there are good reasons. But if you are one of the 33% of the population who consistently report getting less than 8 hours of sleep,[222] there must be at least one thing you can change about your current sleep habits.

---

[220] Psalms 103:14

[221] Psalms 127:2

[222] "1 in 3 Adults Don't Get Enough Sleep." CDC, 1 Jan. 2016, archive.cdc.gov/www_cdc_gov/media/releases/2016/p0215-enough-sleep.html.

Take responsibility for that which is in your power to change. He has given us everything we need for life and godliness; we do not need extra hours in the day.[223] Frankly, I would overfill a 28-hour day as readily as I do a 24-hour one!

If I may mother you for just a minute: go to bed!

I say all of this a little tongue in cheek, as is our way in my family, but I do mean it. Underneath it all, going to sleep is an act of trust in the One who neither slumbers nor sleeps. For the child of God, the discipline of sleep becomes a spiritual declaration of trust. Our house alarms and locked doors are not what keep us safe at night. He is.[224] Would you allow Him to hold all the things unfinished, all the things out of your control, all the what-ifs, all the ruminations, embarrassing memories, unsettling traumas, and anything else your brain has to chatter about? Come back to the present. Reinhabit your body. Pay attention to the way the tip of your tongue feels on the roof of your mouth. Every time your mind tries to spin, return to that sensation. If you are still not able to go to sleep, God may have somebody for you to pray for there in the dark. I have received many prayer assignments in the night watch. But then return again to stillness and warmth and rest. Nite! See you tomorrow.

---

223 2 Peter 1:3
224 Psalm 4:8

CHAPTER SEVEN

Desert Lies

What is keeping you wandering?

THE PREMISE OF the whole ministry, Promised Land Living, is based on the idea that many followers of Jesus are in relationship with Christ, doing all they know to do, believing that Jesus Christ is Lord, accepting the authority of Scripture, but still living a life that feels much like wandering in the desert. Instead of experiencing the Promised Land of abundant life, peace that passes understanding, and joy inexpressible, there is no water, no shade, no respite. I don't mean a life abundant with material things. I mean God's kind of life, energy, motivation, or "zoe" in the Greek that is abundant in your soul.[225]

Can you imagine that there is even more waiting for you? What would life look like if you had more zeal and energy?

I asked myself where all of our energy is going. Why are we still acting like we are in arid, dry lands even though we know Jesus? What keeps us wandering? Through the renewing of my own mind in Scripture and the discipleship of those wiser, I realized it all boiled down to one thing—Lies. There are lies deeply rooted in all of us that feel like truth, imitating the truth with a few key knife-twisting changes. We know the most important truth about what Jesus did for us, but we often have distortions of His character or our identity in unexamined, pivotal places. These lies can cause us to make choices or trigger bodily responses that block the rule of peace in our lives. Yes, we have saving

---

[225] "Strong's Greek: 2222. ζωή (Zóé) -- Life." *Biblehub.com*, biblehub.com/greek/2222. htm. John 1:4, John 4:14, John 10:10, Romans 6:4

knowledge of truth. And there is more truth waiting for us to grasp and live from. Training to live an examined life leads to living into the peace that He has already given to us.

Ours is not a fire insurance faith. God does not get us just barely over the threshold of Heaven and dump us there. We are His masterpieces. He wants us to know Him intimately and wants to be near us. He spends our lifetime gently sanctifying us, drawing closer, sanding off edges, releasing us, unburdening us, unblinding us, freeing us, softening us, strengthening us, and making us more like Himself.

And we, as His beloved, get to *participate* in this development of our relationship with Him. Would you like to know how to participate in this process? God promised the land to Abraham, He showed the land to the spies, and He asked the Israelites to conquer the land. We tend to think of abundance the way we picture people's vacations—with fancy drinks in their hands, squinting beyond the white sands to blue waves, relaxing in lounge chairs. We mistakenly equate abundance with being comfortable. This leads to all sorts of "quests" to pursue comfort in a manner that denies us the abundance God promised us![226]

While Joshua and Caleb brought the Israelites into the land, the Israelites had to take the land that God declared was theirs. Kay Arthur, Founder of Precept Ministries, calls this possessing your possessions. Joshua and Caleb understood their inheritance and how to own it for themselves. They didn't apologize for it. They didn't doubt it. *They took it.* Would you like to step into *your* Promised Land like Joshua and Caleb did? To do this, we need to deny any desire to be passive in our faith; otherwise we will stay stuck like a lost child in a house of mirrors..

∞ Distortions ∞

I don't know why carnivals call them fun houses. Enjoying the freedom of kids let loose at a carnival, my sister and I paid our ticket and waited our turn to go into the house of mirrors. We were giggling and holding hands in the sunlight as we ran up the ramp. Immediately

---

[226] Matthew 6:33

upon entering the dark, stuffy labyrinth, I stopped and lost my grip on my sister's hand.

I became disoriented, swallowed up by images of myself everywhere. I did not like it; the sight did funny things to my head. Each mirror created some distorted view of me. My face was terribly misshapen in each reflection. Some mirrors made me short and stout, while others made me long and disturbingly skinny. I started making a beeline for the exit, or I thought I did. I ran into a mirror. I turned, took a couple of steps, and bumped into another.

I wanted out desperately, but in my panic I kept bumping into "myself." I could hear other kids laughing, and I could hear my sister's voice getting further away, but I couldn't figure out how to move through the maze of images of myself that seemed to mock me. The mirrors reflecting each other created an infinite number of repetitions of the same grotesque picture of myself. This was not fun.

I stopped and paid attention to each image surrounding me. There was a way out; I just had to find it. After a few minutes, I realized that I needed to follow the path of non-distortion, *ignoring* all other reflections, and soon, I found my way out. Fresh air, sunshine, and Lauren greeted me at the end of the tunnel. I never went into another funhouse again.

We can find ourselves lost in a funhouse. Lies distort. Lies mock. Lies disorient. And if we see ourselves through that distortion for too long, it starts to feel like reality. Some folks call it stuck. Others call it helpless. Others call it "Just the way I am." The list is endless for what we call it. The reality is, no matter how we dress it up, no matter how we rationalize or battle, "it" is still a lie. Lies are intentionally misleading and leave us wandering. Miserable. There's no shame here, no finger-pointing. Only: Do you want to be well? Are you willing to move out of miserable?

Two questions might come to mind: One, how do we know there is a lie? And two, how do I find it?

We believe that identifying "it" is at the center of all discipleship. It isn't just "it," for there can be many distortions, or as we like to call them, desert lies. But it's not enough to just identify the lie. In fact, many have done a fantastic job of identifying the lie yet still can't seem to pull themselves out of the fun house. They know where it came from, why they believe it, and that it cripples them. They see the lie everywhere they go. They identify with it so strongly and are so used to it that it creates a terrifying but accepted dead end. A painful, repetitive cycle of thoughts and behaviors perpetuates the feeling of being stuck, which creates a sense of powerlessness, and eventually, after a long string of defeats, a sense of hopelessness.

But we don't always know how to combat the lies from a position of rest.[227] Sometimes in pushing hard against it in the way we intuitively respond, we unintentionally strengthen its foothold in our minds. Our strong response chemically reinforces in our brains that this thing is a threat and requires more attention. The web winds tighter.

These lies often block the path between our head and our heart, "knowing in our knower" as we have mentioned before. We know in our heads that Jesus loves us, yet so many landmines are planted in our souls that we are afraid to move at all. We become fundamentally disconnected. We don't even know what we truly look like undistorted. We are in community without experiencing community. We are surrounded by people we love, yet we struggle to feel their love. We attend church and say the right things we think other people want to hear, but we don't know how to represent ourselves, and we find ourselves deeper in our own isolation, staring at a despicable image in the mirror.

The funhouse has swallowed us alive.

But there is good news. So much good news! There is a path out of the funhouse. Do you believe it still? After all your wandering, maybe even 40 years worth of wandering in the desert, so long that the promise of a land flowing with milk and honey is a distant memory passed down by your parents, do you still believe it's there?

While you may have been swallowed alive by the funhouse of lies, you are alive. You are still in Christ. You are still His, and He is still yours. Your temporarily stuck location in the fun house doesn't change your eternal position in Christ.

There is a path. Jesus is the Waymaker. He made a way for us to the Father, and He is the Way of Life. He made a way for us to get out of

---

227 James 4:7, Ephesians 6:12

our eternal pit and a way out of this temporary pit that has us trapped now. He is the path in both cases.

To follow this path, Jesus asks us to leave the familiar. He asks us to let Him set a new pattern for us, a pattern built upon confession. Now we will put this into practice. It's not grueling. He promises that His yoke is easy and His burden is light.

> *To follow this path, Jesus asks us to leave the familiar.*

Selah Moment

Describe what it means to be at peace in yourself. Take your time with this. When I say in yourself, I don't mean *with* yourself; I mean a deep stillness that isn't threatened by outside disturbances. There is harmony between body and soul and their Maker. Find a memory where you experienced peace and maybe journal about what it was like for you. Perhaps the moment of your conversion is the only truly peaceful memory you know; perhaps you have many. Find words for being at peace in yourself.

In that moment of peace, something happens so deep in the soul it is hard to articulate. It's like the moment you stand on the beach and look out at the ocean. Or the moment you pull over the car and pause to take in breathless mountain views. What is <u>that</u>?

I become a beholder of the majesty of God. My soul is quieted. I come back into alignment with my proper place in the order of things. He is the One who holds all these things together. I experience awe at His might and beauty, and wonder that the Maker of these things would be mindful of me and has brought me into His family.[228]

This brings safety. Assurance. Security. The ocean shore comes up to our toes but no further. The mountain stands firm upon immovable

---
228 Psalm 8:4-8

rock, and our feet are anchored upon its strength. Instinctively, we start drawing longer breaths. Our bodies respond to beholding with rest and breath.

The second bit of good news is that the price has already been paid for your peace. Now we spend the rest of our lives learning how to walk in this peace.

My desire at this stage in the journey is to show you this new pattern. But I'm nervous. Nervous that you are resistant. Nervous that you've read so many books you're going to gloss over this. Nervous that you might put the book down now because this is where it becomes a little too real. The work begins here and now.

May I gently reassure you that it won't feel like work in the way you have come to know work? Remember my path out of the fun house? The "work" was to focus on the truth and not the distortions. As soon as I recognized a distortion, I moved my eyes to seek the truth. This is what I want to show you. Does that feel like something you can do? If you look at what you're telling yourself and it doesn't align with what He says, then you know that is not the path of an abundant life.

The framework I am about to introduce to you is based on the biblical principles of confession, taking thoughts captive, renewing our minds, humility, and submitting to the authority of Scripture and the Lordship of Christ. Remember the concept of going from simple to complex back to exquisitely simple? The simple shift methodology or the "how" is based on my experience as a coach over the last thirty years. As I said in Chapter One, the frameworks I introduce to you are just starting points. The steps of the shift themselves don't create change but rather the conversation with the Creator of our souls that the framework facilitates. Sitting with each step as you first learn the process helps to strengthen understanding, because each step builds upon the last like scaffolding.

The shift begins with recognizing you are not at peace. The moment you experience angst of any sort, you're mentally in the fun house, and it's time to look for the way out. Are you ready to let go of the distortions that are all too familiar and courageously face the truth about who God is and who you are?

∞ 7 Step Shift® ∞

We call the path the 7 Step Shift.®

Seven is the number of completion. The shift is a complete turning away from living in distortions to fully acting in the truth. Not just identifying the lie or even acknowledging the truth but acting on it. This is what protects us from wandering and reverting. A complete turn means more than knowing the truth. Knowledge doesn't lead to freedom. Walking, literally moving, in truth does. Jesus instructs on this active participation in truth, bringing greater reality of the same in John 8:30-32. Jesus reveals the path to experiencing freedom. "If you *continue* in my Word, then you will know the truth, and the truth will make you free." He was speaking to those who came to believe Him. He was telling them that the freedom you seek will come from remaining in Whom you believe, not just the initial belief. How do we remain (abide) in that belief? This is where the 7 Step Shift® comes into play. Shifting returns us to our rest in Him. The shift is a freedom cycle that burrows the soul deeper and deeper into understanding of the truth we already know to be true.

I think it will be best if I show you the shift rather than describing it to you. I will give you a couple of windows into my life where I shifted rather significantly, and then we will practice walking through it together.

Step 1: Note the symptoms.

As a young woman, I attended women's ministry meetings. One of the elder's wives, Debbie, remarked at one of these meetings that I was very strong. As she said that, my heart began to race. I became restless. My mind went numb. My body wanted to bolt out of the meeting. My eyes went downward. I could no longer think clearly.

Step 2: Ask, "What I am telling myself?"

I am too much.

Step 3: Ask God, "What is the truth about myself, the other person, my situation, and/or about Him?"

I didn't know what the truth was, but I trusted Debbie enough to call her after the meeting. To my relief, she answered immediately. "Debbie, you mentioned today that I am strong. What did you mean by that?" She told me things about myself that were true that I didn't think anyone saw or could appreciate. And she did not tell me that I was too much. She said they needed a leader like me right now during this transition of the Women's Ministry and that I was handling it in a gentle but firm manner, which made the process we were using trustworthy.

Step 4: Compare what I'm telling myself to what God is saying. Decide if I am willing to tolerate any lies I am believing. If not, then I confess what I was believing OUT LOUD.

This is the hinge that opens the door to freedom right here. "God, I cannot believe how quickly I trash-talked myself when Debbie used the word 'strong.' I am ashamed of my strength. Mom was strong, and she hurt people. I equate strength with hurting people. Can you show me how you can redeem my strength for your glory and the building up of the body of Christ? I am a willing vessel, but I don't know what that looks like or how to go about this."

Step 5: Declare the truth to myself, standing on the authority of Christ.

Debbie continued, "Cheryl, God made you strong, and He needs to be strong in you. You do not need to be strong in yourself. If you want Him to redeem those tough years, you need to let Him do just that. You don't have to make up for something; instead, you have to surrender someone, and that someone is you." I received this truth and declared it to myself then and many times after that. "God made me strong; I will let Him be strong in me."

Step 6: Ask God, "What is one small step I can take in that truth?"

God, I don't want to wander in that old thinking pattern. You have created a new pattern for living for me. Show me what that new pattern looks like around my strength. What is my first step? The Lord offered that I should share my insecurity with Debbie, allowing myself to be vulnerable with her. This. Was. Terrifying.

Step 7: Immediately take the step.

"Debbie, before we get off the phone, may I share something with you? I think the Lord is showing me that I have been afraid of my strength because I didn't want to become like my mom, so I was living in a lot of shame and fighting myself. What you showed me today is that my strength is not the problem, but my view of my strength is the problem. I want to surrender my strength to the Lord and see it as a gift that He will shape and use over time. Would you pray for me about that?"

My friends, I no longer apologize for being strong. I spend that once-wasted, wandering energy on surrendering my strength to the Lord. Every day I get to practice submitting myself to His perfect ways. And I eagerly embrace my admission that I do it imperfectly. Isn't that wonderful? Because if I was strong in myself, I wouldn't be allowed to make mistakes. I wouldn't ever have to apologize. But God healed me of that. Now it is a joy to confess my sins. It is a delightful relationship-building moment when I get to seek forgiveness from another. Grounded in the truth of His love, I don't need to cover for myself anymore.

I've been real. Shall we go for raw now?

Here's a second example of a major shift in my life (trigger warning: suicidal thoughts):

You see, for most of my life, I was looking for an escape route from a difficult upbringing. Part of the difficulty was my controlling mom. And part of it, I can admit as a mature adult in Christ, was my own sensitivity and way of processing.

Below is a brief history of my "I need to escape" story. Some of you will relate and may want to grab some Kleenex. For others, this will be a bit dry and unrelatable. Maybe pop some popcorn then?

Since as early as 4 years old, I can hardly remember a day I lived in that house that I wasn't brought to tears. My mom sent me to a Catholic nursery school. The two nuns were kind and gentle. But I didn't feel safe, so I kept to myself and was unable to respond to their kindness. Their concern led to a parent-teacher meeting. They asked me to stay after all the other kids were picked up. My mom showed up, and I was terrified. But rather than having to face her, I was invited to go out into the play yard with a box of chicks to watch them and feed them. My terror was replaced with the hope that maybe they would talk to Mom about some of the secret troubles at home. Somehow they must have known! I never told them, but I was relieved they had the courage to face my mom.

But life didn't change. The nuns, although kind, couldn't reach my mom and couldn't rescue me. Elementary years brought some relief in the form of babysitters as Mom started working to help Dad make ends meet. Babysitter Debbie left us alone and watched TV. Babysitter Danae spent all her time with me. We did crafts, sang songs, she told me stories, and I dared to share one or two stories of my own, like what it felt like to dance in the wind on the swings. But inevitably I would have to let her go after long hugs and face dinner with Mom. It became unbearable. My next attempt at escaping was to run away. I made it three miles to a local mall. The plan was to stay out of sight, remain overnight, and catch the first bus to my grandma's house in Chicago where I knew I would be safe. I was always safe with Grandma. Tornadoes, police searches, and eventually my sister's tattling thwarted my plans. They found me, but I felt more lost than ever.

By high school I performed well academically and met all expectations of me, but I remained a bit aloof even though I was sought after by those whose tears needed to be wiped, hearts needed to be heard, and minds needed to stop racing. I was growing stronger as I braced against the verbal assaults at home and kept our secrets tucked safely in the soul vault. However, something in me was dying. It wasn't a good strength—it wasn't about resilience and grit. It was about independence and isolation. I was going it alone. Although I would see people look brighter and feel lighter after our conversations, I was getting sucked deeper into a loneliness that all but suffocated me. I needed a new escape path. This time it would be suicide.[229]

I had the entire plan mapped out. My sister confronted me; I'm not sure how she found out. I told her not to worry, I was just having a bad day. But the next day, I was called down to the basement of our

---

[229] Suicide hotline: 988 for English and Spanish, see https://blog.opencounseling.com/suicide-hotlines/ for more languages.

980-square-foot home. It was never a good thing to be called down to the basement. Dad was sitting on the couch. My sister was cowering behind my seething mother.

"Take a seat."

I sat woodenly. The next words ravaged.

"Cheryl, you brought this entirely on yourself. You cannot blame your father or me for anything. You can only blame yourself."

I got my wish. That was the day I died. It was not by my own hand but by the sword of my mom's tongue. I turned into something else, hollowed out, impenetrable.

Throughout life thereafter, I was going to be strong. Steeled against everything. Private with everyone. I would serve and love and listen, but I would remain a stranger to those I heard. I hid behind care and concern. I made one more plan to end my life at 22, but a mysterious Good Samaritan named Cookie interrupted that chain of events. I decided that day that suicide would not be my escape route.

Eventually, while I was no longer seeking to escape life, my body, fatigued from running so hard, collapsed. Lyme disease, mitochondrial dysfunction, growing up with poor nutrition—I could blame it on those things, but underneath it all, I did not believe I could stop and rest. If I did, I would get in a heap of trouble. I could not inconvenience anyone, or I would prove that I had no value. Are you hearing the lie creeping in here? There are probably some things you want to tell me, but the reality is I wouldn't have heard you. I knew my story. And my story was me. I had lived in the house of mirrors too long to know any different or believe there could be anything different. Christ brought me into a place of eternal rest, but Cheryl kept her soul wandering in the temporary torment of a powerful desert lie.

That is until Sybil broke through it all.

Step 1: Note the symptoms.

I was lying in a hospital bed very sick, with no reflexes, unable to swallow, and hooked up to IV Solumedrol 3 times a day. Once again, I was looking for an escape route. My friend, Sybil, who was a nurse at the hospital where I was staying, stopped by at the end of her shift. You'd think I would have been grateful. But frankly, I didn't want Sybil there. I wanted to suffer alone. My symptoms were recognizable after all those years: I needed to get out of there or tell Sybil to get out of there! Sybil was sitting across from me and was scared, but it felt like she had to tell me something. I told her to speak. Because of course, I was going to be strong.

"Hit me with your best shot, Sybil!"

Step 2: Ask, "What am I telling myself?"

Sybil reflected a few things I often said to myself. She then said softly, voice shaking almost imperceptibly, "Cheryl, do you realize that you speak death over yourself all the time?"

I had to agree. I did like to say things like, "Well, if I don't die..." or, "If the proverbial bus doesn't come and hit me..." And I did feel like I was dying, so why not just be blunt about it? It brought me small comfort in the form of artificial control.

Step 3: Ask God, "What is the truth about myself, my circumstances, the other person, and/or about Him?"

When Sybil told me that, I had a choice to make. I could spend a lot of time explaining why that was so, pleading for sympathy, commiseration, and agreement. Or I could ask God what the truth was. I was far enough along in my walk with Jesus that I trusted that His way of thinking was a better path, so I was willing to explore what He had to say. What I heard in that moment was something like this: "Cheryl, I am the God of life. Will you worship me and trust me with the path forward for you rather than trying to create your own path by dancing with death?"

Step 4: Compare what I'm telling myself to what God is saying. Decide if I am willing to tolerate any lies I am believing. If not, then I confess what I am believing OUT LOUD.

"Sybil, you are right. I have made an agreement with death. I thought death was my escape route out of my own misery and pain and the misery and pain I think I cause others. But I confess that I am a new creature in Christ, and I want to think, speak, and live from that inheritance I have in Him." I then turned my attention back to my internal conversation with the Lord.

Step 5: Declare the truth to myself, standing on the authority of Christ.
"God, you are my God. You have preserved and protected me in spite of myself for your good and mysterious reasons. You are the God of life. Of freedom. Of abundance. And you ask me to walk in that truth."

Step 6: Ask God, "What is one small step I can take in that truth?"
I spoke out loud again.
"Sybil, I sense God is wanting me to remove all language of death and dying from my vocabulary. I will no longer say, "If I should live so long or if I don't die tomorrow." Instead, I will position my language and my thinking around the phrase "Lord willing,"[230] which invites the Lord into every decision and discourse."

Step 7: Immediately take the step.
Since *that day*, I have expressed my mortality and the sovereign authority of God over my life with the phrase "Lord willing." Delight.

It was such good news of glad tidings for my soul that had been trampled for so many years by my insecurities and the insecurities of those closest to me—I was free from language that positioned me under the authority of death!

That entire exchange took less than five minutes. Now think about the great lengths we will go: traveling the world, paying enormous amounts of money to experience something that will give us five minutes of pleasure or five minutes of a thrill ride. But what Sybil gave me was the gift of not five minutes, not five years, but a lifetime of freedom from a paradigm that ruled and robbed me for years. I've been on mountaintops in the Swiss Alps with my bestie. It couldn't compare to what happened to me that afternoon. The majestic snow capped view is a beauty that I see and take in. The other is beauty that is shaped within and now pours out to others.

I hope now that I get to be Sybil for you.

---

[230] James 4:15

You now have an overview of the 7 Step Shift® process. I also offered two real examples from my life.

Would you be willing to walk through your own 7 Step Shift® ? You can do this alone or have someone go through the process with you.

Ready? Gulp. That's a scary word, isn't it? I wonder if there is a better question to ask.

Ready to receive?

Ready to release?

Ready to humble yourself?

Ready to experience relief?

What are you ready for? Your response can then become your motivation for the next 15 minutes we work together.

Each progressive step is designed to walk the path of Jesus. To die to ourselves and to be resurrected into new life. In doing so, we will move from glory to glory in Christ Jesus. What do I mean when I say that? When I'm moving from glory to glory in Christ Jesus, I'm experiencing transformation of my soul that begins with my salvation, continues through my sanctification, and carries me into eternal glorification with Christ Himself! I experience spiritual lightness, like a robin singing her evening song to the setting sun. A lightness that defies the world's pull towards its vortex of sin and pride. I'm above my circumstances such that my spiritual eyes can see God's hand moving and His purposes unfolding through little ol' me! When I keep short accounts – God receives glory. When I give God credit for my growing humility – more glory to God. When I resist telling a white lie to make life easier or to make me look good – Glory to my Father! When I share what God revealed to me about my weakness and His ample mercy and grace to cover me – I give glory to God! And when I say that I will refuse to live in shame, which is nothing more than pride wrapped in self-disgust, and choose to fire the lies that are choking out His abundant life in me – God receives all the glory![231] Imagine, God gets the glory for my abundant life! Paul talked about this, too, when he declared under tremendous duress (sometimes despairing even to the point of wanting to die):[232]

---

[231] Reimer, Rob. *Soul Care 7 Transformational Principles for a Healthy Soul.* Carpenters Son Pub, 2016.

[232] 2 Corinthians 1:8

And the Lord will rescue me from every evil action and bring me safely into His heavenly kingdom. To Him be the glory forever and ever. Amen. 1 Timothy 4:18

The 7 Step Shift® is a method by which we elevate what is happening in us to a conscious level for the purpose of aligning with God and His truth. Choosing to align with God's truth and then acting upon it is a crucial part of our sanctification in Christ. It enables cooperation with the Holy Spirit. It quiets the demands of the flesh. It opens the heart to divine revelation for how to walk in this moment and the next moment and the next. And it honors the very personal 1-1 relationship we have with God. Excited? Me too! If you get stuck, pause and pray rather than give up. It's not a complicated process, but it will take practice.

Step 1: Note the symptoms.

(Romans 12:1-2, Psalm 32:3-4, 1 Corinthians 6:19-20, Proverbs 4:20-22, Proverbs 17:22)

Sit with yourself for a moment and describe what is going on in your body. Mind racing, jaw clenched, heart racing, lightheaded… What might be your "symptoms?"

Tip for Step 1: Refrain from using diagnostic language like I'm stressed, I'm feeling anxious… Keep the identification of symptoms very concrete. No labels.

My symptoms:

Step 2: Ask, "What am I telling myself?

(Proverbs 4:23, James 1:6-8)

Write down what you are saying to yourself. Don't edit or evaluate it. Just write it down.

Tip for Step 2: Keep this short. This is where people tend to cycle and get stuck in the story. No more than 2-4 sentences. Then try to narrow to the strongest statement (e.g., It's up to me, I'm guaranteed to get hurt, I'm not safe).

My story:

Step 3: Ask God, "What is the truth about myself, my circumstances, the other person, and/or about Him?"

(Psalm 25:4-5, Psalm 32:8, Psalm 139:17-18)

Spend as much time as you want writing down truth. It may take a while at first to access it, but even after a few minutes, Holy Spirit will begin to show you.

Tip: Don't ask *yourself* what the truth is—ask God. There is no shifting or shadow with Him.[233] No distortions.

God's truth:

Step 4: Compare what you're telling yourself to what God is saying. Decide if you are willing to tolerate any lies you are believing.

(John 17:17, Psalm 139:23-24, Proverbs 3:5-6, 1 John 1:9, Psalm 32:5)

If not, then confess the lie that you have been believing OUT LOUD.

(Genesis 3:9-10, James 5:16, Romans 10:10)

This is the surrender step. This is the step that unleashes God's redemptive power in you. *Lord, I confess I have been believing* _____.

Tip: Even if you are alone, pray this out loud. There is something

---

[233] James 1:7

that doubles the TNT of our confession when we can hear our own words: Once spoken, twice heard.

After praying your confession out loud, write down some of what you said. Not before. Wait until after you pray.

Step 5: Declare the truth to yourself, standing on the authority of Christ.

(2 Corinthians 10:5, Zechariah 8:16, Philippians 4:8, Acts 4:31, Ephesians 6:19-20, Matthew 28:18)

After we go through the comparison, decision making, and confession process, it's time to take the wobble out of any residual doubt that might be lingering. Speak the truth to yourself clearly and succinctly.

Tip: If you take too long with this step, your flesh will tend to create complications. Don't let it.

What is the declared truth?

Step 6: Ask God, "What is one small step I can take in that truth?"

(Psalms 86:11, James 1:5, 1 John 1:7, Psalm 25:4-5)

Maybe you've heard the phrase that God gives us just enough light for the next step on the path. This is the practicality of that phrase. We refuse to deny ourselves the opportunity for God to reveal His goodness to us.

Tip: The step will align with the truth but will often go counter to your natural inclinations or instincts. Old thinking wants to creep in. That's normal, and yet, in this moment, you choose to continue to listen to the bell of truth. You choose to trust God with outcomes. You choose to trust God with your attitude. You choose to trust God with your security. This type of trust leads to obedience. Obedience is powerfully freeing.

What is the small step God is asking you to take?

Step 7: Immediately take the step.

(John 14:15, John 14:23, 1 Samuel 15:22, 3 John 1:3)

Do not hesitate. Do not question. Be like the child who chooses first-time obedience.

Tip: Take the step.[234]

∞ A Moment of Decision ∞

What did you experience? As you try this for yourself, I feel the need to warn you about a common pitfall. The shift is a door to freedom. Many people have tried to go through it without step four: Confess the lie. Confession is at the heart of finding rest. Confessing truth. Confessing lies. Confessing good. Confessing bad. Confessing. Ah, the cleansing work of confession. While step four can feel a little redundant, it is crucial because it is where the will is activated. Remember our discussion about cooperating or contending with God? Step four is the moment of decision. This is the point where you answer the questions honestly for yourself in your heart: Do you want to be well? Do you want abundance?

It also brings the lie under submission to the authority you have over your mind and, more importantly, under the authority of God. In Chapter 5 I connected confession and rest. This confession pulls the lie out from under the coverings of self-pity or rationalizations that allow it to stay, much like the biofilms that the Lyme spirochete created for itself in my body; it made itself look like a non foreign entity to my

---

[234] See Appendix D for a quick 7 Step Shift Reference page

immune system. The layers over our lies make them harder to recognize, harder to kill. But if you are willing, truly willing to let it go, there is such freedom. Your willing desire is the key that unlocks the door but only if you are hungry for it.[235]

∞ Not One and Done (Again) ∞

I have always loved getting my hands in the dirt. Some of my sweeter memories with my mom are planting little rows of tiny carrot seeds in the dirt behind the house on our "littlest acre" of land. We would make a line in which to drop the seeds, barely a furrow in the ground, maybe one that a beetle could plow, just took the tip of a finger.

We tried to plant tulips too, but the sunlight was dappled in our yard, and year after year only the green shoots came up. No blooms, try as we did, digging up the bulbs and refrigerating them for the winter just in case our outdoor temperatures were too frigid or not cold enough. The second scenario is unlikely though, in Chicago. Mom liked to have flowers on the table, and I did too, although she only allowed the flowers we grew, nothing wild.

When Tom and I bought our own house, I started filling the space in front of our porch with bushes and then flowers. It was fun to be able to grow things just because I liked them. This was one of the first things that made me feel I was making my house a home. This is a quiet thing that has grown in me since becoming a mother—the desire to make beautiful and peaceful spaces for people I love. Once I filled the front, I started filling the sides of the house, then all along the fence. Now everywhere I look, there are lovely growing things year-round. I made sure to choose a variety of plants so something would always be blooming.

Have you ever pulled out a particularly stubborn weed by the roots? It is satisfying when you get the whole thing, isn't it? If you leave even a little, you may rest assured that within a few days or a week, that darn thing is going to be poking back up out of the ground again. Once

---

235 Psalms 143:10, Philippians 2:13

there was a thistle that had grown up in my garden while I was away that had a stem as thick as both of my thumbs put together. I started to pull on it with one hand, but it was too embedded to pull out that easily. I dug around it, pulled off some of the lower leaves, squared up to it with my feet on either side of it, grabbed it with both hands, and squatted up with all my might until it came out of the ground, and I fell backward. I was satisfied to see that I had most of it, but there was still a white end at the bottom of the hole the exhumed plant had left, so I got my long weeding tool and pulled the last of it out. It never grew in that spot again.

There are other weeds like nut grass or chickweed that return and multiply every time I pull them up. I pulled one out of one of my container gardens where the dirt was still very loose to find the main root was about two feet long, spiraled like a stretched-out phone cord from the days of landlines, and wrapped around a stick at the bottom. No wonder they kept coming back! And the crabgrass, my goodness, the way it spreads and puts down roots at each juncture is so frustrating.

When my neighbor lost her husband tragically, I planted a garden of flowers for her to the left of her drive. We don't talk much, but we genuinely love one another and look out for each other. The garden greets her every day with a reminder that she is loved. It was easy to plant the garden. The hard part is keeping the crabgrass and clover from choking the beautiful and delicate blooms.

When we first clear our heart of the lies, it feels so good. Everything is in order, the good things in our lives are free to grow, and our resources go towards the things that matter to us.

Everything is in alignment, working synergistically. But have you ever heard of a garden that you only had to weed once? The 7 Step Shift® is not something you do just once or twice or even 10 times. It's not a "one and done." It is a tool we use, just like a garden trowel digging at stubborn roots, to take thoughts captive and bring them under obedience to Christ continuously. The 7 Step Shift® is something we can use to renew our minds and cooperate with the transformative work of the Holy Spirit in our lives. God tells us that it's not sacrifice that pleases Him. It is an obedient heart, a humble and contrite heart that pleases Him.[236] When we seize those thoughts, uproot them in obedience to Christ, and reseed our hearts with thoughts in agreement with God about His truth, we are practicing profound humility and intimate relating to the Father.

Sometimes it is a lifelong process to get all the way underneath the root of a lie. So we keep pulling it, keep shifting into the truth every time we see it pop up. And if it has been a little while and the weeds have grown tall, it's alright. Just start pulling one at a time.

---

[236] 1 Samuel 15:22, Psalms 51:16-17

CHAPTER EIGHT

Identity

Who are you, really?

I HAVE COME to believe all lies we get to shift out of are rooted in one of these two thoughts: God is not enough, or I have to be more. That second umbrella includes the attacks on who you are. Have you experienced those accusations that you have to be better, do more, control more, achieve more, have more to get what you want? There are many ways our identity can be distorted, like those mirrors in the funhouse distorted my face. When we think God is not enough, we stop trusting. That leaves us to have to trust ourselves, and that converts to the exhausting belief that we have to be more such that we either step fully into the belief, living frenetic martyrish lives, or retreat from the belief and become maddenly passive. It's quite the lethal combination. Suddenly we find ourselves surrounded by desert sand once again.

I accidentally caught a glimpse of myself in the mirror the other day while I was deep in thought. It reminded me of when the kids would catch that same look on my face and wonder if I was mad about something. I had to explain that I was just concentrating, but it made me aware of how much even a simple facial expression can change the emotional landscape of the environment around me with the ones I love. I was so grateful for the relationship I had with the boys that they could inquire what was going on for me. But let's imagine that we didn't have that relationship. They would walk around continuously wondering why Mommy was mad, and I know that at least one of my boys would have spent much of his time trying to help me not be mad.

This, too, is distortion.

Noticing this behavior in him, it would've then been easy for me to interpret it as a confirmation of my fear that perhaps I was like my mother after all. I would've shrunk myself as a mother, desperately trying not to traumatize my boys but still playing out the old ways. My decisions would not have been motivated by good parenting principles but would have been based on tremendous insecurity. Distortion robs us of delight. If I gave in to those insecurities, I could not delight in my son because my son would become only a reflection of my shortcomings. Such thinking is insidious, to say the least.

There was also a time when I believed that if I allowed myself to have too much fun, I would have the rug ripped out from under me. The left-field verbal punches my mother would throw caught me off guard so many times, I learned to be on guard always. There was no predicting how she would act or how she would interpret my behavior. It was comforting to me to believe this, to have some kind of rule that I felt would protect me, but in reality, it took its toll on me. We can make lies our identity, wrap them around ourselves like that Linus blanket, and tell ourselves we can't do life without them. I made myself smaller and smaller and tried to define myself by anything that was not her. But at some point we have to define ourselves by what we are, not by what we are not. I am so grateful we are able to leave the old patterns behind.

How much pain from distortion could we avoid if we would just talk to God about it?

It's not that it won't get disorienting at times. It's that we get caught in the disorientation, and it starts to sound or look true. Each stage of life has its own opportunities for distortion and identity crisis. And at every stage we are developing our identity. We try to reflect this identity journey in our unique logo. This is so important; it's a huge part of each person's journey. When we surrender this treasure of ourselves fully to the Lord in any given moment, then we blossom more fully into all He has created us to be.

∞ Boundless Life ∞

In our logo, you can see the representation of the growth of the individual. We start as the small speck, which is navy blue (the logo is available in full color on our website). This is the version of us governed by the flesh; it is our starting point. Sin nature rules and we stay very small, our vision myopic. Then we begin to become a little more self-aware, and we hide the sinful nature–the deception, the pride, the self-serving intentions, represented by the first blade that points to the left. This is often as far as self-help and religious rituals can get us. We have added layers and layers of fig leaves to compensate for the parts of ourselves that make us feel ashamed.

But if we surrender and let go of the old self (ie: thought patterns, behavioral habits), Holy Spirit brings new life and redeems all the things He placed in us from the beginning in more beautiful ways than we ever could have created for ourselves. That is what the largest and middle blade, bright yellow in color represents—God's Word cutting through all our best and worst intentions, all the lies, all the striving, all the death and slavery. Then there is opportunity for new growth in new directions like the final blade on the right representing energy. This blade is the same color as our starting point because it is you and I redeemed. Boundless life now becomes available to us and we no longer live in hiding

This can represent the first time He enters your life or countless smaller areas we let Him into later as we surrender more and more to His Lordship. It has to be an act of the will, though; it will not be an unbidden lightning bolt.

Take my strength for example. In the last chapter I told you about how Debbie had called out the strength she saw in me. I was so afraid of being like my mother, I denied any part of myself that could be like her.

I hid.

Because I was afraid of my strength, I denied the idea of motherhood completely for the first six years of my marriage. I swore I would never have children because I did not want to allow the remotest possibility of inflicting the pain I experienced on my own child. I was terrified of what I saw in that imaginary and yes, distorted future, afraid I would crush a child. This is the fear I referenced at the beginning of the chapter. Misdirected fear will lead to distortions. Always.

> *Misdirected fear will lead to distortions. Always.*

I still remember the day we made the decision to become parents anyway. I was scared, but something had shifted in me. I didn't yet understand who I was, the lies He would dispel, and who I would become, but with time and distance I was able to see my mom in a different light. This was many years before I knew the Lord, but He was already working. When I moved away from Mom and Chicago, I got a little space from the tension. I was able to play and relax more without her over my shoulder, and I had room to bud into my own person. I developed this curiosity about her. My hate was beginning to be replaced with compassion, which was the beginning of the process of allowing love to take root in me. The more the hate quieted and love fanned, the more I was able to open my heart to the idea of children. This was a small flash of yellow.

I loved pregnancy. For all the foolishness my body would put me through later, it took to pregnancy like a dream. I walked 5 miles every day up until the day I delivered, and I adored every kick and turn they took in my womb. The love and tenderness that grew for them every day that they grew surprised me, softened me, bolstered me, and took me over.

The woman I became as a mother and a Lyme survivor would've been completely unrecognizable to the woman who finally made the decision to have children that day. I grew into and accepted my strength; I stopped putting it in a locked box. I let it make me protective, and I took on leadership roles.

We joined our church in Florida when my oldest was a newborn, and one of the women in the welcoming small group from Chapter 1 became my role model. Her name was Elizabeth; I even loved her name. I was so interested in everything about her. I went over to her house almost every day, just watching how she kept her house, raised her children, made her meals. I had so many questions. I had finally found someone to model my mothering after instead of just trying to do "not" like mom, and I was like a little puppy, following every move she made. One day in frustration, she put her hands on the counter and said, "What else do you want from me, Cheryl?" I just smiled and asked to continue being allowed to watch her, taking note in my heart that godly women were allowed to get frustrated sometimes. I am so grateful to her. It is impossible to trace how many ways she has influenced my way of living.

I didn't do everything right, but I broke the pattern. I did not pass down the pain I inherited from my mother. And I would later become a safe mother figure for a season to many people trying to find their way. Mothering is an integral part of my identity, and I am so grateful God did not allow that part of me to remain locked away. He replaced my distortions with the truth of His design for me as a woman. It was beautiful. I was beautiful. And although the two boy toddler season was straining physically, I was indeed at rest in my role.

However, not long after my second son, David, was born in 1995, the Lyme struggle began. I had barely begun to find my voice as a person when I literally lost my voice – there are probably still recordings somewhere from that time of the slurring, shaking, thin voice that couldn't find the words I wanted. I had to reframe my motherhood, this thing suddenly so precious to me, and the way I was there for my children on the days I couldn't hold them and couldn't stand to hear their voices.

The paralysis overtook more and more of my body until I needed assistance with every life function. I remember one afternoon that stands out from the blur of countless days like it. I was lying in bed, like every day (I could not go anywhere without being moved there by another) and I called out to be taken to the bathroom. Tom had left. I was alone in the house. Eventually, I knew that I had lost the battle of holding my bladder. I imagined my husband's reaction when he came home to find the mess.

I was in so much pain, I couldn't think, pray, or praise. I could only pee. Tears filled my eyes as I experienced my absolute helplessness. I couldn't even raise my hand to wipe my tears.

Suddenly, out of nowhere, my sense of helplessness was replaced with an absolute and total peace beyond anything I had ever experienced before or since. I sensed the Lord's pleasure in me when I was completely useless to the world. I felt myself being wrapped by a warm spiritual blanket of eternal comfort that was so tactile that to this day, I can still remember the sensation.

"Be still and know that I am God"[237] came to mind. I laughed a little because what else could I do? And I rested in my complete and utter dependence on Him for everything. As I lay there resting in Him, I was awestruck that His pleasure in me could be known in such a compromised and useless state. It was so palpable, I could sense Him smiling at me. I could do nothing for Him, and He loved me. All else was stripped away; my identity was simply in being His child. Laying there in my own filth, unable to clean myself or wipe my tears, He saw me, cradled me, and delighted in me.

The New York CEO, stripped away. The tennis player competing for a top spot on the 3.5 ladder, stripped away. The drum major of the Marching Illini, stripped away. The co-women's minister of a church of 5,000 members, stripped away. The person who served everyone else and accepted no help for herself, stripped away. Everything I thought reflected my faith in God and love for His people evaporated in the heat of this crucible. And He still loved me, the one He made, the thing I will never have to prove or work for. He loved ME.

Treatments came that allowed me to regain some function and strength. By some, I mean truly starting at square one. I relearned how to do nearly everything. I had swallowing therapy, speech therapy, physical therapy, and occupational therapy. I spent months practicing the simplest movements and then so many more with multi-colored exercise bands. My quest to regain strength continues to this day; my tiny dog can still run away with me on a walk, but hey, I can take him on a walk.

Long before I ever got sick, I was terrified of Lyme. It was not a battle I would have chosen for myself. I knew it was difficult to diagnose, it

---

237 Psalm 46:10

was painful, and it was difficult to find doctors who were willing to treat it. When we lived in New York, I would yell out "tick check" every ten minutes on a hike and expect all my friends to check their ankles and behind their ears to make sure they didn't have any unwanted hitchhikers. I was so obnoxious about it, that my husband took a picture of everyone checking their ankles on a hike in the Adirondacks one day because it was a more accurate representation of the trip than any of the vistas. None of my friends from New York contracted Lyme, only me. What I feared the most came upon me.[238]

But something changed in those years of illness. Lyme was no longer my greatest fear. I could have been afraid of relapses or other mysterious illnesses, but once I started to feel like I was really starting to heal, my biggest fear was that I would return to the person I was before. While I was sick, my relationship with the Lord was so sweet. There were so many tender moments with Him and with my family.

As I started to regain function, it was not a linear progression. There were days when all I could do was sit with my head packed in ice. That was okay. There were days when I could put one load of laundry in the washer. That was okay. There were days when I was found collapsed somewhere because I tried to do too much. Okay – that was not okay! As my energy allowed me to attempt to return to normal life activities, I learned over time to ask the question, "What would You have me do with the strength You have given me today?" I was declaring back to Him that my strength came from Him, and I was surrendering to living in alignment with Him that day. It didn't happen on day one of my illness; however, time and training made that the only question that would determine/regulate my activity for the day. Each day became a day of worshiping God, no matter what I got done that day. I had no guilt, no sense of not being enough.

"What would You have me do with the strength You have given me today?"

But as time went on, I started to return to the old ways, my flesh. I was picking up pride, picking up self-reliance, picking up anger, impatience, and selfishness. I ignored it for a while. I wasn't willing to admit it was happening. It wasn't painful enough to really get my attention. But finally, as my soul started feeling like the plant on my

---

238 Job 3:25

windowsill I forgot to water, I went to God about it. I asked Him, "What happened?? This is what I was afraid of the most!"

Almost before I could finish the words, He replied in my heart, "You changed your question."

I had to pause when I heard that. It reoriented me. It stopped me in my tracks. All I did was turn to Him in my "what I feared the most came upon me" moment, and He ran to me. He was right, something had changed as my days filled up again. I had, at some point, turned the question into a command. "Lord, give me the strength to do everything I need to get done today."

It wasn't until my will was tired of being self-willed and I willed it back to the Father that the yellow cut through my life and parted the waters *again*.

The Father's voice and manner of ordering things obliterated the old way, and I was able to receive inexpressible blessing. Delight.

How long do you think the prodigal son needed to be gone before the father would've been ready to receive him back home? Not long, right? As soon as he left, as soon as he broke the relationship, the father wanted him back. But the son had to make the choice to come home. God's desire is there, but He waits until our will has turned towards Him.

> *It wasn't until my will was tired of being self-willed and I willed it back to the Father that the yellow cut through my life and parted the waters again.*

And the lovely thing is, we don't even have to clean up the pigsty; we just leave it.

Just come home.

To this day, I still order my days this way. "Lord, what would you have me do with the strength You have given me today?" It is a simple but powerfully orienting question for me. I am connected to His complete sufficiency (God is enough), and I surrender myself to Him who loves me regardless of how much "usefulness" I have to offer (I don't have to be more).

I discovered important things about my identity, both as a child of God as well as hidden treasures about myself that He designed in my unique nature to reflect Him. Let's talk about your journey with your identity.

∞ Who Are You Surrendering? ∞

This is one place I believe the church has some work to do. We have created many helpful lists that define who you are in Christ. Let's just post a few of those items here:

I am adopted.

I am holy.

I am a treasure in an earthen vessel.

I am loved.

And yet, who is this person that is adopted, holy, a treasure in an earthen vessel that is loved?

That is a question we explore in depth at Promised Land Living. I may know who I am *in Christ* but who *am I* in Christ?

Sometimes we go on a long journey to find ourselves. It is a season when "going slow to go fast" is especially important. We can't rely on automatic responses to define ourselves such as where we work or how many children we have. If we don't do the deeper work, we tend to go back to hiding. I believe Jesus is often trying to pull that facade off of us. Yes, sin still lives in our bodies,[239] and we are weak.[240] And yet, I am now hidden in Christ.[241] Who is this "I" that is now hidden in Him?

If you're like me, you long to understand why you are here, and you want to know that your life "counts." And maybe, let's make this even more personal – not only do we want to know it counts, but we want to know our uniqueness. What helps me stand out from the sea of humanity? These are not bad questions. These are questions of longing. However, if not explored within the context of God's love and design, they can also be paralyzing questions.[242]

---

239 Romans 7:23
240 Hebrews 5:2
241 Colossians 3:3
242 Romans 1:23, 1 Corinthians 10:31

Add to this desire the instruction to surrender ourselves to the Lord. What am I surrendering when I don't even know who I am? It can begin to feel quite contrived and/or confusing, both of which are dangerous and unnecessary responses to a supernatural design God created. Yet, if we rush the process, expect an immediate answer to our questions, or are afraid the answers will never come, we find ourselves creating a persona to help us ease the discomfort of these unanswered longings.

This persona, over time, becomes quite dissatisfying and, as energy wanes or life confronts it, we now face a critical juncture of continuing to feed the persona or invite God to cut through that and allow Him to begin to show us the person who He knitted and formed in our mother's womb.

I have met many brothers and sisters who mistakenly thought that dying to self meant denying who they were. One woman fought so hard against herself, thinking her extrovertedness was "bad" that she became a mere shadow of herself.

One evening, we were making our way through the identity module of a PLL group. Shelly had this very puzzled look on her face. I kept looking over to her to check in. About three-quarters of the way through the night, her face changed to have a "eureka" look. She turned on her microphone to share.

"Oh my goodness… For all these years I thought surrendering myself and picking up my cross was to literally deny and push down all the ways God had created me. I thought unique qualities in me were antagonistic to God working in my life. I've been living for years telling myself "I can't do this; I can't do that' instead of bringing these good things God created under the restraint of the Holy Spirit."

She realized that as she was sanctified, she would still be recognizable as Shelly as she was being brought into the image of Christ.

I directed our group to look at the apostle Paul. "What are some words to describe him after Christ?" When I ask a group this question, these are the kinds of answers I get:

"Zealous."

"Perfectionist."

"Strong orator."

"Sense of authority; passion for what he was doing."

All of those qualities were also true *before* he knew Christ. Before Christ he persecuted the church, and after he was persecuted for Christ. He was so recognizable as Paul that when the disciples tried to bring him into the church, the people didn't want him.[243] They knew he was there when Stephen was stoned.[244] The disciples had to assert that Paul had received the Holy Spirit and was now "one of us." What did "us" mean? The body of Christ with the Holy Spirit guiding, restraining, and empowering us to do the good work ordained for us from the beginning of time.

That which we deny is the flesh. The desire to serve self, protect self at the cost of others, stroke the ego, chase cravings, and all the ways sin has corrupted is the flesh. But the person God created you to be is as unique as your fingerprint. He has not made anyone just like you, and He has entrusted you to reflect His image in your unique way. A quick example – when I was learning to pray, I tried to pray like my prayer partner, but it felt contrived and stiff. Soon, however, I found my own prayer voice, Cheryl's prayer voice. He delights to see you finding those gifts He left just for you inside you. He is as excited by you becoming His intended creation as a composer is when the french horns and the clarinets and the cellos all play their parts just right. They were never intended to play the exact same thing – that would be a very boring symphony! They may take turns playing the melody but even then in their own voice and timbre. The symphony becomes one voice through powerful instrumentation as we become one body through God's powerful orchestration by the Holy Spirit.

Let's look at Peter, impetuous Peter. He jumped out of more than one boat, told Jesus to call him to walk on water, and was the first to declare Jesus as the Messiah. He was also the one who reportedly told his tormentors to crucify him upside down because he felt he did not deserve to die in the same manner as his Savior. This is the man who denied Jesus three times in fear of being crucified with Him. Now that the one thing he most feared was upon him again, what was different? Not Peter. He was still very much Peter, but now he was filled with the Holy Spirit. His priorities had changed, and his fears were supplanted with a boldness for presenting the gospel to those around him. The

---

243 Acts 9:26
244 Acts 7:58-60

servant girl's pointed finger[245] didn't have the same power over Peter as he grew in his faith. But throughout his journey, impetuous Peter we got to know and love was recognizable through the very end of his life.

We, too, are recognizable. Scripture indicates we will recognize people in heaven.[246] We don't kill the person God created in us; we kill the desires of the flesh blocking the transformation of the beautiful creation God made to come forth.

I am so tired of people apologizing for who they are, for their tears, for their passion, or for their strength. Stop saying you're sorry! Those things are nothing to apologize for. God does not make sorry goods. And that's where Shelly was, living an "I'm sorry" life. "I'm sorry I am who I am." No!

We have to stop saying what God made is junk. We tease out the differences as we mature. Who I am in the flesh when unrestrained causes great harm, but who I am in Christ can do great good!

That raw material is what we identify in PLL as our heartland. Just like Caleb took his mountain, we each have property in God's Promised Land. That land is how He has formed us and knitted us *for His good purposes*. We consider the heartland phrase to be putting words to the essence of who you are.

∞ Essence ∞

When I walked into my grandmother's house, there was a warm cinnamon smell that was part laundry detergent, part her cooking, part the wood of the house, part her perfume; it all came together as her essence. My mother had a very sweet smell; it was a light, floral scent. After she died, I had a pair of her pajamas that I saved in my closet. I would go smell it when I was overwhelmed with missing her. It was the closest thing I could get to Mom once she had gone home to Jesus. It was an echo of her essence.

---

245 Matthew 26:69
246 1 Thessalonians 2:19-20 (Paul expects to recognize those he ministered to when Jesus comes), Matthew 17:1-8 (Elijah and Moses are recognizable in their imperishable bodies)

There is an essence of who you are that is going to show up everywhere you go; you can't help it! You can try to kill it, tame it, dress it up, or dress it down, but it is always there. "Wherever I go, there I am." We call this the heartland statement, a way to put words to the herb mix that describes your essence. It may be very calm, or curmudgeonly, or floral, or passionate, or adventurous; you fill in the blank. Essence.

Meet LaShanda. She is beautiful, funny, creative, tender, and clever. When we met, she said that she felt like she was fuzzy and clouded to herself. There were so many voices telling her who she should be and how she should act. She was always in someone else's shadow and defined as someone's daughter or granddaughter. No one ever called her by her name.

She went by "Shawna" most of the time because it was easier to say, and nobody had to bother with how to spell it or how to pronounce it. This was a metaphor for how she did everything. She felt like she was inconveniencing others simply by existing. But as she went through this heartland process with us, she was able to quiet all those other voices. She was able to connect to the God who made her, loved her, and called her by name before the foundation of the earth.[247]

After this, she decided that she wanted to be called by her given name, LaShanda. She practiced going by her name in the course with us, and then began introducing herself as LaShanda in more contexts as she became comfortable in this new space. She stopped apologizing, stopped trying to appease, and became more confident in the essence of who she is.

There's a quote from my dear friend, Tracy: "God's gift to us is who we are; our gift to God is who we become." It's those things imbued in us, not spiritual gifts. We are digging down to what was there in us in the very beginning.

This is a unique process that we have taken many people through. My best friend's husband had taken every single personality, strengths, animal, color, type assessment known to man as a highly recognized corporate sales executive before going through this. We all want to know that there is something unique about each of us, and Jack was no different. He wanted to know he was special, and there's nothing

---

247 Ephesians 1:4, Revelation 13:8

wrong with wanting to know you are special. Otherwise, why would God spend so much time telling Israel they are the apple of His eye and the great purposes He had for them?[248] Why would God tell us He has giftings and callings unique to us?[249]

When Jack saw his heartland statement, he simultaneously felt very special and in awe. In fact, it is the most emotional I had ever seen Jack. It became a moment of worship. Assessments don't do that for us. As we get to know ourselves in the truest sense, in the context of our Creator, the response will be worship because God made a wonderful thing in you. Delight.

I recently watched a talk from a scientist, Professor John Lennox, at Cambridge to a mixed audience, some of whom were very antagonistic to a creation view of the world. He shared, "How can I not believe there is a God who has designed this creation when I look at the order of nature?" He went further to marvel at the way the human mind is able to reason in a way that goes far beyond what a brain evolved for mere survival would achieve. He interpreted this as evidence in itself of a Creator that wanted to be known.[250] Professor Lennox was given an innate curiosity about God's creation. He was given the mind of a scientist. He was bestowed with an ability to ask big questions and to articulate ideas that hold the imagination at attention. These qualities could be used to serve antagonistically against his Creator or as His workmanship, reflecting God's magnificent design. We like to say at PLL that all of us reflect the image of God, though not completely. If you take more and more of the body of Christ and put us together, you get a fuller picture of God. It's a fascinating image, too big for this book. The

> *As we get to know ourselves in the truest sense, in the context of our Creator, the response will be worship because God made a wonderful thing in you.*

---

248 Deuteronomy 32:10, Zechariah 2:8
249 1 Peter 4:10-11, Romans 11:29
250 "Professor John Lennox God DOES Exist." *Oxford Union.* https://youtu.be/otrqzITuSqE?si=BWfUwzrbeNneLcx8

infinite is infused into the finite. The response of awe is spontaneous. This is amazing to me; how else can I help but respond?

One day every knee will have that response.[251] Everyone will see Him and who they always were with the distortions unmasked. Everyone will see what they chose to trust in or fight against their entire life. For the believer, that one day is not some day but now. We bow our knees now. We live into the preferred future God gifted us through His Son. And this preferred future is the way of rest. Rest from proving, deceiving, comparing, hiding, covering, searching, dominating, blaming. In this preferred future we learn to rest from all of it! We are empowered to choose which version of that future we prefer to live into now. When we no longer contend but allow ourselves to be trained to embrace through the restraint of Holy Spirit, we are living in our heartland in the Promised Land.

Sometimes we say, "Oh, if we could just bottle the energy of a toddler." When we say this, we usually mean physical energy, but let's look at that from a different perspective. Toddlers aren't comparing themselves to anyone else. They aren't wasting an ounce of energy trying to be anything but themselves.

Imagine for just a moment that you took back all of the energy you spend comparing yourself to others, trying to be something He never intended, squashing down pieces of yourself. What do you think you would become? How full would your tank be? How easy would it be to get up in the morning? How much less threatening would another person be when they see you or you see them?

There can be a safety and security in who you are in Christ such that when you interact with that person, they cannot threaten you anymore. Yes, they will influence, inform, and give ideas for places to do work, but they cannot shake who you are anymore. It's not possible when you are that sure and that clear. Then you will be like Stephen, who even on the brink of execution stared hate in the face and said like Jesus, "Do not hold this sin against them."[252] He did not shrink back from who he was in Christ and who Christ was in him. Stephen was known for his boldness as a deacon. This boldness landed him before

---

251 Philippians 2:10-11
252 Acts 7:60, Luke 23:34

the Sanhedrin. He did not stop being bold when threatened. Instead, he became the first martyr of the church. Because of that, he was bold in his declaration of Jesus as Messiah and was even able to love his accusers through their hate. He served them the gospel Himself even as they threw rocks at the table set before them.

John the Baptist and Jesus recognized one another before conscious thought. There was knowing in the womb when they were near one another. They were already who they were before they were born, before society or parenting or trauma or blessings or influence. John would become a Nazarite, separating himself from good things in life for the single purpose he knew from the womb when his mute father wrote "His name will be John," a declaration by the earthly father of the Heavenly Father's call on his life.

At the end of his life, in jail, crisis descended. He sent a message to Jesus, "Are you the One, or do we wait for another?" He needed to know his entire life hadn't been for nothing, that he hadn't poured out everything he had for the wrong one. As convinced as he had been, he had a shadow of doubt as death loomed over him. He was reminded of his own words that he spoke in the wilderness: "He is the One who makes the lame walk and the blind see."[253] This One you've been trumpeting and baptizing, He is the One, John. You simply must become less so He can be more. John, your job is done. You can go in peace free of doubt.

I wonder what might come to mind as you consider John. What might be the heartland boundaries of John's life? I might say something like beholding loner, nature enthusiast, ruggedly compassionate, unwavering in purpose. There's an example of a heartland phrase. No other people on the earth would fill that exact description – maybe parts but not all. Can you see John in those words? Those phrases sketch simple lines around this man's complex life. They were him. His life was lived fully and unreservedly for Christ, not himself, but you can still undeniably recognize him as John the Baptist. This is the intention of a heartland statement. It isn't a mission statement. It isn't about what you are going to do. It describes the person you are in whatever you

---

253 Luke 7:18-35

do. Whether you ever come to the Lord or not, these qualities or your essence will always be true of you.

I was told for many years that I needed to be an attorney. People said I belonged in a courtroom because I believed in truth and exemplified power. Imagine what happened initially when I came to know Jesus. Now I knew THE truth and was connected to ultimate power in Jesus Christ. I was a little overzealous in my initial slightly aggressive attempts to share the truth with people. To this day I cringe and laugh simultaneously. I had some things I needed to learn. In my enthusiasm and exuberance, before I hurt too many people too much, I started to see I needed to do some work here. Holy Spirit began to restrain. That heartland quality of "powerful truth" lived in me as a child, just ask my mom! When she tried to say anything even slightly wrong, she had to be ready for a battle. And I was going to win. I was not going to let her say something that was not true. That quality still lives in me now, but it is being transformed into the likeness of Christ.

He has uniquely made you. You can be assured of that. You don't have to wonder or be afraid. Your snowflake looks very different from mine but is equally beautiful.

But my friend, all snowflakes melt. All flowers wither.[254] If my quest in this journey is to prove that I'm unique, then I'm going back to the covering light blue blade from our logo, creating a persona. I'm fighting for something that is already mine. Instead, I simply embrace that I am snow. Beautiful for a season; I will melt, but I will live. I surrender the perishable in exchange for the imperishable.[255] There is something powerful in putting words to and naming your essence so you can stop fighting to prove or demonstrate that it's there. We have seen so much spiritual energy restored in brothers and sisters during this process. This, too, brings rest.

I remember when my bestie took me to Switzerland. We made a couple of stops along the way in France and Germany. I wanted to stop the car every 15 minutes to take in the scenery, watch the swans, grab a cup of French coffee. I insisted we picnic on cheese and bread alongside the road, because that's what the French do. I brought myself

---

254 James 1:11, Isaiah 40:8
255 1 Corinthians 15:53-54

fully into the experience without apology or care. We laughed so hard we cried. We would pause and stand in silence as I tried to take in the views of the Swiss Alps. I never once was concerned about being anything but myself. And Zane delighted in every moment with me. Imagine us beginning to live from that place of complete freedom from all self-consciousness with our Father. Imagine you and the shaping Holy Spirit partnering together training to delight in God and maybe even to be able to laugh at yourself just a little bit.

Little poiema,[256] may you rest in the understanding that God made you. Maybe we can state it more clearly – stop doubting that you are you. Once we understand that, we train to receive Love Himself into who we are, not deflected off a mask or performance, and that expands our ability to now love others authentically with *ourselves*. This is how upfront and personal the body of Christ can be. But I get ahead of myself. We'll talk more about that in the community chapter.

If you find yourself wanting to go deeper after the following Selah moment, I would love to have one of my team members take you on the Promised Land Living journey, which includes Holy Spirit-influenced building of this heartland phrase. If this resonates with you, if you're curious, I hope you'll reach out and talk to one of our team members or join an upcoming discipleship group.

---

[256] "POIEMA – GREEK WORD STUDY." *Preceptaustin*, 24 Sept. 2012, preceptaustin.wordpress.com/2012/09/24/poiema-greek-word-study/.

Selah Moment

Is there a part of you that has believed any variation of the lies that you are "sorry goods"? Nick Vujicic, a quadriplegic, struggled with that, too. He was suicidal by the time he turned twenty years old. But God. Nick knows that you have a Commander in Chief who thinks differently about you! God wants us to do our good works here on earth in the victory that is already His! To do this, we have to decide to walk like we know we are on the right side. I remember a scene from *The Last Rifleman*, when Artie is talking to a German who also fought in WWII. The German admits that the only gut punch worse than knowing they had lost the war was realizing he had been fighting on the wrong side. Sobering confession, isn't it? But for us it's different! The war was won in Christ, and we are on the winning side. Jesus leads us in triumph. He invites us to ride up on the chariot of victory with Him. It's time to start living like we are, instead of walking with our heads down like one defeated (as you do this, remember our battle is not against flesh and blood).[257] Would you be willing to put the 7 Step Shift® tool we discussed in the last chapter to use in this context? As we walk through the process of shifting out of any lie pertaining to your value in your own life, consider asking the One who made you fearfully and wonderfully[258] what He would like you to know about how He sees you.

Feel free to use this space or your own journal to reflect on the things He has brought to mind on this topic:

Step 1: What happens physically to me when I'm having a sense of lack of worth – describe the *physical* symptoms (mind races, sweaty palms, feel the need to run away, etc.)

---

[257] Ephesians 6:12
[258] Psalm 139

Step 2: Pause and ask yourself what you are telling yourself about you, the other person, the situation, or God (but in this example of worthlessness, let's focus on you). Here are some thought joggers to get you started: *See, you keep proving you are worthless. You will never measure up. If you had _____ you could have prevented _____ from happening.* Write down what you hear you telling yourself. You may recognize it's not true; that doesn't matter. It still owns you in this minute – don't rationalize it away so it flees for the moment only to return later; bring it into the light so you can nail it against the cross.

_____

Step 3: Ask God what He says about you. Don't think about asking. Ask! Write down what you hear.

_____

Step 4: Compare what you are saying to yourself with what God is saying. Where you are not aligned with God? Do you want to stay in misalignment or do you want to agree with God? If you are ready to agree with God, then confess what you are believing or saying to yourself that is not true. Then confess the truth. The truth about God, His authority, the work He has accomplished – anything that He brings to your mind. Confess this out loud first, and then record what you remember saying.

_____

Step 5: Declare the truth to yourself before God, standing in His authority.

_____

Step 6: Ask God what is one small step you can take into that truth (to "seal" your alignment with God).

_____

Step 7: Immediately take that step. (This could be anything from writing out a prayer, seeking forgiveness, setting a boundary, smiling – God is very creative!) He will show you the next rock He wants you to step on as you live into the Truth you have declared.

_____

CHAPTER NINE

Skandalon

Who do you need to forgive?

THE DAY I met Tom's mother, Grace, she didn't talk to me. When Tom and I started dating more seriously, I told him, "I don't think your mom likes me that much." He spoke with her privately to try to understand what might be going on. She did not even try to sugarcoat her feelings about me; she told him boldly, "I hate that woman because she is going to steal my son from me."

My entire marriage to Tom, his adoptive mother Grace wanted nothing to do with me through the day she died. It is ironic to me that her name was Grace. While I was fighting Lyme, she was fighting lung cancer. I knew she loved crossword puzzles. Every Sunday, no matter how sick I was, in an effort to love her, I would cut out the crossword puzzle from the newspaper with my own shaking, uncooperative hands and address it to her with my scrawled handwriting. She never mentioned them. Grace had also gotten her daughter, Winks, to hate me. After many years, when I finally formed a relationship with my sister-in-law, Winks was shocked at how I had loved her mother.

How? How could I have loved Grace? I surely did not at first, but while we were still living in Florida, I told Elizabeth about Grace and her contempt towards me. She gave me some very important advice. "Pray blessing over her." That woman? Who makes me miserable? The one who tries to get my husband to turn on me, makes my life harder, and criticizes me at every turn? Her?

But I trusted Elizabeth. From that day forward, instead of thinking about what I thought I deserved, I prayed for blessing over Grace which guarded my heart from hating her. That made it possible for me to love Grace with a genuine love until the day she died of lung cancer. It was never reciprocated, but it never needed to be. I wanted it, not even really for my sake, but for her sake.

Her behavior came from her childhood. In her family, the boys were always favored over the girls. She was a castaway. So she was simply repeating what she knew as she favored Tom and made me a castaway. She came to look like what she had not forgiven. It wasn't conscious.

When Grace died, I bore no grudge against her. I was already free. Was I sad? Yes. But you can be sad and you can be free. The two can coexist with one another.

> *You can be sad and you can be free. The two can coexist with one another.*

After she died, I found a gift that I had sent her. It was a beautiful fourteen-carat gold necklace. She had never even opened the box. She was never able to receive the love she was given. I wasn't sad because of what she did, but I was sad because she could not open the gift of Christ that I represented.

None of my generosity towards Grace could have been possible if I had been carrying any sort of grudge against her. My spiritual mentor, Elizabeth, recognized that I was entrapping myself with my grudge as soon as she heard me describe the situation to her years earlier. What a gift she gave me!

The trapped soul is not at rest; it paces and seethes. The advice Elizabeth gave me was as much for my benefit as it was for Grace's. My extravagant gesture towards Grace, by earthly standards, led to me being able to receive so much more of the love of the Father through His Son. It opened up a storehouse of divine treasure of His good gifts.

Even after she died, the family dynamics would take time to heal. Tom managed to get my sick self to Chicago for a reunion because family is important to us. We were sitting together downstairs with Mike and Winks when the moment became serious. They said they wanted to share something with me.

"We know you think you have Lyme." He was trying to be nice about it. He continued,

"We understand you really believe that you have it. But we see through that. It's a game you're playing to control Tom and get attention."

What could I say to that? How could I possibly respond without making myself appear even more of what he described? So I crawled up to the bathroom and silently wept.

But fast forward: not only did I forgive Winks, but as you know Winks and I have an incredible relationship now. We love each other; we are endeared to one another. There is a new generation of reconciliation that could not have happened if I had clung to my offense. The past does not have to repeat itself in our family; instead, the dysfunction died with Grace.

∞ Offense ∞

So let's talk about this word 'offense' I have been using. There is no word in Scripture for unforgiveness. You don't unforgive someone, instead, you become offended. The word for offense is "skandalon."[259] The literal meaning of that word is: the trigger for a trap, a stick for bait.[260] When you pick up that offense, you have allowed a trap to snap shut on your soul. Maybe your leg is caught in a painful jagged vise, or there is a rope around your neck, or you've found yourself in a cage. It feels good for a second, that anger, like the bait tastes good to the fox, but then the weight and chaos you find in yourself afterward clings tight. You resent the other person for this too, thinking they are the reason your leg hurts so badly and you can't move on. But we are not mindless, trapped animals; we have the means to open the trap.

Let's take it a step further. Skandalon is translated several different ways including "temptation," "stumbling block," "hindrance," and

---

259 Romans 14:13; "G4625 - Skandalon - Strong's Greek Lexicon (Kjv)." *Blue Letter Bible*, www.blueletterbible.org/lexicon/g4625/kjv/tr/0-1/.
260 See previous footnote

"[rock] that makes them fall."[261] It is the very same word that is used for the cross as an offense or a "stumbling block" when describing the way that the shame of the cross and the humility of Jesus were things that caused the religious leaders of the day to miss Jesus as the Messiah and, as a result, miss eternal life with the Lord. They got stuck on their expectations; they were "trapped" in their pride. Anger blinds. Imagine the rage of the Pharisees at this man claiming to be Messiah, this core hope of their identifying faith that made them unable to even consider another perspective. How grave, how deadly of a trap was that offense they picked up against Him. Unforgiveness is only one subset of skandalon; there can be many ways we can get stuck.

This word, skandalon, a trigger for a trap, is ancient. The term "trigger" in the mental health field was first included in the DSM-3 in 1980.[262] The two terms are not the same; there are places where the concepts do not overlap, but there is one that is very relevant, specifically when those traumas are from our relationships. When a person is triggered, they are flooded with the same neurochemicals that were released upon the original trauma. We do not have to be at the mercy of our triggers.

Grace very well could have triggered me again and again; my own mother treated me far worse than Grace did. But I became more "untriggerable" the more I released Grace and the more I forgave my mother. It wasn't that I handled the situation better; it wasn't that I coped with the flood better each time. Jesus healed me such that the flood was no longer occurring every single time. I was becoming less offendable. But I soon learned there was more work to do.

---

261 "Skandalon in the New Testament." *Girardian Lectionary*, 9 Sept. 2020, girardianlectionary.net/learn/skandalon-in-the-new-testament/.

262 Riachi E, Holma J, Laitila A. Psychotherapists' views on triggering factors for psychological disorders. Discov Psychol. 2022;2(1):44. doi: 10.1007/s44202-022-00058-y. Epub 2022 Dec 12. PMCID: PMC9744044.; DSM–III (1980) 3rd ed.

Selah Moment

Can you think of a time when you have been offended? Where do you feel the skandalon or an offense in your body? This can be the beginning of shifting out of unforgiveness into forgiveness. You will have another opportunity at the end of this chapter to make the shift. For now, just identify the wrongdoing and describe how you feel that wrong in your body.

Skandalons can come on the behalf of others, as well. A couple years ago my friend Martha told me that her husband wanted to move again. They were in their 70s, and her husband was fairly immobile, which put all the burden of an unnecessary move on my friend. I was about ready to hop on a plane and haul myself into their home in Texas to have a word (or words) with Vernon. I was mad and also scared for my friend Martha.

I knew this would be too much for her. In her love for me, she said: "I appreciate that you care about me so much, Cheryl, but please don't carry an offense on my behalf with Vernon. It's not good for your soul."

I never realized I could pick up an offense for another person until that day. But as we continued to talk on the phone, I sheepishly and somewhat begrudgingly put down my offense. I knew she was right. It made me feel like I was really caring for her in the moment, but she knew long term I was only hurting myself. Now, that's love!

In one of our men's courses, we had a participant who was a pastor. We reached the part of the course about forgiveness. In the safety of the group, the pastor found the courage to confess that he had not forgiven his mom. He made the moment more real when he admitted that he didn't want to. Our respect for him grew rather than diminished. It takes guts to admit that, especially as clergy.

I paused, gave him space to hear his own words and acknowledged his pain with my face and a nod. The men in the group gave him space as well, suspending their own immediate reactions or judgments.

There was a choice there for all of us. We could respond quickly to fix and tell him, "Well, you know all about forgiveness. You know you need to forgive your mom." But in love and respect for him, we chose to be present with him; we stayed slow. We allowed him to sit in the discomfort of his admission. If we had chosen a pharisaical listening style, ministry would have stopped. If we had picked up an offense on behalf of his mother, ministry would have stopped. We gave him room to continue processing, and more gunk came to the surface.

"But it doesn't matter if I forgive her. She is never going to change her behavior. We will still have to have boundaries with her. It won't change anything." A few seconds of quiet followed as we gave him the floor.

"Honestly, I don't think she is worthy of my forgiveness…" There it was, the vulnerable naked truth.

Gentle inquiry brought him back to the Scriptures, brought him back to the cross. As a group, we mentally climbed the hill to Golgotha together. We imagined we formed a circle under the base of the cross and brought our senses into it. Can you feel the sweat and blood dripping on you? Can you smell the blood and the stench of death coming? From this place, in the context of the reality of what was done for you and your forgiveness, are you telling me you are unable to forgive her? It was still a struggle. He had preached forgiveness from the pulpit. He had held people's hands through their own forgiveness journeys in counseling sessions in his office. But now when it came down to it for himself, he felt his own sweat beading down his face. He was disconnected from himself, disconnected from his Savior. But there at the foot of the cross, the burden had to fall; there was no more distraction or distance from the truth of his own need for forgiveness and the love that had given it to him. It was now unavoidably, intensely personal. He was finally able to uncurl his fingers and let it go. And in that moment of choosing to forgive, the pastor finally found rest for his weary, offended soul.

Another example – a senior pastor's wife who was so kind and loved by many, but when anyone tried to get close in a real way, she was closed off and unavailable. What finally came out in PLL was that she was still angry at God. She had prayed that God would heal her brother and he died. Forty years after the loss, she was still holding an offense against God.

There was a trap there for her. She never needed to forgive God. He doesn't require that. In fact, it is impossible to forgive God. It's actually blasphemous to think He needs forgiveness. God does not owe us a debt, nor has He ever sinned against us. That theology is ripe for an ego-centric view of a lowercase g "god." But she does need to seek His forgiveness for holding an offense and allow Him to minister to her in her sorrow instead of shutting Him out and holding Him responsible.

> *Allow Him to minister to you in your sorrow instead of shutting Him out and holding Him responsible.*

This is happening for the pastor's wife right now as I write to you. I don't know what the outcome will be. I pray that she will find comfort in His arms.

When Job was struck with loss and illness, his wife held an offense against God and encouraged him to do the same, telling him to "Curse God and die," but Job would not.[263] He lamented, he was confused, he even wished he had never been born,[264] but he would not carry an offense against God. Carrying an offense against God causes spiritual illness in a person.

Our job is to forgive others as Christ has forgiven us. Our job is to receive Christ's forgiveness for our own mess and to recognize that when we are holding an offense against God we need to spend some time with Him. It does not hurt Him; it only hurts us. It cuts us off from the source of comfort and healing.

∞ Who Do You Look Like? ∞

Maybe you don't feel especially trapped. Maybe you still feel that clinging to these hurts is the only way to maintain your sense of self. But I will tell you something else, something sobering and terrifying.

---

263 Job 2:9-10
264 Job 3:1-7

When we cling to these wounds, we are not looking like the Father; we start to look like those whom we have not forgiven.

This is the principle behind what is described by mental health professionals as generational cycles. We repeat what has happened to us. We raise our children the way we were raised unless we choose not to and work hard at new patterns. This repetition is not just limited to parenting. Children who are abused tend to inflict the abuse they received on younger, weaker children. We find words coming out of our mouths we swore we'd never use on people we love after hearing them as a child and with the ones we most desire to love. Heartbreaking. This is what we do as humans unless the cycle is interrupted. We pass on our pain.

But we don't have to. I have shared some stories from other people, and I've shared a difficult relationship of my own, but what about those deepest wounds? What about the ones that are unforgivable?

Without Jesus, yes, there are unforgivable people. Corrie Ten Boom has much worse stories than I do; she had many unforgivable encounters. Elisabeth Elliot faced the people who killed her husband. Brother Yun faced unimaginable suffering.[265] Look up their stories if you are not familiar with them. Their faith humbles and encourages me.

The person who wounded me the most was my mother. I've shared a little bit about her, and I will pull the curtain back a little further now.

I was a little girl, around 8 years old, playing on the living room floor, and my mother called me, "Come upstairs, and close your eyes! I have a surprise for you!" I jumped up, took her hand, and innocently hurried up the stairs, happy little bare toes bouncing off the carpet. She sat me down in the bathroom on the toilet lid and told me to close my eyes. I immediately obeyed without hesitation or peeking, my heart rate increasing with excited anticipation.

"Now open your mouth, and take a bite."

I opened my mouth so wide and bit down so hard--into a bar of soap. My "surprise" was some kind of punishment for an unknown "misbehavior." I looked up at her, beautiful and cold, my smile replaced with sour spitting, and my view of her changed as tears filled my eyes. I didn't

---

[265] Wikipedia Contributors. "Brother Yun." *Wikipedia*, Wikimedia Foundation, 2 Sept. 2024, en.wikipedia.org/wiki/Brother_Yun.

know it then, but I would never again close my eyes without peeking; I would never again trust her voice. The soap story was an introduction to her increasing control as I tried to become more independent. She would reinforce that "lesson" again and again around my appearance, how I ironed shirts, anything fun I found to do, and especially about how I made her look to our community. Another incident that reflected our dynamic happened the day I inconvenienced her by falling off a top bunk head first onto a concrete floor at a summer camp in elementary school. I was found unconscious the next morning. I did not receive any medical attention for the concussion.

I want to let you into this part of my history a little bit because more ministry has happened and continues to happen through my broken places than through my strong places as I allow Him to redeem it all.

A little over 6 years later, I made a plan to kill myself as I told you in chapter seven. What I didn't tell you is how I wondered if she would miss me, if she would know that it was her that made this life no longer worth living for me. I was going to finally show her how much she had hurt me. Maybe in my absence, she would understand what she had done to me. And it would finally stop. I could finally get away from her.

Those words, "You can only blame yourself," delivered with such fury did slay one version of me, but with it my hope to ever get her to love me. I had my answers. She would not understand what she had done. And she would not miss me. My life was suddenly mine. Why should I waste it on her? Why should I scream my loudest and most painfully raw message when this, too, was just screaming into the void? This would not give me what I wanted. So I stopped trying to get her to love me. Not only did I stop trying to get her to love me; I was also unwilling to receive any love from her. My offense fueled my self-destructive fury. I ducked my head and took what she dished out in a calculated exchange for the choices I made, and I got out of the house for good as soon as I could.

I love open windows and doors now, because my mother used to close them before verbally ripping me apart. I still, at 60, dread my birthday because the stress on her of putting on any kind of party was always my fault, and the fallout was never worth it. My name was a curse. I mentally flinched when hearing my name long into adulthood because it had always been the prelude to a tongue-lashing. I ran away from home at 7, I tried to end my life at 16 and again at 21. But God.

Friend, I do not blame my mom. I miss her every day. The scars I have with me today are things I have to work through, but they are by no means reasons to hate her. The memories I carry with me are the mornings she would sing to me and open our curtains. On the rare days that she was truly happy, I would know it because she called me "Sherry Berry." Because of forgiveness, I do not think about soap; I think about slow days snuggling in the bed together and the way she would gently rub the inside of my forearm. Or how she would let her toes touch my toes when we sat facing each other on the couch. I remember making the most of our last days together by laughing about wigs for her instead of crying about the illness they were there to cover. Laughing through her insistence on eating fries even though we both knew she would soon regret them.

I can do this because I have forgiven her. I do not hold her responsible. Because I am more than safe and vindicated in Jesus, and my rights are bound up in His life, I have surrendered my right to a safe childhood. I can see her in a light that I could not see before I released her to the justice of God.

What I could not have seen back then was her own crushing responsibility to hold an entire extended family together, and that her need to control herself and her children under such a firm and suffocating hand was coming from her own fears. She even loved me in her own way, but I didn't believe that until much later than I could have. She didn't know how to love me, but she did care about me, and that means a lot to me now. None of these statements are excuses; they don't erase her transgressions against me. What she did was not okay. She should have been my haven; it was her job to make my world safe. But I can say these things out of an understanding born of compassion rather than my own needs, resentment, or even any loss.

When I understood the depth of the forgiveness I received from Jesus, the very first thing I did was call her to tell her I forgave her. No one told me to do this; it wasn't something I tried to do; it was just the natural result of the lightness of my own forgiveness. I could no longer hold anything against her. I forgave her fully and freely. She wouldn't accept my forgiveness then, but I was free. Delight.

The acknowledgment I wanted at five came decades later, but I forgave her years before I received it. If I had still demanded acknowledgment, I would have been giving my power away. My dear friend, Donna, understands this. Both she and her brother were sexually molested over a period of years by a neighbor. Their parents could not acknowledge what happened. Her brother committed suicide as an adult after suffering a long time the weight of feelings of guilt and shame. Donna is now a woman of more grace and mercy than any other person I know in my life. It was a long journey to get to this moment, including taking a trusted friend with her to the scene of the repeated crime. But to talk to Donna now, she operates in an authority that is so powerful she does not need her parents to admit their mistakes. She simply wants to love them in their pain and woundedness. In her own words:

> *I see this as His work, not mine. I just get to walk in it. He defined who I was. I chose to accept it. Then mercy, sweet mercy came. That took everyone off the hook. I didn't need retribution to know who I was. I didn't need to please anyone to know who I was. It took time for it to sink in. But once it did, radiant colors replaced my black and white world.*

I could have waited far too long to be free, and could still be waiting today. I had the choice in my hands to spiritually walk out of my childhood house, or stay inside ignored and bleeding on the carpet, demanding something over which I had no control and that she could not give me. It was a losing battle.

If I had still demanded acknowledgment, I would be giving my power away.

Like Donna, you also do not need to defend your right to feel wounded. You know what happened, and God knows. You do not need to explain it. But you do not have to carry it so closely anymore. He knows, dear one. There are battles we were not meant to fight.

There was a time when I thought I could not be whole apart from Mom admitting her error, but that gave her too much power and authority. When I released the need for confirmation, I shifted the authority back over to the Father and what he says about my value and the situation. I am now at rest because I live from my wholeness not for my wholeness. I stopped using so much unnecessary energy, and I found such gentleness from the heavenly Father. And from THERE, He gave me the grace to love her with unconditional love. Even though her communication style didn't change with time, her barbs and jabs didn't sting as much anymore. I was still freer. She couldn't trigger me nearly as much anymore.

I had all of her moves down. No matter what she threw at me, I was unflappable. Until one day she did something new. When we were home for Christmas in 1996, I went upstairs and overheard her apologize for something to my sister. I sneaked back downstairs and became very worried. My mom never said she was sorry. My mom could not be wrong. That was how she protected herself. This was incredibly out of character for my mother, and my radar was up.

Shortly after the holidays, we discovered that she had pancreatic cancer. She would be 55 in a month. There was a softening happening in her heart as she faced this monster. My prayer for her soul then became, "Please do not let her have the heart of Pharaoh. Soften her heart to receive You fully." I knew that she knew about the crucified Christ as a Catholic. She was painfully aware of her sin. But she did not know the empty grave and the resurrected victorious Christ.

Over the next several years my Aunt Cathi and I prayed for her daily. My aunt had uprooted her life and moved to Chicago from California to care for my mother in these days of illness. One day, three months before her death, my mother was rocking furiously in her rocking chair. Cathi looked up from the clothes she was ironing and noticed a change in Mom's countenance.

In her typical commanding way, Mom called, "Cathi. Cathi, come over here. I need to pray right now."

So Cathi came over, held her hand, and started praying.

"No! I have to pray."

Now no one had ever told Carol to do this. She had never set foot in an evangelistic church. She had never heard an altar call. She didn't know there was such a thing as a sinner's prayer.

She said, "Jesus, I'm ready to surrender everything, including myself, to you. I give you everything. I receive your forgiveness. Please receive me as your child."

From that day forward, all my mom wanted to do was to pick up the phone and seek forgiveness from everyone around her. That sheepish "I'm sorry" that she gave Lauren in that guest room at Christmas was a foreshock of a tectonic shift that would happen in my mom's soul that would open to the forgiveness and mercy of Christ.

People would come into my mom's room expecting to see death, but they would leave with nothing but the evidence of the new life that was overflowing from her. She was no longer hiding. The Lord had cut through, and all you could see was new growth. Communion with the Eucharistic Minister who visited her home every Sunday took on new meaning. Bible verses leapt off the page and quickened her heart. She was voraciously hungry for His Truth even as her body was wasting away from cancer starvation. This is where my story of forgiveness with her continues.

It eventually became my turn to receive one of her apologies. She asked for my forgiveness, and I told her that I already forgave her. She was dissatisfied with the conversation; she felt that I didn't understand what she was asking. I was uncomfortable and didn't want to discuss it. The relationship was still breached.

But God.

The next week when I returned to visit her, my mother called me to her bedside. She had cut out an article from a magazine that detailed a story like ours. The mother of an adult daughter wrote of her deep regret about the way she had wounded her daughter with the way she had spoken to her throughout childhood. She could see what it had done to her daughter when earnest attempts to please were constantly met with fierce criticism, shame, and accusations of malicious motivations in an attempt to control behavior and prevent feared outcomes.

She held it up to me with tears in her eyes. "This is what I did to you... I am so sorry."

This was a decision moment for me. Would I allow the next step of repair? I had already done the work of forgiving her, I didn't even need her to be sorry, but God's ministry of reconciliation was moving and I needed to decide how I would respond.

I tore up the article in front of her.

"What are you doing??" she exclaimed.

"Oh Mom, THIS is what I forgave you for when I made that phone call so long ago."

I didn't need to lean into that moment and make her understand the depth of my pain. This was time for rebuilding. She was forgiven the day I called her on the phone, but the relationship remained broken until she was ready to do what she needed to do to move toward me and attempt a repair. Healing comes from confessing our sins one to another, and as uncomfortable as the moment was for me, it was important that I enter into it for her healing.

By the way, there is a big difference between forgiveness and reconciliation. Forgiveness does not mean trusting an untrustworthy person. You can forgive someone from a safe distance behind strong boundaries.

That day gave us a precious and sweet gift of reconciliation. My mom's transformation permitted us to develop, for those few short weeks left in her life, a relationship we otherwise could never have known. Grace and I never reconciled, although she was forgiven. Mom and I reconciled 16 years after she was forgiven. I didn't get to control either outcome; I just tried to let Jesus' ministry of reconciliation guide me during each relationship.

∞ Key to the Trap ∞

There is another important caveat to this freedom I am sharing with you: Before we can forgive, we must acknowledge our pain.

What is forgiveness, really? How does it work? What is it when the offense seems unforgivable? Do I just say everything is okay even if it isn't? No. We all have things that have been done to us that are miles from okay. We have violations of our rights and wounds to the holy and precious spirit God created in our person. These things demand justice.

We are so good at avoiding pain. Instead of going to God with that pain when we've been hurt or when we hurt others, we cover the pain with anger. Anger anesthetizes the pain, so we don't feel it anymore. But the problem is, now it's festering. The wound is not closed, it is just numbed. You can't go through a forgiveness process without facing the pain and acknowledging the full extent of what was taken from you. You cannot release what you have not mourned. We bury these feelings alive. Once buried, they turn and eat away at every good thing around them like a parasite. It's time to give them an eviction notice.

To really understand offense, we have to take a step backward and understand rights. We get offended when we have a right that is not honored by another person. I had a right to a safe childhood. My mother violated my childhood; she neglected me in ways that still have physical health consequences to this day, and she left countless scars on my heart. When I became a mother and felt the overwhelming love I had for my children, it showed me everything I could have received from my mother, and I grieved for those things. In those tears in my grieving and processing with the Lord and sisters in Christ, I was able to release all of those feelings. And I will release them again if they return.

He is always healing us; even now as I write about this in hindsight, I am changing the way I tell the story three years after writing the first draft. I get to lay down more of the weight, more of the offense; it doesn't pain me so much. I get to change my narrative, the way I view what happened because of how I see God and how He sees me. When I grew in my understanding of agape love and understood it to be the only love that is not transactional, God expanded my ability to also forgive my husband at deeper and deeper levels. This led me to more ropes that tie me to this world burning in the crucible of covenant relationship.

There is justice for every single moment of abuse and neglect. Not because they made those injuries right, but because Jesus did. The justice I require was exacted on the body of Jesus.

He forgave me of so much. God had a right that I obey Him as His created being. People I have wounded had a right to be treated better than that. The justice He requires was all satisfied in the body of Jesus. He took these offenses on Himself in His body on the cross. So my rights also are vindicated in that sacrifice. His death was enough for the wrath of God, and it is enough for mine. So Jesus, go between me and the Father when I sin. Jesus, go between me and my mother. Jesus, go between me and my husband. Jesus, go between me and everyone who has hurt me. Jesus, go between me and everyone I have hurt. You, indeed, are our mediator.[266]

Selah Moment

Remember the offense against you brought up earlier in the chapter? Are you ready to walk out of that trap? Is it possible that it is time to entrust them into God's hands and God's justice? If your heart is ready, put their name in the blank here.

Dear Lord, I thank You for the power of forgiveness [Colossians 3:13], and thank You for forgiving me when I was far from You. I entrust _____ into your hands, Jesus. Go between me and _____ [2 Corinthians 5:19]. Because of your ministry of reconciliation to me, I choose to forgive _____ who has hurt me [2 Corinthians 5:18]. I choose to forgive them for _____. Father, help me set _____ free and release them to You [Romans 12:19]. I release my right for justice by my own hands. Instead, train me to now bless him/her who has hurt me [Romans 12:14]. You are the cleanser! [1 John 1:9] Now cleansed, help me walk in righteousness, peace, and joy, demonstrating Your life here on earth. I choose to be kind and compassionate, forgiving others, just as You forgave me [Ephesians 4:32]. In Jesus' name, amen.

---

266 1 Timothy 2:5

CHAPTER TEN

Shadow of the Almighty

What is left to surrender?

REMEMBER MY FRIEND from Chapter 5 who did not have assurance of salvation? This question "what is left to surrender?" finally unlocked peace for her. It may not be assurance for you, but if you are still unable to connect to rest even a little at this point in our journey, I wonder if there could be something left to surrender for you.

We move into the shadow when we try to grasp for control of things that were never ours to control, those things we know we cannot control. There is an opportunity here to move from the shadow of darkness into the light and then under the protective shadow of His wings.[267] This is another kind of "beyond." Beyond control. Beyond comprehension. Into His compassion. "He who dwells in the shelter of the Most High will abide in the shadow of the Almighty."[268] Those verses have prompted me to ask my team at one of our trainings: How close do you want to live to the Almighty?

Is there anything that you hold back from Him, something you'd rather just take care of yourself? I wonder what that back room holds for you. It could be reputation, compulsive busyness, or asking why. For another young person, it was their desire for marriage. For me, it was my self-reliance in the arena of my children. I thought I had everything sorted out; surrendering was something I'd done when I started following Jesus, and I had surely released my red cape through

---

267 Psalm 57:1
268 Psalm 91

Lyme. I thought it was a one (or two) and done. As small as my heart is, I had no idea how many secret chambers it held that still needed to be handed to my Savior and Lord.

∞ Shaking My Foot at the Wind ∞

When he was a little boy, my oldest son, Michael, was playing catch in sandals with Tom in the driveway. It was a cute father-son moment, lots of laughing and little challenges. I loved seeing the pride on Michael's face every time he caught the ball and looked to his father to share it with him. I headed inside to clean up some morning dishes.

The next thing I know, Tom is walking in from the garage carrying Michael. He was shielding Michael's face. On one "go long" Michael's sandal got stuck on the pavement as he tried to turn and run for the catch. His mouth hit the pavement first with the full weight and momentum of his body. There was so much blood and he was crying hard.

When I saw his mangled face something ferocious reared up in me. A rage that I didn't know existed in my soul. I wasn't mad at Tom, I wasn't mad at Michael. I wasn't even mad. I was experiencing a consuming rage that was wildly destructive and protective.

The hot ball of energy welling up in me needed to go somewhere. The fridge was closest. With all the energy of my fury, I kicked it with my bare foot. The next thing I felt was a searing wave of pain shooting through my foot and up my lower leg that brought back my parental sobriety. That whole scene lasted less than five seconds. Five seconds that showed me something in myself I didn't know was there.

I think the Lord gives us glimpses of how He feels about us in our love for our children. I love Michael, my firstborn, my lionheart, so much my heart could explode sometimes. I love David, my baby, my wise beyond years, deep water musician just as much. They are everything to me. Their pain is my pain. Their joy is my joy. Not because I live vicariously through them, but because my heart so yearns that they be whole and well and good. I want Shalom for them, even if that were to cost my own wholeness. It reminds me of Paul's words where he says he is willing to die if it would lead his Jewish brothers into the arms of Jesus.[269]

I feel true rage whenever I am witness to a child being hurt. Any child. But when I experienced my son's pain for the first time, it was nearly overwhelming.

I do not presume to say that the Lord feels exactly like I did in that moment, but I do see His responses to His people's cries in Scripture. Perhaps it is something like that for Him. Jesus saw people being taken advantage of in the temple, the one place where they ought to be safe from greed and predation, and He flipped tables.[270] In Psalms when He hears the cry of the righteous, the earth trembles and quakes, the foundations of the mountains shake and tremble because He is angry.[271] When He heard the cries of His people under Egyptian slavery, He moved mightily to deliver.[272] I was a helpless mother shaking my fist (foot) at the wind, but He could do something about it. He was and is and will continue to be my Deliverer.

That night, I limped up the stairs to the hallway outside our bedrooms. I paced. Back and forth down our hall. The wrestling was real. The seethe still fueled my path back and forth between our bedroom and theirs.

But soon, I started to get tired. And soon I found myself talking to God. My consuming anger released into prayer to my Father. I didn't want to talk to Him. I wanted to be in charge. I wanted assurance that my children would be okay. I wanted to declare the future and have it be so. And I recognized that this was exactly the source of my fury. I finally came face to face with my lack of control. Not just lack of control but zero control.

I looked at the entrance into the boys room, took a deep breath, and very slowly walked into the darkened room.

I quietly walked over to Michael's bed first. I took a deep breath as I listened to his even breathing. I knelt on the soft, slightly prickly carpet right beside him, laid my hand gently on his tummy and whispered a prayer of surrender as tears quietly washed away any residual attempts

---

269 Romans 9:3
270 Matthew 21:12-13
271 Psalm 18:6-8
272 Exodus 3:7-8

to cling to a position that was not mine. Yes, I am their mother. Yes, I am their protector and guardian. *And*, I realized that I can't protect them from everything and everyone.

"Thank you for entrusting these precious souls to my care. I entrust them back to You, the only One who loves them even more than I do. You hold them in Your hands. Watch over them, protect them, and teach them to know You."

As a mother, I so wanted to spare my boys pain, I would rather they never have to face their vulnerabilities or experience the dark nights of the soul. That is not within my power, try as I might, and that is my view when I'm focused on the temporal. But when my eyes are lifted and I am aware of my position in eternity, my fears shrink and my faith expands on behalf of not just myself but those I love the most. And in fact, I recognize I would be removing their own power to decide, to determine, to discover, and to overcome.

Sometimes as they got older, I saw hurt I had to pretend not to see because they did not want to share it. They each have to go on their own journeys. It was mine to give them the best start that I could under my wings, then mine to release them, and now my privilege to witness them on their path and walk next to them as long as the Lord allows.

What is left to surrender? We can try to do an inventory. That's not a bad thing to do; however, it's really when the primal cry wells up at a point of profound vulnerability that we have the opportunity to yield that room in our soul that has just been violently thrown open by an unwanted perpetrator. We come to admit we are desperate for something different, and we won't do that if we are still comfortable with where we are in any way. These moments cut through so that we stop fooling ourselves about what we do or don't want. They turn us to want Someone who is sovereign, Who has our highest and best good, Who has not left us as orphans even as we live in a messed up world. It invites the question: How desperate are we for that rest? Will we surrender to Him?

Often, this is the last thing we want to do. We want to fight. We want to curl up and die. We want to curse. We want to blame. But surrender?? The Lord's ways truly are so much higher than ours. We are so scared of being manipulated, of being controlled, of being thought weak, of being considered a fool. Paul understood this! Paul is the one that taught us that when we are weak, God is strong. He even admitted that if Christ had not died and been resurrected, Christians should be most pitied among all men.[273] He helped us face that hidden fear of being thought a fool with the bold declaration and evidence of the resurrection.

Surrender does not mean we give up living; it doesn't mean we give up hoping; it doesn't mean we give up praying fervently for the good of those loved ones. Surrender simply means we acknowledge that God is ultimately in charge and that He is working in ways we don't yet understand or see. He is our Commander-in-Chief. And when we fight, we fight with the weapons He hands us. The world's weapons are defensiveness, self-reliance, blame shifting – so many things we've talked about that are absolutely exhausting. They are too heavy for our hearts. Too unwieldy for our spiritual hands to navigate. Too complex for our mind to keep track of. But God says to you, His anointed one,[274] to take off that silly armor and pick up your sling and your stone. Each time I lay down my self-made weapons and pick up God's, I expand my ability to trust because I'm declaring my willingness to trust Him. "The battle is the Lord's" doesn't mean we never fight; it simply means we only fight the battles He puts in front of us, with His weapons of warfare.

Ultimately, spiritual surrender is an act of faith; it's a transferring of control to your heavenly Father for those burdens that are just too big for your shoulders to carry. It doesn't mean you won't do amazing things with God. It doesn't mean God doesn't have incredible work He wants to do through you, great victories to take together. It means, as we learned in Chapter 6 on Responsibility, that any right you thought you had to any outcome is relinquished. You simply walk in faith, knowing that your heavenly Father is at work. That's right side column living.

> *Each time I surrender, I expand my ability to trust with my declaration of willingness to trust Him.*

---

273 1 Corinthians 15:14-19
274 1 John 2:20; 27, 2 Corinthians 1:21-22

Staying in that right side column is impossible. We waiver, we forget, we doubt. But we return. That's the key: we shift back into that state of abiding through surrender over and over again.

∞ Testing of Faith ∞

That early moment of surrender was tested with both of my sons many times. When David was in middle school, he was hiking in Pisgah National Forest with Tom and his Boy Scout Troop, 217. I was still very sick, so Tom would make it a point to check on me every night, even if out of town. The troop leader's wife, Lisa, called me. It was about 7:30 pm. She asked if Tom had called. I said no. She said that was odd, because her husband, Charlie, hadn't called her either.

"Lisa, they are lost."

"What, Cheryl? How do you know?"

"Because Tom would have called me. I know they are lost."

Lisa and I put a plan in place to notify the church and to gather up several of us in the van to head out to the mountains. Michael would come with me to help ensure I didn't become a liability to the crew.

After hanging up the phone, I got on my knees, and prayed: *"Lord, you are good. You give and you take away. If now is when You choose to take away my husband and my son, I will still declare with every breath that You are good. Blessed be Your name, forever!"*

Those words came from a heart that was at peace, even though my body was shaking like I had too much caffeine. I had to pray those words first, before I went to battle, on my knees and with our search party for their protection and safe return. I had to declare His sovereignty to Him and myself to remain at peace and at rest. Those words came from a soul that knew her Savior and her Lord and refused to call upon any other name than that one. Those words came from a woman who had not yet been rescued from the refiner's fire of Lyme pain and suffering yet had come to know just how good and faithful her God was, is and always would be. A guttural praise welled up from the bowels of a child of the Most High God that determined all she had was all she needed in Him.

Next, I called my sister-in-law. "Winks. Tom and David are lost in Pisgah National Forest."

She was overwhelmed with worry for me.

I shared what I prayed with her to comfort her. As of this writing, Winks does not know Jesus the way I do, but she said that is one of the most profound acts of trust she ever witnessed. To God be the glory. I didn't say it to save her. I didn't declare it to witness to her. I testified only of my own journey, and I invited her into that journey. I was in Him and He was in me, activating, guiding, fortifying, consoling, shaping, securing. All the things I wanted, but on my own could not experience.

"We are headed out to activate a Search and Rescue (SAR) for them, now. I'll keep you posted."

Within 24 hours, the Lord mercifully allowed the entire troop to be found, safe and sound.

Still, God wasn't done in this area of my life. A couple years later, we were on vacation in Cocoa Beach, and Michael snapped at me while we were putting kayaks in the Banana River. He never snapped at me.

"Michael, son, are you okay?"

"Yes, sorry Mom."

My mommy radar was up.

The kids returned from the trip, and Michael was very off. His headache, confusion, and fever escalated such that by early morning he was taken by ambulance to the local hospital. We drove behind and arrived shortly after. The nurse returned from doing a spinal tap and was so shaken she couldn't speak to us.

Lord, I need your strength.

"Nurse, what is happening?"

"Your son's spinal fluid is so thick with infection that we are not sure if he will make it. He is being transported by helicopter to the Children's Hospital in Orlando."

The nurse gave us directions to the hospital. Michael was placed on the transport gurney.

I prayed protection and healing over my unconscious son, and then

I told him, "Michael, you fight with all you have, son, and we will see you at that hospital. God's got you!"

We drove to the north side of Orlando. Unfortunately, we found out that the nurse, in her distress, gave us directions to the wrong hospital. We had to now drive south through Orlando to get to the correct hospital. This particular day was the day of the Tea Party political demonstrations.[275] The roads were so thick with cars that I could walk faster than the car was moving. The urgency inside me was confounded by the creeping pace of the car. Every second that passed while we remained in the same spot made the scream build in my throat. I told Tom to stop just for a second.

"Why, honey?"

"I need to get out and pray and move!"

As Tom continued to navigate traffic, I walked along the sidewalk, dodging people, hands lifted in the air, praying, praising, weeping, crying out. I didn't care who saw me. I only cared about one thing, and that was clinging to my Savior and Lord. I was powerless, and I had to be prepared for whatever He would allow me to see and experience if we could ever get out of this traffic jam.

By the time we arrived at Arnold Palmer Hospital for Children, Michael was already admitted and in a room. Admittance spoke so slowly. Elevators moved so slowly. I moved too slowly. I don't doubt I held my breath from the moment we entered the hospital until the moment I was able to see Michael with my own eyes.

There he was, alert, talking with an attendant. The attendant said that Michael somehow had rallied and was able to provide all necessary information about himself upon admittance, even though just 30 minutes earlier he had been unconscious.

Thank you, Lord!!!

It was a long climb back from bacterial meningitis. Michael and I spent two weeks at the hospital in Florida while Tom tried to give David some sense of normalcy back up in NC. But as a family, we weathered the storm. As a community, people came together and loved us.

If this situation had happened ten years earlier I would have lost my

---

275 "More than 4,000 Attend Orlando Tea Party." *Public Advocate of the U.S.*, 2025, www.publicadvocateusa.org/news/article.php?article=4454.

cool with the poor nurse who gave us the news. Now, I had no rage, but I did have a fire in my belly. So much so that when Michael started seizing in the hospital bed one day such that his head was banging against the wall, I found the strength in my normally very weak arms to drag the entire unit away from the wall. But I was not angry in my soul. Healing was happening.

I was tested. Both of my children whom I surrendered that night after Michael's fall were allowed to suffer. My children were tested and allowed to go through their own refiner's fires.

Life wasn't done with me. And God would be with me, through it all. So much of life's journey, I was learning, was a journey of surrender.

I had to pray a very similar prayer over my granddaughter when she was still in her mother's womb. My first grandchild. My baby's baby. My daughter-in-love had an accident around the house with an electric shock that went up her arms. After speaking with appropriate medical resources, she called her mother. Her mother is a wise woman of faith and prayer who reminded her of Moses' mother, Jochebed, surrendering her baby in the basket on the Nile. Just like Jochebed, we mothers learn to surrender our children to the mightier Hand as they grow up and leave our protective wings; she just got to start early.

I stayed up all night sick to my stomach, pacing another hallway, praying that the electricity had not interrupted that tiny heartbeat. I gave her into the Lord's hands again and again as I fought against instinct to take her back into my own hands and control. I never want to pass a night like that again. It took me all night. Wrestling like Jacob. It may take you all night, literally or metaphorically. It is our work to surrender more and more to Him, to make Him the Lord of every nook and cranny of our hearts. God is so good that He will engage with us, even be willing to wrestle with us. At the end of that wrestling we may have a new name and a limp, but we will be at rest again.[276]

Did it mean I didn't learn "my lesson" earlier? I don't know the answer to that, and the Lord will show me when I am with Him. But what I can tell you is I knew to turn to Him. My anxiety was high, so my surrender took hours of inviting Him into the room that electrical current blew open. It was a room I didn't even know was there. It would

---

276 Genesis 32:22-32

happen again and again when both she and my younger grandson started their lives in the Neonatal Intensive Care Unit. It happened over and over. I wasn't in a canoe on a lake with all my loved ones safe in the cabin behind me. Though that image from the introduction was just an imagination, the peace I described is very real. How could I find peace when my loved ones were not safe at all? By yielding to that Mighty Hand.

Rest has a significant yielding component to it. We often think of yield in terms of interest earned or crops from a harvest, but the yielding I'm referring to is a humble holy submission to the eternal when the temporal screams its demands. And in this yielding, we may trust that God produces a harvest beyond wildest expectations, much of which we cannot see with our eyes or perceive. That is rest to me. It is not up to me to yield that harvest. It is only for me to yield myself, my control.

What is left for you to surrender? Maybe you are beginning to get a sense of what room it is you've bolted a hundred times over and plastered with your do not enter sign. Maybe you don't even remember what is in that room. That's okay. I'm not asking you to figure it out right now if nothing has come to mind. When the Lord chooses to allow life to blow up the door, I pray you won't be afraid to go in there with Him and let Him do the dirty work of house cleaning and wiping your tears away and even dealing with a little fist banging against His chest if that is necessary. He is big enough to handle your temper tantrum. Just have it with Him. And then let Him carry you out of there once it's all out of you.

> ### Optional Selah Moment
>
> For a deeper dive, see Appendix C for a collection of manmade methods that create barriers to trusting God for people historically throughout the life of the ministry. These are often activities and mindsets that we put "stock" in to help create a sense of self worth.

∞ Firm Foundation ∞

When the big earthquakes shake us to our very core, there is no going back. We cannot wish for things as they were before. The sooner we learn to adapt to the new normal the better off we will be. Longing for things put right is only human. We know what right looks like to us. The Zealots of Jesus' day also knew what right looked like. They were sure an overthrow of the Roman government was their right. To the Pharisees, following every jot and tittle of the Law was what right looked like.[277] We all have a sense of what is right. And when that sense of right is threatened or wronged, we wrestle.

Fortification of our hearts does not come from returning to a sense of control. It comes from that upon which we stand. My husband recently came home from a half day retreat. He simply sat with God. He was asked two questions when he started his time of fellowship with the Lord: "Why did you come today?" and "What is the state of your soul today?" His response to the second was that he felt shaky and a bit anxious. There were things he wanted set right in his life.

The reading for this sit with the Lord was Psalm 62. The Lord met my husband. Consider pausing to read and simply circle or underline the different ways the Lord addresses our anxiety inside of this Psalm:

> Our soul finds rest in God;
> my salvation comes from him (the writer is Cooperating with God!);
> Truly He is my rock and my salvation;
> He is my fortress, I will never be shaken.

The first time that is written, the Psalmist is declaring a truth. Look what happens the second time he writes in verses 5-6.

> Yes, my soul, find rest in God;
> my hope comes from Him.
> Truly He is my rock and my salvation;
> He is my fortress; I will not be shaken.

---

[277] Matthew 5:18

The first time the Psalmist reminds himself where his rest comes from. The second time the Psalmist tells his soul to rest in God. The Psalmist declares the truth then shifts into that truth. And fortification of the heart comes!

The longer we cling to what is lost or what we are afraid to lose, the more despair and anxiety take root. Weeping can last for an evening, but joy can be our morning companion.[278] How is that possible? Relationship with the Lord is the short answer. Paul wrote that in the midst of horrific suffering; he was sorrowful yet always rejoicing.[279] Again, we see joy and loss coexisting, joy even overcoming the sorrow. We return to abiding, just as the Psalmist writes about his rest being in the Lord.

Psychologists have come to understand that the worst trauma is that which is experienced alone.[280] Paul was humiliated, but he wasn't alone. Paul was ostracized, beaten, and shipwrecked, but he wasn't alone. Everywhere he went he chose to remain united in Christ, both in His death and, soon, in His resurrection. He writes that just as the sufferings of Christ overflow to us, so also through Christ our comfort overflows.[281]

---

278 Psalm 30:5
279 2 Corinthians 6:10
280 Social support is well-established as a major protective factor following potentially traumatic events (i.e., exposure to "death, threatened death, actual or threatened serious injury, or actual or threatened sexual violence") [1] American Psychiatric Association. Diagnostic and Statistical Manual of Mental Disorders, 5th ed. Author: Washington, DC, USA. 2013.
Calhoun, Casey D., et al. "The Role of Social Support in Coping with Psychological Trauma: An Integrated Biopsychosocial Model for Posttraumatic Stress Recovery." *Psychiatric Quarterly*, vol. 93, no. 4, 5 Oct. 2022, pp. 949–970, pmc.ncbi.nlm.nih.gov/articles/PMC9534006/, https://doi.org/10.1007/s11126-022-10003-w.
281 2 Corinthians 1:5

∞ Unshakable ∞

I don't know what you have lost. My dear friend Wende lost her son to suicide. My spiritual mentor, Elizabeth's son, died in her arms at age 11. My mom lost her dad at the tender age of 18. My father lost his bride at age 57 to pancreatic cancer. My friend, Julie, had several miscarriages. Another friend, also named Julie, lost her missionary husband to a plane accident. My friend, Lisa, lost her oldest son to a drowning and then her husband to suicide. There isn't a friend in my life who hasn't experienced death blows to the soul. It doesn't take but a nanosecond to find that which causes our hearts to ache.

Paul felt this, too! He faced this, too. And he wrote about it in 1 Corinthians chapter 15. This chapter became my promise chapter. It helped me to know I wasn't insane when I allowed sorrow and rejoicing to coexist in my soul. It fueled me to cling to Jesus no matter the trial, testing, temptation, or torment. Below is a picture of my page – I did this many years ago but still return to it often. Light gray reflects that which is of the flesh. Dark gray reflects that which is of heaven. Look at how Paul compares and contrasts the two conditions that somehow co-exist. The flesh must die. The soul will live on. Death will be swallowed up by life.

In the end Paul summarizes that which fortifies his soul through every loss in 2 Corinthians 4:16-18. If I had a life verse, it would probably be this one. It is the rudder that has sustained me through all pain. It pulls my eyes away from my circumstances and helps me to look at Jesus again when I'm scared, suffering, lost, confused, frustrated, ashamed.

> "Therefore we do not lose heart. Though our outer self is wasting away, yet our inner self is being renewed day by day. For our light and momentary affliction is producing for us an eternal glory that is far beyond comparison. So we fix our eyes not on what is seen, but on what is unseen. For what is seen is temporary, but what is unseen is eternal."[282]

---

[282] 2 Corinthians 4:16-18 (NIV)

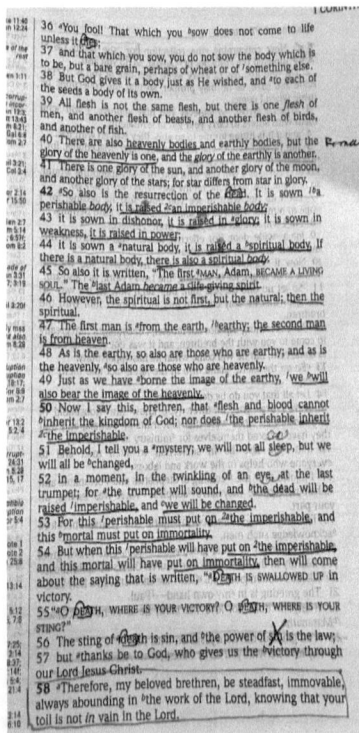

No matter how long or how painful my suffering, it cannot be compared to the eternal weight of glory that awaits in Jesus Christ, my Savior and my Lord. All that I did, do and will suffer is momentary. All of it – compared to the eternal weight of glory that is in Christ Jesus. The last enemy to be abolished will be death.[283] Death will be swallowed up in life.

We will outlive our longings. We will outlive our sufferings. We will not be overcome by those who are determined to shut us down. Life is hard, then we die. That is a true statement. Life is hard and then we live. That is also a true statement. The seed of our flesh will fall. The soul will rise.

Each loss creates opportunity for a spiritual redirect. And each decision to spiritually redirect fortifies our hearts. We do not lose heart. Yes, I sure do in a moment sometimes, but then Jesus grabs hold, and I redirect my eyes that were looking away and say, okay, Jesus, I am looking at You. I know You are acquainted with this, too. I know You don't want me to walk through this alone, either. I invite You into my pain.

Tears fill my eyes as I write this to you because I don't know what you have lost. But I will give you the treasures I have found, the only things that give me breath sometimes.

I found the above passage in 2 Corinthians because of Elizabeth in the midst of Lyme. I had already begun a journey of surrendering so many things to the Lord's hands and would continue it. As I suffered

---

283 1 Corinthians 15:26

with the illness, people would tell me things like, "It's good; it's the refiner's fire, Cheryl. It's just the refiner's fire." In the throes of it, I would wish to say to them, "If it's so good, why don't you jump in here with me?" But I *was* in the Refiner's fire. I was just tired of people telling me that.

Then one day, I heard from Elizabeth! It had been several years since I talked to her and her voice has always been balm to my aching soul. She knew to be brief on the call as she could hear my pain.

She said, *"Cheryl, I want you to know that you are in the refiner's fire…"*

For a moment my heart was crushed – here, even Elizabeth was going to give me such weak and immaterial consolation for the pain as if I were a burnt offering. But I refused to shut my ears (remember that chapter on open listening?).

Her next words rang sweet and pure to my soul: *"…and remember, Cheryl – the only thing the fire will burn – the only things it will burn, are the ropes that bind you to this world."*

There it was – hope in the midst of the prolonged, agonizing suffering that I know Elizabeth suffered as well, when her son died in her arms. (For more about her story, please look up Journey for the Heart ministries.)[284] Elizabeth's words shifted me from asking how long I would be required to suffer to wondering how free I would become on the other side of whatever ropes were being burned at that point in time. My joy returned tenfold after that conversation. Delight.

As one who has been so tired, I say to you fellow sojourner– the only thing the refiner's fire will burn are the things which bind you to this world. Remember what comes out of the refiner's fire? Silver. Gold.

> *The only things the Refiner's fire will burn are the things which bind you to this world.*

Who we are in the Lord is beautiful. That fire will eventually give way to the fullness of His presence, and all that remains will be your priceless, eternal offering to your Lord.

Those things that are most precious to us, the real things, are precious

---

[284] "Elizabeth Mitchell - Devotional and Bookstore." *Elizabeth Mitchell*, 15 Jan. 2025, elizabethamitchell.com/.

to the Father, too. I surrender even the ones I love most to His loving strong hands.

Years after my diagnosis but prior to my shift away from speaking death over myself as I continued down that long road, the pain was wearing me down intensely, and I had almost died several times. I despaired to the point of death. I was ready to die. I was done fighting. Done with the surviving and the treatments and the struggling and the trying and the striving and the suffering. Done done. I told God, "I am ready to die. Take me home." I had it all planned out. I would lay in my place in the bed, Tom would lay next to me, morning would come, I would wake up in Heaven, and Tom would be the one to find me. I finally found a way to fall asleep in the excruciating pain by imagining my release from it, looking forward to seeing God before the sun rose.

However, the next morning I woke up alive, in my bed, with my body screaming in pain at me. I was mad. Tom asked me if I wanted to go to church; it was a Sunday.

"Yeah…" I grumped. I knew that my flesh was mad, but I also knew this was not the time to turn away from God or to live in my feelings.

We threw me into the wheelchair, heaved me into the car, and rolled my butt into church. What I found there was a video testimony from a woman in Canada. She was a cancer survivor. She had been through a center to receive painful bone marrow treatments, so painful she wanted to die. My ears perked up at this. She continued, "I kept looking at the phone, knowing that if I picked it up and called my daddy, he would come get me, and I wouldn't have to do it anymore. But I didn't pick up the phone. I finished the treatments, God let me live, and I'm here today."

Tears sprang to my eyes. But I did pick up the phone!! I picked up the phone, and my Daddy didn't answer.

God spoke to me in my heart then that He wasn't done, that my story wasn't done yet. That was 20 years ago almost to the day of writing that sentence. That's something for me to make that connection as we take this journey together.

To live is Christ, to die is gain. I'm hard pressed to know what I want more, but it is for your sake that I am still here (paraphrased).[285]

---

[285] Philippians 1:21

Instead of being discouraged by the Corinthians verse above, as some can be, it encouraged me that no matter how long I was afflicted, it was momentary.[286] No matter how hard it was, it was light in comparison with the weight of the glory that is coming. Christ became the backdrop for whatever was going on. He is my hope, the giver of breath, and the lifter of my countenance.

∞ God is Stronger ∞

And I get to be reminded over and over again that it's okay to surrender myself to God.

One night we were staying at my father's house. This was shortly after I broke my back during a horseback riding accident. I had one of the horrific headaches that are a part of my autoimmune issues. I was writhing in pain, moaning like a dying cow. I was lost, absolutely consumed by the pain. Up to this point, I had always protected my father from seeing this scene. He is a tender-hearted soul. And, of course, he hurts for his children. But this ill-timed headache wouldn't allow me even that small gift of continuing to protect him from my private journey with pain. I was grieving, I was hurting, I was embarrassed, and I was scared that I might have to live through yet another horrific experience. Suddenly a strong hand grabbed my hand. It was my father's 86-year-old hand.

"God is stronger than this. He has you."

My father's words washed all the sewage filling my soul with that one reminder. God is with me. Relationship. Fortification of the soul. My earthly father's hand became the bridge to my heavenly Father's hand. All that I said I believed, and all that I lived that I believed had been momentarily lost to profound discouragement. And my Pops grounded me once again in the truth.

I am still being shaken. And so are you. It's okay to be shaken. God loves us too much to allow those ropes that bind us to the world to remain. Sometimes that shaking is nothing more than a quiver, a slight

---

286 2 Corinthians 4:17-18

tremor under our feet. At other times it feels so violent that we don't believe we will be able to withstand it and instead we'll be swallowed up whole. This is part of our journey of faith. Hebrews promises us that everything that can be shaken will be shaken.[287] As the refiner's fire burns the cords that hold us to this earth, the shaking only removes what can be shaken to reveal that which is unshakable. When we fix our eyes on the temporal, the shaking is terrifying. But if we can focus on eternity, things look much steadier. And I don't just mean Heaven after death.

We have been trained to think about eternal life as something that happens later, at the end of days. But friends, if we are in Christ we have eternal life now. Heaven will be a continuation of the relationship we already have with the joyful relief of being free of the burdens that living in this sin-tainted and time-bound world we sojourn in for now. We are still living in bodies that moan and ache. Most of us will, by the end of this life, groan with creation for the return of our Lord. But our souls are already home in Jesus. It is this security that makes our suffering light and momentary. We are training to live from that rest that is in us—Jesus Himself.

The hope offered in these verses about great shaking is that we are receiving a Kingdom that is unshakable. There will come a day when all the shaking is done, and we have been made into people who can live in an unshakable kingdom. And He will wipe every tear from our eyes.[288] Thank you, Father, for making us into an unshakable people.

Though the mountains may be moved and the hills may shake, Abba wants to take your hand and remind you,[289] "I am stronger than this. Let Me be your strength."[290]

---

287 Hebrews 12:26-29
288 Revelation 21:4
289 Isaiah 54:10
290 Psalm 73:26

Selah Moment

The ultimate and most expensive exchange in this life occurs when you exchange your filthy rags for His righteous robes (Titus 3:5). You become justified before God. This is a one time forever exchange. Now, as we learn how to walk in this preferred future of righteousness in Christ, we are in training to put off the old man and live from the new.[291] This is called sanctification, which reflects an *ongoing* exchange. We exchange those secret places where we feel we need to be strong or walled off, trading them for God's strength and hedge of protection. We are learning how to enter more fully into His rest. Are you ready to make God your strength in that place you feel you need to be strong?

Perhaps you've become aware of a weapon of warfare crafted over time that belongs to this world and needs to be put down. What is that weapon defending? If you were to give that secret chamber in your heart a name, what might you call it?

- Feeling important.
- Feeling safe.
- Knowing I'm loved.
- Being assured I won't be laughed at.
- Can't afford to waste a minute of my life.
- Better make sure my life counts for something.
- I'll rest when I get to heaven.

Check out the list of Barriers in Appendix C and see if that doesn't help you with identifying whatever "it" is. If you are ready to let the Father into your secret room, how could you make the conversation exchange more personal for you? Lying prostrate on your face? Kneeling in your prayer closet? Maybe

---

291 Ephesians 4:22-24

you need to pace somewhere like I did for a while. You might be better journaling, or maybe even writing a song, like my son, David. It's worth the risk of losing a bit of momentum for just a moment to Selah here. What is the impact of the work you've done as you consider moving more fully into the shadow of the Almighty? Would a 7 Step Shift® help you here? (See the end of Appendix C)

Father, I confess that for too long I believed the only way to survive in this world was to put on my red cape and leap from tall buildings. I've crashed more times than I can count. But that cape keeps calling my name. I confess that it is not what You ask me to wear. You ask me to wear your peace and your pace. You invite me to a gentler approach to activity and serving. I refuse to be B.U.S.Y. anymore. I want my days to be filled with an increased consciousness of You and a perpetual invitation for You to show me how to live. I want to abide in a deeper, more mature way. I want to become more dependent upon You. I trust you will show me how to do this. And as a declaration of this decision, I'm giving you my red cape to burn. I'm taking it out of the secret place in my heart. Now it can't be put on anymore. I just want to put on more of You. Thank you for this sanctifying exchange where You will increase and I will decrease! Amen.

CHAPTER ELEVEN

Community

What do you need?

THE UBER PULLED up to the hotel sometime in the evening after a speaking engagement. I couldn't even remember what city I was in. I was so tired, but not from traveling. I was tired from pouring out; I had poured everything I had into the ministry of the day. I felt alone. I needed a deep connection moment with God, and frankly, I was too tired to seek it out on my own.

I thanked my driver and trudged into the hotel. It smelled like rain, asphalt, and cigarettes. The computer bag in my hand was pulling on my shoulders; all I could think about was putting it down.

The elevators were down a long, tan hallway to the left. On the right, something caught my eye. It was a blue banner. I don't know why I was drawn to it; I see banners for conferences at hotels all the time. I turned right, temporarily forgetting how heavy my bag and body felt.

As I slowly walked closer, I could see that it was a kind of celebration put on by a group of ministers from several local Black churches. I still wasn't completely sure what I was reading, but I meandered over to the table and said hello to the lady behind it. She was dressed exquisitely from her hat to her matching blouse and skirt to her hose and heels. Her smile was warm and her eyes bright. I asked her what was happening tonight.

She responded, "Oh! We are having a service later this evening. Would you like to join us?" There was not an ounce of hesitation in her voice. I was dressed casually, Caucasian, and visibly exhausted, but none of those observations factored into her decision to eagerly embrace my presence at their worship that night.

I suddenly felt awkward. I didn't have clothes with me to wear that would show respect.

She told me it did not matter, "Just come!"

My heart felt a bit lighter at the invitation and the anticipation of worshiping with these dear sisters. Although my fatigue was bone-deep, I sensed I needed to be there. After getting my bags packed for an early morning flight and taking a brief nap, I headed back down to the conference room. Only two other people were sitting in the rows. The drummer was setting up and the leadership was discussing logistics. I sat peacefully – alone but not feeling an ounce of loneliness. A woman chose to sit next to me in the emptiness of that large room. We struck up an easy conversation. I apologized for my outfit. She was just glad I was there.

The rows slowly filled, and someone eventually stepped up to the stage to welcome us to the service. The music began. My friend, there is nothing like the music when you are in a Black church. I sang with absolute abandonment to the joy and love in the room and experienced an infusion of Holy Spirit energy as I shouted words of truth over myself and every person there. I lost myself in worship. I forgot where I was, but I knew who I was with – my family. My own spiritual body. We knew the same Lord. We loved the same Lord. We worshiped the same Lord.

And then it happened. It was time for the offering. I remembered too late the tradition of each person going up to put their offering in the basket at the front of the church. I had nothing to give! My pockets were empty. I was devastated that after what these kind people had done for me, I could not demonstrate gratitude in the giving of even a single dollar. As our row turned to begin our journey from the back to the front of the room, I followed, anticipating walking past the basket empty-handed. One of the ministers at the back saw me as I moved past her and grabbed my hand. She split her offering and gave me half, so that I could give to the basket.

The Lord saw to every detail. The congregation provided every need. I came with empty pockets. I had nothing to offer. Yet community "covered" for my lack.

Sometimes I create community. Perhaps it is by sharing a meal, telling a story, inviting someone else to share their story, or giving some refrigerator rights in my home. Sometimes I painstakingly build it over many years. Other times, I am invited to enter into a community that someone else has created. This time I received a beautiful, refreshing gift from a thriving community of the Lord that I may not encounter again until Heaven. It was an example of a quote by Bonhoeffer who describes community as an "unspeakable gift" in one of my favorite books on Christian community. The oneness I got to experience was, as he puts it, "not an ideal, but a divine reality."[292] Sometimes our humanity gets in the way of that oneness, but we are still one in Jesus.

Unity does sometimes feel like an ideal, a lofty, possibly even unachievable, one. But what if we reframed it? What if oneness isn't something in which we've fallen short and been disappointed by but something we may grow into? A good gift that we may partake in now as much as we are able? As all the leaves on the tree in my backyard are a part of the same tree, so are we are a part of the same plant, drawing strength from the same vine, no matter how far apart each leaf may find itself.

He is the Vine, and we are the branches. We abide in Him. We spent some time talking about abiding in our individual walks in Chapter 5, and now it is time to talk about abiding in the context of these other branches. As beautiful as one branch can be alone, it can never compare with the beauty and fruitfulness of the plant as a whole.

What if oneness isn't something in which we've fallen short and been disappointed by, but something we may grow into?

I visited a smaller church recently with a lower ceiling and a pared down worship team. I didn't experience the same sweeping away that I did in that hotel ballroom, but what I heard there warmed my heart. I heard the voice of the Church. I could hear the soprano of the young mother next to me, the smooth, softer sincerity of the woman on my other side, the bass of the older man two rows ahead of me, all blending

---

292 Dietrich Bonhoeffer. Life Together: A Discussion of Christian Fellowship. San Francisco, Harpersanfrancisco, 1954. Pg. 26.

together as one sound, unique to itself, filling up the room with praise to our God. All of us in our various stages of life, a couple bent with age and still holding hands, young parents frequently bending down to instruct their toddlers, a sister in a wheelchair fitting into the spot cut out just for her in the pew, new couples and single friends, and a few empty nesters like myself. I couldn't see where all of their hearts were, but in that moment we were all one. It didn't matter what else we had in common save this one, most important thing: we belonged to Jesus, and we were worshipping Him together.

You may be lonely, isolated from Christian brothers and sisters, longing for just one fellow Christ-follower in your life. Or, you may be so spoiled for community that you no longer want it, church wounds and disillusionment making "community" feel more like a burden than the gift of God to us weary pilgrims.

Before we discuss this topic further, please take a moment to write down what the word "community" means to you currently. Sometimes there are very positive connotations for groups within a wider culture in which people find mutual understanding and support. Sometimes there are negative connotations if the word has been used to put weight on you to show up and serve, not out of compulsion but obligation. There are some contexts in which it's so overused, the word has lost all meaning whatsoever.

The Trinity is the model of community into which we are invited. We experience the highest form of community when we are in the center of the relationship of the Triune God. When I allow myself to be caught up in the love of the Father through the redemptive work of the Son and the indwelling presence of the Spirit, I am brought into the perfect community of Father, Son, and Holy Spirit. We learn to join in the perfect unity, the unity that said, "Let us create man in our image."[293]

Jesus' desire in His last prayer in John 17 before His crucifixion was that we be one, even as He and the Father are one.[294] That is community. We get to be in the "let us." In 1 Corinthians, Paul makes a massive appeal: "Let there be no divisions among you, be united in your

---

293 Genesis 1:26
294 John 17:21

mind."[295] Brother Yun reported that in China the underground church was united and expanding in an explosive way, but then well-meaning Americans sent their books[296] and suddenly there were factions following one denomination's ideology or another, following the equivalent of "Apollos" vs. "Paul."[297]

I abide *in* Jesus, and I abide *among* my brothers and sisters. My experiences in worship at the beginning of the chapter refreshed me and brought me the rest I could not quite reach on my own. We are the body of Christ; we pour out to the world; we serve and wash feet. And we get tired. We also must be the body of Christ to other members of our body! When we sprain an ankle, we use our hands to bind it up, and we use our arms to bear that extra weight on crutches for a little while. That is what my Black sisters did for me that night, down to the offering. They brought me to the living water in my time of deep thirst. Remember Jesus' attitude towards the bruised reed from Chapter One? These women were His warm hand straightening the bruised reed. I needed community that night, and I have needed it many times. In some ways, this chapter is the application of all the others, because we work out all of these concepts and principles in the context of one another.

In fact, community has been the catalyst for some of the deepest healing in my life. If you'll notice, both of my shifts described in Chapter 7 were initiated because of conversations with other people. My ability to forgive was taught to me by Elizabeth over a messy counter with six noisy children in the background. Lyme cracked open my walls such that I had to allow the love of my church community to keep my family afloat. My physical healing came at the suggestion of my husband and the corporate prayer of other followers of Jesus, and I had a second healing of the nerve issues in my leg at a PLL retreat when another leader knelt down in front of me to pray, right there in the midst of our casual coffee conversation after I came back limping from a morning walk. The wounds from my mother have been soothed in the context of close female Christian relationships, beginning with Elizabeth, and worked out further with others as each stage of life brought them.

---

295 1 Corinthians 1:10
296 Yun, Brother. *Heavenly Man.* 2020.
297 1 Corinthians 3

It's happened enough times for me that I now believe healing happens primarily in the context of community. Perhaps this is why the Lord tells us to confess to one another that we may be healed.[298] I have mentioned the long process and the work my husband and I have done in our marriage. We did not truly begin to heal in the deepest places until we were seen in that space by close, safe community, as I will share below.

∞ Healing in Community ∞

On December 18, 2020, I broke my back. I tried to go horseback riding in a moment of overconfidence about my body's healing and strength, and I was quickly thrown from my high horse. After 5 days in the hospital with no pain medication (allergies), narrowly avoiding emergency surgery, and isolated from family due to COVID protocols, I was finally, mercifully home.

My son, David, his wife, Brianna, and my chosen family friend, Nicki, stayed at the house to help with the caretaking as I recovered. This was all hands on deck situation, as I could not change, bathe, toilet, or even sleep independently for the first several weeks.

This was already community in that Nicki and Brianna are women whom I had discipled over the last 5-10 years, at the time. I had been "Christian community" for them with the support flowing more from me to them, and, of course, with my son throughout his life. Now I would experience the support flowing back towards me.

My injury completely shattered privacy, not only in the practical sense, but also in our personal affairs for better or worse. Even with these people who knew us as well as I'd let anyone know us, I had hidden the situation with Tom. I could no longer cover for the fact that he was conspicuously not caring for me, and would in fact get in the way or be careless with my body.

I wasn't upset with Tom anymore, though. I was praying for Tom. Praying hard for him. I was doing what I often call "battle in the

---

[298] James 5:16

heavenlies" on his behalf. I prayed that somehow this situation, my breaking, would bring healing for him. I prayed that he would experience the love of Jesus in a way that was so much deeper than he was able to receive up until this point. I prayed that the fears I saw in his eyes would be quieted and cast out in that perfect love.[299] I prayed that the wounded child behind the man I loved would be made whole and would feel safe.

Tom's anger rose at me several times over the course of these days, once exploding in a way that put our issues on full, unmistakable display for all to hear. It broke my heart most that David witnessed the strain. I was fully planning to go to my grave with the secret of our dysfunction.

But Jesus is Lord. He reigns in my wellness and illness, and He was calling us out of the hiding in which we were so deeply buried. He orchestrated this time of my breaking with the time these people who loved us could be with us. Our cover was blown. We were known.

We received a hollow apology the day after one such blow up. Tom gathered us in the living room and read a Scripture about Jonah. The apology itself didn't hold much water; I was about ready for him to be swallowed by a fish and spit out in the right direction, but I forgave him again. He is my husband, and I have promised never will I ever leave him, and I will show him the love of my Jesus until death do us part. He and I were in new territory, though; we now had multiple witnesses, one of them being our son. And each of these young people looked him in the eyes and told him they loved him still. He had shown his darkness, and was not rejected. This little community who was trying to love my body back together rallied around the injury in our marriage too.

He started asking questions. He was aware that his face was blank when the others were soft in the presence of my pain. He started trying to understand their emotions. He still held my needs at a distance, still saw me as an unfair burden, and these mindsets continued to manifest in the way he treated me. But he was beginning to wake up.

Days turned into weeks. I started sleeping closer to 7 hours rather than 5. My moaning was traded in for silliness to get the kids to giggle at me, and we would play sudoku in the evenings. I still had many needs,

---

[299] 1 John 4:18

and I was not at all ready for them to go, but I wanted to release David and Brianna if they were starting to feel the itch to leave. I told them I thought Tom could cover what needed to be done if they wanted to go. The two of them talked it over by themselves over the course of the afternoon, and they returned to me the next day.

"We do not feel like you are safe alone with Tom."

I drew in a breath. There it was. Someone else could see what I felt—I was not safe with my husband. This was crucial for me, too; that they were able to still love him, but they weren't willing to tolerate his treatment of me. I was very grateful that they were able to see and still love. Now that they knew, they were going to make sure I was protected until I was strong enough to take care of myself again.

Tom began to come alive in small ways in our little community during the remaining time they spent with us; he no longer had to hide, and he could be himself at the same time he was a "work in progress." And truly, all of us are a "work in progress." I got to come alive in new ways, as well. I finally felt safe. Once I got through the initial grief of my son facing Tom's darkness, I was able to enjoy the relief that came with their knowing. I had admitted to myself that I was in a difficult marriage at that point, but letting my family into the struggle felt impossible. It was my door to open, but it was as though it was locked from the outside. Not having to figure out how to break the news or continue to hide the situation was a weight off my soul. God simply allowed them to see. He loved both Tom and me by ending the silence.

That truly was a watershed moment for us. There was no more of the dichotomy of believing our own cover story when convenient and experiencing the reality in private. Community brought it up from the realm of shifting shadows into the light. It woke Tom up for a time, and was my first relief from the constant hypervigilant eggshell way I had to live with him.

Even after the kids left several weeks later, we continued to work on our relationship. With Tom's permission, we brought my sister and her husband into the community surrounding our marriage. This brought him peer male accountability, and offered me one more step into the free air. We took another step into the light as we submitted ourselves to the PLL marriage course and brought those couples into our journey.

The gentle refining of that time helped us both to identify lies we had brought into the marriage that had helped us cope and survive but needed to go if we were to truly heal. Take no mercy on your lies. They take no mercy on you.

> *Take no mercy on your lies. They take no mercy on you.*

With each person I let in, I got to experience a little bit more freedom, a little less self-gaslighting, a little more re-integration of my soul. Not everyone has responded the way I might have wanted, but that's okay. I stopped needing that as I got more practice. I started standing up for myself more. Perhaps not perfectly, but I was learning to honor both myself and whomever I was conversing with in each attempt.

Tom and I spent an intense couple of years hammering out the first draft of a new marriage dynamic on the forge of real communication, temporarily increased boundaries, and near constant feedback. It was exhausting. But I have to give Tom credit. This was very difficult for him. He could have walked away, but he decided to keep trying to figure things out. He started going to counseling and doing some serious introspection. Little by little, conflict by conflict, we got to have some times that we could enjoy one another and relax..

I had been delivering a business owner retreat for several years for a group of men who became the next group who got to know the stories I've shared with you as I worked through how to be in myself in my situations, learning how to be open, integrating the personal and the professional. They had their own feelings about the story, and I watched them work through it. In his concern for me, one gentleman counseled me to leave and get out of the abuse. Some were so angry with Tom that they couldn't speak or minister. Still, a couple of the men invited Tom to join me at their retreat the following year.

Tom bravely took them up on the invitation. These men, full of compassion and truth, received him as though he was one of their own. As I watched several of them one by one engage in both light hearted and deeper conversations, these men helped me to see my husband in the light of Christ's love through them. It was as though they were sharing the burden with me of loving him. This was another way that community, this time Christian brotherhood, really brought him in and built him up in his unfinished "work in progress" state. The community around our marriage was continuing to expand, bracing and resetting the displacement like the clamshell brace set my back. The "pressure" was good and healing although not always comfortable. The more people we allowed in, the less opportunity there was for the dysfunction to continue.

One morning one of the guys started the day with a devotional. He prompted us with Revelation 2:17 and 3:12, which references the new name we will be given in the end. One of the exercises instructed each of us to tell our spouse how we could bless them using God's character qualities as a guide. Then we were to tell our spouse what we thought our new name could be, calling out what God is doing in our lives and encouraging each other.

Tom and I went off by ourselves to do the devotional together, but we didn't even get to step one. I'll never forget where we were standing when he took my hand and said, "I want to become your Boaz."

Tom's world as he knew it had been turned upside down. This work was disorienting and uncomfortable for him, and yet in it he had experienced the love of his family, other believers, and now this community. Shame was overcome by a glimpse of a godly vision for who he could be in our marriage.

We invited more into the community, but not all would understand or engage well. While in Florida celebrating the life of a friend who sadly committed suicide, we took two more folks we had known well into our fold, sharing just a bit of the story. The man immediately "took sides" with Tom and began accusing, investigating what I might be doing to exacerbate the situation.

This was one of the dangerous triggers in our marriage. If one person defended Tom, then he would quickly use it to villainize me, abdicating his own responsibility for his actions and the pain he caused. I had been dreading the possibility of this happening here and realized I would soon feel the negative effects of the temptation for Tom to make me the bad guy again. But that didn't mean they weren't trying to love us. And that didn't mean we wouldn't work through the triggering moment for Tom, which we did. The boundaries I had set for the marriage helped us to weather that blip on the radar of healing. Tom came to agree that when we shared our situation more openly, he would encourage people not to defend his position because that defense does not help our covenant cause.

In the winter, I found myself duking it out with some bad shrimp after what had been a fun night out. Now this was not a dainty or polite case of food poisoning; all guns were blazing. And my husband, who used to be angry when my health would cause inconvenience, held my hair, and stayed up all night with me. I experienced true compassion from him, true tenderness. That night was the first time I could lean on him.

A short time after the bad shrimp incident, we were sitting on the front porch with my dad, and he remarked gruffly in his way, "You guys are doing better, aren't ya?"

This from the man of one liners. He doesn't say much, but when he does, I listen. Once again, community speaks and healing happens. As of today, Tom and I are not "done" struggling. Since that day, it hasn't been happily ever after. My story, like your story, on any given day has new twists and turns to it, but that's the beauty of covenant, it's steadfast and foundational regardless of what the day brings. We are not where we were, and we are not yet where we will be. I put my hope in God for the full redemption of our marriage whether here on earth or in ways I will only understand in Heaven, and I am grateful for the community that has surrounded us. We finally stopped hiding. Walking in the light has led to relief for me, and the beginning of a healing journey for Tom. We are receiving the love of Jesus *through* community. The love we receive from our brothers and sisters in Christ is a reflection of His love. "As I have loved you, so love one another."[300] But even the best earthly community is still just a shadow of Jesus' perfect love.

---

300 John 13:34

∞ Agape ∞

Thirty African women are seated in a handmade brick building in Uganda with one of PLL's coaches named Sherrie. They are quiet. Sherrie is looking them in the eyes and asking God to show her how she can reach them. These women sing their hearts out to the Lord. They can quote so many Scriptures. But when she tries to talk to them about the love of Jesus for them, she gets nothing but blank stares. How could she bridge the disconnect for these sisters in the faith?

After a few moments like this, she starts asking some questions about what love meant to them. She starts with some of the deepest loves in her own life, such as her spouse, and the responses from the women surprise her. One shrugged and said that she knows her husband loves her when he beats her. Sherrie is the only woman in the room who is shocked, which then deepens her sadness and her own feelings of inadequacy for this work.

This time, when she shares Jesus' profound love for them, she lets the moment stretch, meeting each set of eyes one by one. She knows they are stuck, and she knows only the Holy Spirit can move them from that place. She feels her heart beat a few times in the silence, waiting on the Lord. Then in a moment she knows exactly what she must do as He brings a memory of His love to her mind, and she moves towards one of the more vocal women. Without a word, Sherrie kneels on the ground and begins to demonstrate washing her feet.

The interpreter is silent because this gesture needs no explanation. The room is breathless. The woman is visibly uncomfortable, but her eyes stay fixed on Sherrie. The other women's eyes are transfixed on the scene before them.

After a moment, Sherrie gets up and meets their eyes again. "This is how Jesus loves. Jesus does *not* beat you to show you that He loves you."

Voice shaking, she takes a breath as her eyes begin to mist over, "Jesus gets down on his hands and knees and washes your feet, and He tends to your wounds. *That* is how Jesus loves you."

She looks around the room. There are no more blank stares now. She sees surprise, a little confusion, but mostly curiosity and thirst.

Now there is movement. Now there is an opportunity to partner with the Holy Spirit to really get them unstuck.

Sherrie called me that evening. We had a long conversation with prayer about next steps to help these women get unstuck.

We realized that the first step was inviting them into a place of vulnerability. In order for that to happen, it was time for Sherrie to share her own story– how for her entire life she didn't think God loved her.

Sherrie fell in love with God as early as 10 years old when she first prayed to receive Christ. She desired to know Him and about Him but had no sense of how He felt about her. She studied the Scriptures hungrily throughout her young adulthood. The more she learned, the more she realized how much there was to learn. After homeschooling her children, she went to seminary where she pursued a master's in Christian Education and after that a master's in Theology. Through all of this, all of the knowledge she gained, she still felt that God didn't love her. She could have told you all the verses in the Bible that mentioned God's love, but she did not experience it herself.

When I met Sherrie, she was in a place where she felt dejected and forgotten. She was the butt of her mother's angry dementia, two of her adopted children divorced their family when they reconnected with their birth parents, and she was ostracized at the church where she worked because everyone felt threatened by her education. She had started to feel like she was the one person who had ever been born that God couldn't love. She participated in PLL under my dear friend Pam's coaching. Through that process, and through the one anothering in the course, the Lord showed her that the feeling was a lie, one she had been under for most of her life. He showed her that Romans 8:35-38 were true *for her*. She was able to know deeply in her knower at long last that God did love her and nothing in heaven, on earth, or under it could stop that.

How do you define love? These women have had their view of love so distorted. Sherrie tried to show the woman who spoke how Jesus would approach her body as led by the Spirit, humbly and gently. Instead of delivering a beating, Jesus took on a gruesome beating in her place and mine before His crucifixion. A beating so horrific, people who study the Shroud of Turin reported that the movie,[301] "The Passion of the Christ,"[302] as bloody as it is, still portrays less violence than He experienced.[303] Love does not beat you.

Love is hard to put into words sometimes. Often we have to define it in moments. The ultimate moment is Jesus' choice to endure the cross for the joy set before Him. That joy was closing the gulf between you and Him. That joy was knowing you, being close to you, being known by you, and bringing you home to Heaven. This relationship is what it has all always been about.

Scripture often describes love in the things you will see Love doing, the kinds of moments you will have with Him.[304] He is patient with you. He is kind to you. He does not dishonor you. He is selfless with you. He is not easily angered by you. He always protects, He always perseveres. He will never leave you nor forsake you, no not ever. Even if you forsake Him, He will not forsake you. Even if you are not faithful, He will be faithful to you. He has sworn by Himself, unshakable, unchangeable, and unbreakable, that He will bless you.[305]

Maybe this is landing with you; maybe it isn't just yet. Sometimes we need to experience His love mirrored from each other to allow His love deeper into our souls. How could He choose to do such a thing without expecting anything in return, without a side truckload of guilt or obligation?

I often choose to explain my love to my family for the very purpose of undoing some of the expectations earthly love can leave on us. I once brought out a bucket of ice water to my pregnant daughter-in-love for her feet in the summertime. She was touched by the thoughtfulness,

---

301 Hector. "Was Jesus the Man on the Shroud of Turin? — Walking Humbly with God." *Walking Humbly with God*, 21 Nov. 2023, www.walkinghumblywithgod.com/blog/2023/11/21/was-jesus-the-man-on-the-shroud-of-turin/.
302 BrioTV. "The Passion of the Christ - Full Movie." *Vimeo*, 30 Apr. 2020, vimeo.com/413740746.
303 D'Muhala, Tom. *The Authenticity of the Resurrection*. 2010.; Background information: "The Catholic Transcript 24 November 1978 — the Catholic News Archive." *Thecatholicnewsarchive.org*, 2025, thecatholicnewsarchive.org/?a=d&d=CTR19781124-01.2.2&e=-------en-20--1--txt-txIN--------.
304 1 Corinthians 13:4-8
305 Hebrews 6:18

felt a little bashful, and thanked me maybe a little too much. When we were alone later, I asked her why she thought I brought her the water.

I offered some options including, "or maybe because you're carrying my grandchild?"

She shrugged, not knowing where I was going with the line of questioning. She stopped meeting my eyes.

I continued, "I did it because I love *you*."

One reassurance of love for me from the Lord came at the end of a hospital visit after yet another health storm in 2016. I got the flu, and in the cytokine storm from my overactive immune system, I experienced a cardiac effusion that progressed to a cardiac tamponade. This is when fluid builds up in the sac around the heart, crushing it. In the emergency procedure to save my life, they forcibly shoved a tube between my ribs and into the sac. Over 1.5 liters of fluid drained from my heart. Seven different attending physicians remarked in their own style and bedside manner that they were amazed I survived the incident.

As the initial shock wore off, I found myself quickly upgraded from the Cardiac Intensive Care Unit to a regular hospital room, and it was time to think about going home. I now felt as though my emotional heart was being crushed as much as my physical heart had been. This is the only time I can remember being truly mad at God. I wasn't angry that the emergency had happened but that I had come so close to death, and yet again, "woke up alive." I just wished He would take me home and be done with it. I felt played with. I felt anything but loved.

These emotions scared me, so I turned to prayer. I found a semi-secluded spot by a window in a hallway and got on my knees. I was so angry, I could hardly talk to Him. It was mostly just crying. I imagine these are the kinds of moments when Holy Spirit uses the groanings too deep for words in His interceding for us. The journey had been so long. I was so tired. It felt so unfair. I felt so incredibly alone.

I don't know how long I was on the floor there, but I was eventually able to form something to say to Him, "Father – I listen to people all day long, every day. If You're going to leave me here, I just need someone to listen to me."

The next day, I was just a few minutes from going home, dressed in normal clothes, putting the last of my things in a bag.

This woman came in and greeted me with a very nice voice, "Hello!"

"Hello." I barked back. I had no time for her; I was hoping she would wrap up whatever she was doing and get out.

She absorbed my tone and continued in her kind one, "Is there a patient in the room?"

"I'm the patient [dummy]." I snipped.

She was unphased by me and my exasperating behavior and continued, "That's good news that you're dressed; that means you're going home!"

For whatever reason, I decided to be a little bit more transparent, "I'm going to the wrong home..."

"What do you mean?" She cocked her head a little.

I became a bit vulnerable and started to try to explain that I'd been through so much, and I just want to go *home,* but I hardened again because I didn't think she would understand.

I cut off my heart and instead asked her, "Why are you here?"

She opened her hands and said these exact words, "I'm here just to listen to you."

She was a hospital chaplain.

I turned into a puddle in response to that, all defenses and anger falling to the floor. Maybe it wasn't the mercy I most wanted of a whole and well body, or a chariot ride home, but it was a tender, tender mercy all the same. He sent me an ambassador, a member of the community of the body of Christ. He has His purposes for my body's struggles, and I trust Him with that. But He is not far from me. He doesn't expect me to carry any of it on my own. He might as well have walked up beside me and held me, Himself.

After I got control of myself and wiped my eyes and nose, I told her what I had prayed the day before. She began crying then.

"This is my rodeo! Why are you crying?!" We both laughed.

She told me that she missed the morning rounds with the nurses, so she didn't know who the patients were (or that I had checked I didn't want to be visited by a chaplain). She had to rely on the Lord's leading to know which room to visit, and He kept bringing her to mine even though it didn't appear that there was a patient in the room. He was also ministering to her in confirming that He spoke to her and used her "one anothering." She brought holy community to me even though we may never see one another again on this side. It was a big agape fest in that room. Delight. To this day, I have not been angry with God again.

We love because He first loved us.[306] Our love is limited by our understanding of His love for us. I do not tell you this to try to squeeze some more love out of you for others. Our love for others is merely an outward sign; I have no agenda to affect your outward sign, just to draw your attention to it. I tell you this because knowing His love for you is an end in itself. Your relationship, your community with Him, the Triune God, is the most important one in your whole life; developing it is the most life-giving, the strongest agent against this bone-wearying life. Jesus is the friend who sticks closer than a brother. How is your community with Him? Can you talk freely and honestly with Him? Are you listening? Are you recognizing that you don't have to run? You may rest in His love. Community, in many surprising forms, lets a little more of His love in. Sometimes you will knock on someone else's door. Sometimes they will knock on your door.

∞ Koinonia ∞

Love is the foundation for all of this, specifically agape love, the unconditional, selfless love of God. It is entirely "other" to the world. It makes no sense; it confounds. It is a new way. If we walk in the way of rest, love is the path, the very ground on which we walk. We build our community like the Philippian church, on a groundswell of love from Christ. We fellowship with the Father, and we express our rest within the body of His church. We are commanded not to forsake fellowshipping one with another.[307] It is no coincidence that the way Jesus asked us to remember Him in communion is a liturgy done in community. He wants us to break bread together, to encourage each other in songs and hymns; this is where we live out our rest together.

Koinonia means "participation fellowship — the act of sharing in

---

306 1 John 4:19
307 Hebrews 10:25

the activities or privileges of an intimate association or group; especially used of marriage and churches" (Lexham Research Lexicon of the Greek New Testament). The communion of the Spirit goes beyond mere participation to the deep, intimate, interconnected sense of community that is a quality of our relationship with Holy Spirit."[308] It is a special privilege, and it is created only by Holy Spirit.

There have been hundreds of times I have dragged my butt to church. But there have been less than a dozen times that I left church dragging. Something of the fellowship with Christ is encountered when I remember someone's name in the hall or make eye contact with one I know well or am meeting for the first time. The high five given to the rambunctious three year old boy ready to bolt transfers stored energy of this love and communion. I am bolstered. His mom gets a nano second of respite.

Koinonia is the experience of the oneness we have in Christ that we discussed at the beginning of the chapter. That is not to say that we do not also create community with those who do not know Jesus at this time. Jesus and John the Baptist both call the Pharisees broods of vipers because they were not unified with the people. They were among the common people, yet they were not ministering to the common people. They separated themselves and made their own little way about their works. May we never separate ourselves from the commonness of our body in Christ! We partake in koinonia and take that love with us to every circle in which we find ourselves.

The church is intended to be this home base for us, the place where we come home to koinonia so that we may more abundantly carry it with us to every other circle of life. If that isn't the case for you, take heart; you may still encounter it with brothers and sisters who love Jesus in different circles in your life. The church is not a building. It is the people of Christ. Find them and let them find you.

At one point I felt like I had to hide our marriage issues from the church authorities. I had experienced first hand what happens when you become too vulnerable. During that debilitating Lyme season, a

---

[308] "What Does It Mean to Have the Communion of the Holy Spirit (2 Corinthians 13:14)?" *GotQuestions.Org*, Got Questions Ministries, 20 Aug. 2024, www.gotquestions.org/communion-of-the-Holy-Spirit.html.

woman from the church suddenly showed up in my bedroom. She was there to visit me and asked if she could use the bathroom while there. Several years later, I learned that this same woman had a drug addiction and would visit the sick only to steal their narcotics.

We were one of the victims. We were told that we could not confront the woman, that we needed to forgive her and to not hold onto any anger. I explained that she was forgiven, but I had every right to have a conversation with her so that we could both heal. But church leadership declined our request. Instead, we never experienced resolution with this person. Sadly, this is not an uncommon experience. There is much unresolved in relationships within the church that one day will be fully redeemed.

One of my daughters in love, Cassie, has given me permission to share her story of similar pain. Her biological father (she calls him her sperm donor) told her mom to choose him or choose the baby, but she won't have both of them. This man was a so-called Christian. Thankfully, Cassie is married to my son who truly loves the Lord, and we are watching redemption happen. In fact, at a baby shower we had for her and Michael, we prayed over them and the baby. Forty people prayed over their little family. And Cassie cried. There was softness and tenderness towards the love of the Father being poured out to her even while her earthly father had abandoned their family. Healing was happening in the same community that had hurt her.

I don't want to rush past this part. You may be very wounded by the church or other close community. One of our participants had to completely cut herself off from her family of origin. The culture was that of climbing and clawing on each other's backs rather than holding each other up on their shoulders.

It's very difficult to try again when we have been betrayed or otherwise let down by community. It makes us very gun shy when our need for others and the longing for togetherness rises up; it makes it feel like it would be easier to just take care of ourselves by ourselves. We get caught in the eddy of our own questions. Where would you find people? How do you make those bonds? How do you know you've chosen the right ones? How do you know they won't disappoint you and leave you worse off than you were before?

We don't know that people won't hurt us, but when we live apart from community, we are already hurting. I understand that this feels preferable sometimes. I remember when I felt that way. And when I felt that way, I truly could not imagine what it could feel like to be nestled in community.

When we are apart from God, we live this wandering, clawing, individualistic, right-in-my-own-eyes, wrestling, restless state.[309] Some of those patterns can persist even after we come to know Him. The individualistic part of that can feel right in my own eyes. It's this "I'm not burdening anyone," "I'm not relying on anyone," "I'm pulling myself up by my own bootstraps" sort of mindset.

This is where Cain lived. He shed blood in anger, and it cut him off from community. He became quite successful but restless. He had a bounty on his head. We are all living that way, in a spiritual sense, outside of community.

When I'm in survival mode, my thinking starts to sound like: "how am I going to avoid regrets?", "make sure I don't mess up," "ensure past failures don't come back to haunt me." There is no community in that kind of hiding. There is no rest in that because we are running backwards.

When I come back to "let us," I let down my guard because I remember that there is no longer enmity between God and me; I am looked upon with love, and I can receive that love. Once I settle it in my knower that I am no longer under judgment from God, I don't need to worry about the judgment of man. When I'm no longer running and hiding, I can heal. When I'm no longer defending and rationalizing, I can heal. That can happen when I'm no longer in survival mode. There is a very physical aspect to this too: fight or flight vs. rest and digest.

Leaving survival mode requires trust. We let our walls down with Jesus first. We allow Jesus to remake those places of our heart where others have wounded or disappointed us, accept the risk of pain, and let others in anyway. We allow ourselves to be seen by others, firmly rooted in the love with which Jesus surrounds us. Even if we are rejected, even if our worst fears of abandonment are realized, we are safe in the full acceptance and presence of Jesus. Our peace becomes a safe place

---

309 Isaiah 53:6

for other people. Our healed places become the place from which we are able to most pour out blessing on others, and we receive blessing from others.

Hurt people hurt people. Where I am still wounded, I will lash out. When God is allowed to come in, there is healing. And that healing can look like breaking sometimes. When the kids saw Tom and me as we were, it felt like breaking. When I had big blowout fights with my friends out of my abandonment wounds from my mother after which I got to experience them not abandoning me, it felt like breaking at first. When I let Jesus into more of those scary places, those places get broken, my pride gets broken, my self-protection gets broken. Our wounded places become, as I like to call them, "broken" instead; there is still history there, but wholeness, too. It's a crack out of which love and grace can most freely pour out because Jesus first poured those things in at the breach. Wounded people hurt people, broken people pour out.

Where I am wounded, I will lash out, Where I am broken, I will pour out.

I have included a graphic illustrating the realignment that happens when we allow Jesus to minister to us in those wounded places. He is working healing into those places, and He brings wholeness. Our wounds are not just the strikes we receive from others but the painful places in us where the lies are still running. When we remain under the lie, for example, that "I don't need anyone," the flesh and its self-protectiveness walls off the soul and denies the work that the Spirit would do.

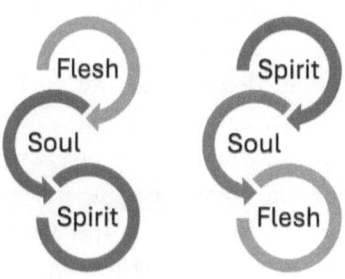

Realignment

But when Jesus is allowed to do His work, His Spirit, the Holy Spirit, is in charge, which refreshes the soul and animates the body and its actions. We are able through that same hurt place to give deeper compassion, understanding, and practical support when we see that they hurt in the same way that we do. Others need Jesus in us working through the places we are weak just as much or more than the places we are strong. Even if another strike comes, what pours out of that crack is forgiveness and grace rather than poison and vitriol.

It's scary to allow people in, even a little bit. We are out of practice, it seems. Being out of practice doesn't change the need for it. God designed us for community. One anothering is a pillar of our faith. Generosity is to become as natural as breathing for us. Fellowship awakens our connectedness to the Father, expanding our hearts to receive. As Francis of Assisi put it – quite often it is in giving that we receive.[310] Receiving sometimes is about pouring out and giving. Something lies dormant in us without it. Community creates the opportunity for connection that brings warmth and healing to our souls while simultaneously giving us a canvas to express our generosity. Do I get hurt at times? Yes. Do people take advantage of me? Yes. Do people sometimes get too clingy? Yes. I can choose to avoid those and endless other possible discomforts, or I can enter the sea of humanity and practice loving and receiving love, watching my little vessel expand its ability to take in the Infinite.

"To love at all is to be vulnerable. Love anything and your heart will be wrung and possibly broken. If you want to make sure of keeping it intact you must give it to no one, not even an animal. Wrap it carefully round with hobbies and little luxuries; avoid all entanglements. Lock it up safe in the casket or coffin of your selfishness. But in that casket, safe, dark, motionless, airless, it will change. It will not be broken; it will become unbreakable, impenetrable, irredeemable. To love is to be vulnerable."[311]

How do we do this? So much of what we do in PLL is preparing our little vessels to expand and receive. The finite is trying to receive the infinite. If you've ever had a moment in which you've experienced such a burst of love or profound loss you feel your heart will break, that is a time when our finite frame is struggling to receive the infinite. It's

---

310 "The Peace Prayer of Saint Francis." *Journey with Jesus*, 2025, www.journeywithjesus.net/poemsandprayers/554-saint-francis-of-assisi.
311 Lewis, C.S. *The Four Loves*. San Francisco, Harperone, 1960.

different than looking upon a gorgeous waterfall or mountain because we are simply beholders of that beauty, but we don't become a part of it. But in community you can partake. You could sit on the sideline and just behold, but you can't receive that way. We feel safe sidelined in a self-protective kind of way. No one can hurt us there, but neither can God use His community of love to heal you.

You receive by acknowledging your need for that community, as messed up and screwed up as they may be. You need them, and they need you, as screwed up as you may be. I started this chapter with the question "What do you need?" to connect us to this aspect of community that allows us to stop having it all together. This question helps us acknowledge to ourselves that we do need others and prepares us to be vulnerable with them. It also prepares us to take the appropriate amount of responsibility for ourselves in interactions with others. It prevents the unhealthy dynamic of expecting others to solve the mystery of our emotions and needs. This question helps us to show up authentically to our interactions with others. Then we may have the space to pay attention to what the person in front of us may need.

I spend a good bit of time on this "receiving" piece because it is where I got stuck. I described for you how I became a safe place for others, I did give and pour out, I became very needed, and I made sure I needed no one. My emotional walls were too high, no one could get in to harm me, but no one could get in to help me. "I won't let you hurt me" also means, "I won't let God use you to heal me." Longsuffering is not for the impatient.

Through Lyme disease, God taught me how to let go. I didn't know how to receive the fullness of community, but God allowed me to be in a lowly position that taught me how to receive. I don't believe that my illness was "punishment" for personal shortcomings (this concept can so easily get twisted) but I do believe He can redeem and use anything. No suffering is ever wasted by God.[312]

Today, allowing others in means I allow my tears to fall. It means letting those I teach know when they have taught me something (which is quite often) and striking up conversation with a new face because I need the companionship as much as they do, even though my little

---

[312] Psalm 56, 2 Corinthians 1:3-4, Romans 8:28-29

introverted heart would sometimes rather just stay inside. It means choosing a different pattern than I would have during the "undercover" Lyme days when one of my kids asks how my health is.

It can also mean allowing somebody into how tired you are. That you can't be "on," but you need people. One PLL participant made the decision to re-enter church community after some significant betrayal from her home church. She went somewhere new, so there were no expectations of who she had been, and she showed up to a small group. She did not say a word. She picked a spot on a squishy couch and sank into it with crossed arms. She showed up the next week and sat on that couch. She showed up the week after that and sat on that couch. She did not speak to anyone for three months, and they let her. Her porcupine quills slowly relaxed, and she began to slowly ever so slowly make friends. This sort of thing has happened with many PLL participants. PLL is not competing with the church; we view ourselves as being the church. And in that process of practicing being the church with a smaller community, sometimes a person who hasn't been in church a long time will find themselves having the courage to go back to church.

When I'm worn out, like the story I shared at the beginning of the book, I do not have the bandwidth for a wider community. At that time, I couldn't start something new. I didn't have the capacity to interface with some of my more give-heavy relationships. But I did need my team. I had been going it alone. When I admitted I needed help, they rallied around me, they helped me delegate, and they propped me up like Aaron and Hur propped up Moses' arms when he got tired in Exodus.[313] He couldn't do it alone, and neither could I.

When we are in community, as "Life Together" describes, and a member is absent, we truly miss them. It isn't "too bad they aren't here." There is a real ache. We long to hear their voice, to understand what's happening with them, and to have them ask questions about us. It is hard to experience the fullness of our story without that person being in our life.

You may ache to feel that kind of togetherness with people, even with just one person. I want to caution you against the trap of waiting to find your community because, most of the time, it isn't something

---

[313] Exodus 17:11-12

that independently exists; it's something that we create or build into right where we are. If you wait to find the people who are just right that you can accept and you expect to accept you, you will be looking for a needle in a haystack the size of Alaska. Instead, bring love and humble curiosity into all your circles, and you will find that you have more community than you know what to do with.

When we moved to Raleigh from Florida, we didn't have any family nearby. I knew we needed people, so I set to work on making our neighborhood our new community, making my own door open. I loved how I had neighbors growing up in Chicago who didn't have to knock on our door, and I didn't have to knock on theirs. I wanted that for my boys, so I tried to be that kind of neighbor myself.

Our bonds with our new Raleigh neighbors did not happen by accident. We set out to know them, and very importantly, allow ourselves to be known. I didn't realize how crucial it would be for us at the onset of this effort, but backyard neighbor Brenda wound up being the one who found me collapsed in the side yard. Neighbors were the ones that made sure that the damage from hurricane Fran was sorted out while Tom and I were at the hospital for one of my health episodes. Georgi would not let the power company leave the neighborhood until they had fixed our outside electrical box as well as hers after we all went a week without power. Nancy grabbed our packages from the front porch when we were out of town. We cut her lawn and took out her garbage to remind her that we saw her. Pastor Lucian's wife had cancer, so we took extra meals over to them periodically to remind them they are seen. Contractor Scott helped us move furniture. We blew the oak leaves off the driveway for a newly-single neighbor. Retired Jim and my husband would catch up as they leaned against their rakes. I checked on recently widowed Libby just to say hi. Over the years, our neighbors became a community, one touch point at a time. Now, most of the neighbors would describe our street as family.

The parents' of our sons' friends at school became second parents to them; they rotated spending nights between about 6 houses, sometimes multiple different ones in a week, so Tom could be at the hospital with me or so they didn't see their mother battling one of the waves at home. And we had the privilege of walking with them through their dark valleys of loss and struggle. The sons of this group are still best friends to this day; they have brought spouses and children into this circle that is every bit as loyal and loving as an extended family.

Just start with one step towards more real connection. One touch point at a time. And my dear reader, train your little vessel to receive. Let down your drawbridge, and leave your pride by the door. You will not be loved perfectly. Your toes are going to be stepped on. They're going to say it wrong, they're going to hug too tight. That's all part of receiving love. Let them in.

Selah Moment

I want to create space for a moment here for you to bring any reluctance to come back into community before the Lord. There is often some sort of lie keeping us in hiding or survival mode. Would you be willing to sit a moment with the Lord and go through the Shift process to see if there is anything there for you? I have included thought joggers to prime the pump. They are not intended to influence or shape your responses.

Step 1. What physically happens in your body when you think about participating in community?
　Thought joggers: *Get physically tired. Heart races. Panic wells up in my throat.*

Step 2. What are you telling yourself as those symptoms manifest in your body?
　Thought joggers: *I'm going to be rejected. It's not worth the pain. I don't know how to be myself in community.*

Step 3. What does God's truth say about you, community, and Him?

If you would like a thought jogger on this step, please see the footnote. I have not included here to give you a chance to feel the open space with the Lord.[314]

Step 4. Comparing what you are telling yourself with what God is telling you, are you willing to confess any lie you are believing as well as declare the truth – out loud?

Thought joggers: *Lord, I see that I'm not trusting and having fellowship with You first. In fact, I'm isolating myself from You before I isolate from others. I confess that I want to be back in fellowship with You and want to be a vibrant part of the body of Christ. I don't know how to do that yet, but I trust that You will guide me.*

Step 5. If you complete step 4, now declare the truth with God's authority back to yourself.

Thought joggers: *God you are about community and you will teach me how to reenter community. You will heal me through community and you will heal others through my engagement in community.*

Step 6. Ask God what is one small step you can take into community.

Thought joggers: *Lord, where do I begin to engage in community again?*

Step 7. Take that step without hesitation or reservation.

---

314 Thought joggers: *If you are in Me, you are already in community. You will learn more about Me as you fellowship with others. You will learn more about yourself as you fellowship with others. I can help you through the pains and disappointments that come with community if you will trust Me and fellowship with Me first.*

CHAPTER TWELVE

Shalom

How do we experience the abundant life now?[315]

AS WE PERPETUALLY acknowledge and live under the authority of our Savior, we experience Shabbat rest.

- Rest from hiding our sin, justifying our sin
- Rest from proving we were worthy of the gift of mercy
- Rest from hyperfunctioning to try to earn His grace
- Rest from condemnation because of our confession that we are sinners who are saved
- Rest from the entrapment of carrying offense
- Rest from wondering if there is purpose and good that could come from our suffering, because we know our our Prince of Peace to be good
- Rest when we are bone tired, because our Prince of Peace does not chastise for the infirmity of human frailty and weakness; rather, He comforts and consoles in our moments of testing and trial and tumbles
- Rest in the community of the Father, Son, and Holy Spirit, even in times when circumstances put us in cells of isolation, because we know the Prince of Peace is interceding on our behalf and will mysteriously move others to do the same, even those whose faces and names we don't know

---

315   John 10:10

As this rest begins to manifest more in my life, I find myself walking a little bit more like Jesus. I walk the path of shalom. Shalom is my favorite word right now in Scripture.[316] It was the final gift Jesus gave to His disciples as He neared the end of His earthly ministry in John 14:27.

Jesus is our Prince of Peace, or more accurately stated, our Prince of Shalom! Isaiah tells us that the one whose mind is stayed on God is kept in perfect shalom. Shalom could be considered the outgrowth of rest. As we abide or even delight in our position in Him, (feel free to search on the many points in the journey where I use the word delight) we are moving deeper into rest and experiencing this profound and delightful shalom wholeness. Still elusive, yet more easily identified. Still not fulfilled continually in an eternal sense, yet experienced in a way that quiets the cravings that antagonize and threaten to trample the soul's well being.

The work is not yet complete, but as we yield to Jesus, change slowly happens. Sometimes, we can gaslight ourselves out of our own spiritual experiences because change isn't always immediately obvious. But we get to move to a place where we do not doubt our belief, and when we do not doubt our belief we have peace. If we stand upon the assurance of provision in our faith that God has given us everything we need for life and godliness, then we can trust the transformative process.[317] Even Jesus himself grew in wisdom and stature when He walked here.[318] Community can help us practice celebrating every step along the way towards Christlikeness.

This celebration practice is so important in our growth. Sometimes we see the gap between where we want to be and where we are, and it feels like too much. I remember one afternoon in the high school gym, one of my color guard girls, Ava, had a problem with the way I was running the rehearsal. She struggled to word her disagreement in a way that wasn't blatantly defiant and disrespectful. She did not succeed, but I thanked her and entered the conversation with her.

Later one of my guard captains asked me why I thanked her. From the outside, Ava had been incredibly disrespectful to me. I smiled and

---

316 "E6: Hesed & Shalom. חסד שולשו | Illuminationhebrewinsights.com." *Illuminationhebrewinsights.com*, 2024, illuminationhebrewinsights.com/2024/09/25/hesed-shalom-.
317 2 Peter 1:3
318 Luke 2:52

said, "Because that was much better than what she would have said a month ago. I want to celebrate her progress and effort without expecting her to become perfect overnight." This was food for thought for my captain, too, who had always been very dutiful and often expected herself not to make mistakes. I hope perhaps for her this was a perspective that could open up the possibility that she might be able to also allow herself to be a work in progress.

It bears repeating just one last time – We are always in draft form. I wonder if you could settle into being both glorious and yet still unfinished, as well. We find rest there.

In Colossians it talks about being wise in the way we conduct ourselves.[319] Conduct ourselves is another way of describing how we occupy our space. It is what your soul exudes. Imagine walking with Jesus, or Paul, or Peter – what do you think their soul exuded? What would be some words you might use to describe them? Or get more specific – how was Paul occupying his space when he was comforting his followers who were trying to convince him not to go to Jerusalem or when he cast the demon out of the annoying 16-year old servant girl? This is more what I'm thinking about here. Do we fill our space with insecurity and doubt, avoidant with our eyes down, leaving others wondering and us wallowing? Do we fill our space with cocky, thoughtless words and actions to ensure a strong presence that runs over others? I think about Judas and wonder how he filled his space, maybe with a bit of suspicion and distance. Or I think about Job and how he occupied his space, maybe with the subtle air of a statesman yet the humility of a servant. Do we exude a quiet confidence of assurance of the provision and relationship with the Lord?

When we choose the latter mode (and it is a choice), we are practicing the expression of our faith, and as we do that we grow in wisdom. This wisdom then creates a stronger shalom peace for our souls. I am wiser now than before I started writing, before an altercation with a loved one, before points of conflict and tension. As I access the provision He has for me in all those moments, He pours it out lavishly and wisdom grows. Wisdom then occupies more of my space, leading to greater shalom. As shalom nourishes, my need to justify my existence is gone. I am wrapped up in Him and His love and good purposes. Delight.

---

319 Colossians 4:5-6

I remember a beautiful, eager soul the Lord brought into my life to disciple. I was an Elizabeth to her, she was a Cheryl to me. Every waking moment she followed me. She listened in on my conversations; we sat for our hours on the porch rocking the night away, she followed me to places where I taught or spoke; she sat in on my fights with Tom; she watched how I made messes in the kitchen without concern; she questioned how I could enter conflict with someone and not lose sleep; she wondered how I served while in excruciating pain and not feel resentful. And on and on the dialogue went.

One particularly significant and ongoing discussion was around making decisions and representing ourselves. One day she said, exasperated, "Does this ever get any easier?!" I was able to reassure that the training is very robust early on, especially with one so hungry, yet over time the internalization will create the roadmap of wisdom by which she will be able to walk and take others, as well. She will find shalom taking hold as she responds to God's steadfast love with a steadfast commitment to draw life from the True Vine.[320] Now, almost eight years later, this young lady navigates life like an old soul. Wisdom is carrying her along, she walks in shalom more frequently, and her confidence in navigating uncharted or rough waters in life grows daily.

Elizabeth filled her space with a quiet confidence even during the years following her son's passing that continued to draw people to her. Our shalom will be attractive to others who are searching. They will want to drink from the well we are drinking from, and they drink *through* us for a time. How the church will strengthen as we allow others to drink from our well! The command was to go and make disciples, teaching them all that Jesus commanded. We partner with God in the making of those followers of Jesus. What a glorious job given to us! It is the highest and most honoring work as bearers in His royal priesthood.

What causes us to shy away from this work, I wonder?

- Perhaps we know our water is tainted with offense or hatred or judgment. That, indeed, becomes an opportunity to return to our source, abide, and let him clear the toxins from the stream.

---

[320] 1 Thessalonians 3:8, John 15:1-8

- Another reason may be that you just don't feel like you have enough water for you and for everyone else. I still get empty, too. Some days what I'm pouring out is more than what is pouring in. That is when I need to return to rest. That reason also leads us back to abiding. I can't promise you won't ever get tired again, but it will get easier to return to rest as you practice.
- Perhaps we ourselves are not living as Christ commanded. What a wonderful opportunity for confession and returning, not in being perfect ourselves, but being perfected in Him.
- Finally, perhaps we're not sure it's worth the risk. What if the person doesn't really take hold of the truth, and we're afraid we've wasted our time? When battling this mindset, simply return to the truth that we do not control the outcomes. There are folks that I let go. They came to me wanting to be discipled and nurtured. In the end, they desired me to be the decider and the sole nourishment for their soul. I can't do either, and so I gently let those beautiful souls continue on their journey without me, trusting that another discipler will enter their life to then continue the work. Free will.

Inevitably, just about the time it seems I'm wrapping up the intense stage of one discipleship relationship, another beautiful soul enters my life. Most recently, it came in the form of a distant family member who is learning how to follow Jesus and wants to spend time with me but doesn't want to be a bother. Quite the animated conversation followed when Jesus in me met Jesus in another believer. It brings me back to Jesus and John dancing in their mother's wombs as they met. You may be wondering, when are we ready to "make disciples"? Simply put, when we are living as a disciple ourselves and when we are willing to share our life with another, we are ready to jump into the "making" work. I remember both Elizabeth and another discipler saying the same thing to me. I would say, "May I ask you a question?" and the response I received from both of them was the same: "Cheryl, you can ask me any question you would like, and I will answer it to the best of my ability." I've shared my life with you here. You have a life that is meant to be shared, as well. Redemptive fruit comes in sharing our lives with one another. Through the tears, the joys, the hardships… it all becomes relevant to a disciple's journey, for God makes everything work together for good for those of us who are learning to love Him and choose to call upon His name.

We will receive our final and complete unburdening in Heaven, but the light yoke is what Jesus does for us in this life. I have walked without Him, I have walked in contention with Him, and I have walked with Him. I can attest to the fact that walking with Him and cooperating with Him (right side column page 92) is the lightest way to walk even during the most weighted times in my life. His way is the way of rest. The longer I walk, the more falls from me. I am freer today than I was even six months ago. Praise God!

Selah Moment

I wonder – where are you now as we bring our journey together to a close? Is your answer to the question "Where are you?" different than it was at the beginning of this book? Is your voice stronger now? Is your pot still empty? Take some time to reflect here. What word would describe where you are now?

If you're having trouble finding a word, here are a few more questions to jog your memory about our journey together.

- What has God shown you about Himself through this time?
- What have you learned about yourself?
- Where do you sense you are starting to shift from toil to labor?

As we row back to the bank where the parting of ways awaits us, I feel the ache to talk to you, wishing I could hear your voice and what you would say about this journey we have taken together. Perhaps you began your journey with Him for the first time, or maybe you are an old saint who found some refreshment, lightness, or deepening. As we leave the canoe and still waters behind us, I am so glad you decided to row on with me to the bank here, our last chapter, and a final stretch of flat dirt path to the place our walks will diverge.

∞ Fix Your Eyes ∞

There is so much to celebrate in what the Lord is doing, and at the same time we still walk in a fallen world. I pray that you may hold fast to His sovereignty and the good things, that though the waves buffet, you may always be able to return to a joyful shalom.

Ann is one of our leaders as of this writing. She came into PLL a couple years ago, hurting and quiet. Her manner was stifled and very measured. A suicidal son, a dying mom, and an ill husband are just a few of the many challenges facing this dear woman of God. Having experienced horrific sexual abuse as a child, she resorted to a way of living that required extreme control over herself and others around her to get through this life. She walked through life fueled by anger. By the end of PLL she decided to release her idol of control in exchange for His joy. There isn't a time I speak to Ann, read something she has written, get an encouraging text from her that does not include the phrase "choose joy." I hope one day she writes a book about that.

Each day brings an opportunity to choose. For her, she has simplified it down to one word – joy.

There is something profoundly wise in simplifying. It can help us to carry treasured things along with us and shed the unnecessary. Remember our journey with complexity from Chapter 2?

Naive Simplicity → Complexity → Exquisite Simplicity

Simplicity must give way to complexity at first, because simplicity doesn't take into consideration the nuances of each of our personal lives and situations. That mindset can prompt us to ignore the pain, the challenges. We deny our places of contribution to our situation, and we hyper excuse or hyper blame those around us. God's work in each of us is tender, powerful, and unique. It is unpredictable and yet always for our good. He is the same yesterday today and forever, complex and consistent.[321] He made the universe with mysteries that mathematicians and physicists still pursue today, and yet He says it is best to enter His kingdom like a child.[322]

Through the PLL journey we open the door to the complexity of our lives within the boundaries of God's love and truth. As Ann did this, she became vulnerable to herself and to God and, eventually, to us. We had the opportunity to live in her complexity for those few weeks together. On the other side of that journey emerged the simplicity of a single phrase – choose joy. It honored her unique personhood. It anchored her in her faith. It gave great depth and meaning to her suffering. She has reasons to weep, and she has reasons to sing. As we have explored, these two states of being are not mutually exclusive. Lament has its place in Scripture and in life. There is no toxic positivity; she isn't denying her pain or forcing a smile on her face. But she has an unflappable hope, and she truly has peace that does not make sense. The smile that teases onto her face even as we talk about some of her hardest things is like a flame that somehow stays still and unflickering in the presence of wind and rain. This is the kind of wholeness, shalom, that I want for you, that I invite you into.

I wonder if this book made things a little complicated for you for a while. The questions asked. The challenges offered. The perspective lended. And now it's time to consider – what is on the other side of that complexity?

You can experience wholeness while you are being buffeted, while the flesh is failing, while friends are dying, while spouse or friend doesn't understand, or even while imprisoned. I feel a responsibility so deep within my members to prepare the church for shaking, so we know how to endure. God's ways are not our ways. He does not see our circumstances as we do. He cares about our ability to walk in His presence and peace through testing, trials and tribulations. My altar call for believers is not that you raise your hand again, walk the aisle, and check on your faith fire insurance, but rather that you raise an anthem

---

321 Hebrews 13:8
322 Mathew 18:3

of praise to Him no matter what you face. That you would continue to choose to deepen your trust in Him. That you declare Christ resurrected within you, living and overcoming through you, surrendering your own strength and taking up His. We can actively participate in rest through our celebration of Christ's victory over death and of your victory with Him in your life.

As we savor our last chapter together, I would like to speak shalom to you. I pray it over you. I call it out from you. You are leaving this serene locale, but you are taking the Prince of Peace with you. I pray it is filling that pot of yours, more and more until it overflows, until it leaves no more room for anything else but the perfect love that casts out all fear.[323]

> *My altar call for believers is not that you raise your hand again, but that you raise an anthem of praise to Him no matter what you face.*

Shalom is the peace of God, perfect peace,[324] peace that passes all understanding.[325] It is all things set right. Shalom being worked in our hearts is the kingdom now. Shalom is how eternity kisses the mortal. We see it being worked in our world through one person at a time being redeemed and set free, in long-time chains breaking, and unhealable wounds healing. It is an unrelenting force turning things for good in a world that is set on entropy towards chaos and darkness. Shalom reigns in the hearts of those who belong to Jesus.

This is the reality we have the privilege of living into at all times. Even if you are surrounded by chaos like Ann, living in the midst of a major war like Anna, dealing with your increasingly feeble parent who refuses to acknowledge their errors like Sharon, experiencing a threat to your business by the economy, living in a body that is failing you, or your marriage is falling apart, experiencing fear of the government, or being surrounded by any other threat, there can be shalom. I am not interested in focusing on the circumstances; I want to embrace my

---

323 1 John 4:18
324 Isaiah 26:3
325 Phillipians 4:7

Lord in the moments of intense pain, confusion, betrayal, surprise. My exquisitely simple in suffering emerged over time – focus on Him not on my circumstances. Where else could I turn, Lord, for you have the words of eternal life.[326] It truly is the "but God" life.

As our finite expands to receive the infinite, this reality of the kingdom of God is more real than anything we see with our eyes.[327] We can choose to fix our eyes on the surrounding waves like Peter when he sank,[328] or we can choose to fix our eyes on Jesus, the author and finisher of our faith who has passed through the veil before us.[329] When the sky is pulled back like a scroll, we will see with our eyes the things which our faith convicts us of now.[330] Our security in Him is more sure than the security we feel as we pull the covers over us in bed at night. His sovereignty is complete and eternal unlike any temporary authority over us or any attempt to harm us in its finite and restrained affliction. Jesus is Lord!

∞ Join the Chorus ∞

Thousands of believers across the globe are singing in all things. Whether in the midst of war or peace, imprisonment or freedom, in plenty or in want, they are singing to our Savior because of the peace of Jesus.[331] Not as the world gives,[332] but as only the Spirit can give, if we will only turn to Him. If we will participate with Him by taking our thoughts captive to the obedience of Christ, we experience the abundance of the Promised Land rest. I get to see shalom breaking through in the lives of people who are empowered to join the song almost every day in Promised Land Living; may you be as encouraged by their stories as I am. How beautiful is the church, His bride!

---

326 John 6:68
327 Luke 17:20-21, 2 Corinthians 4:18
328 Matthew 14:30
329 Hebrews 12:2, Hebrews 10:20, Matthew 27:51
330 Revelation 6:14, Hebrews 11:1
331 Philippians 4:11-13
332 John 14:27

Anna in Ukraine is standing at the gateway to the world, comforting and empowering refugees with the gospel. William in India is courageously obeying the Lord's voice with his wife. Samira came to the United States for one year, met Jesus, and took Him back home to her mother in India where they are praying for the rest of their family and community together. Believers in Taiwan are a witness for others that offense doesn't have to mean the end of a relationship, that there can be forgiveness between men because of our forgiveness from God. They are receiving Christ's honor in place of their shame. The women of Ghana are singing about the love of Jesus who holds them tenderly.

Christians in predominantly Buddhist countries are celebrating the reversal of the dynamic they had been taught about God and man. Instead of worshipping in order to receive protection or favor, they know they have everything given to them in Christ because of His obedience, regardless of how well they serve Him.

One man reported, "I now recognize that God sees and loves me more deeply than I had let myself believe. He has an intention in the way that He created me."

An older woman who journeyed with us encouraged the rest of us that the unfolding and growing of shalom never stops, "It just gets sweeter. And you never quit learning. I think I learned more about who I am in Christ during this. There is just a more settled confidence. There is better reliance on His presence, His provision, His compassion, His sufficiency. It just keeps getting better and better and better."

A singer who had forgotten his love of music in the decades of the demands of life found himself singing again during his quiet times and whistling throughout his day.

A rector who was so tired he could hardly speak left the group writing songs, enjoying spiritual retreats and leading his family on a foundation of love rather than resentment.

An engineer came to rest not only in the beautiful design of the universe but even more deeply in the unique design of his identity by the Father. Another man said, "I'm still on the same mountain but looking at it very differently."

At our last meeting, another participant shared that she hasn't been this excited about her faith since she first came to know the Lord. She says she has her joy back. She is truly living again.

God is the Waymaker – He makes the way in the desert! He parts the waters in the sea so we can safely pass through. He does the seemingly impossible, for His kingdom's sake. Jack experienced shalom. He joins the chorus of God's children who experience the world's problems with a peace that passes understanding. Delight.

It's okay if shalom is elusive. What is not okay is to say that what God wants to give you is impossible to receive. Notice I say receive, not achieve. In PLL we often say, "Come explore the seemingly impossible with us!" The great adventure with God awaits. It will include beholding, confessing, and receiving good gifts better than any gift you hoped for under the Christmas tree as a child. He is giving you His peace, for He is your Prince of Peace. As you turn your eyes toward Him, find reason to give thanks in everything, and that peace will return. We are the ones that squelch it, not the world. It doesn't actually have the power to take it from you. He says that in this world you will have trouble, but fret not: I have overcome the world.[333] There is shalom. The ones who are blameless are the ones who stand on His promises.

I desire that you would add your voice to this chorus wherever you are; sing to the Lord! I desire that you would be strengthened in who you are in Christ, that you would become unshakeable, no matter what hits you. Stand on your firm foundation in Christ. He is your Prince of Peace now.

---

333 John 16:33

∞ Bye for Now ∞

Our lives, ministries, and families are waiting for us. Here we are at the end of our journey together. My only regret is not having been able to look into your eyes and hear your stories, as well; that is one limitation of this particular medium. I pray that shalom has begun to replace your weariness. I pray that your cup is filling with living water. Maybe forgiveness or surrender have lightened your load, maybe some new boundaries have been set, maybe you have let community help you, maybe you have found ways to get a little more sleep, or maybe the Shift process has helped you quiet a destructive inner voice that does not reflect the voice of the Father. He is the One who says in many different ways throughout Scripture, "For I will satisfy the weary soul, and every languishing soul I will replenish."[334]

I love the concept of walking with God at His pace as expressed by Koysuke Koyama. "Jesus, who is God, walked at three miles per hour. God, who is love, walks at three miles per hour."[335] As you journey on from here with Him, may you keep in step with Him. May your ears be open to His voice and your heart to His touch.

And I hope that you will walk lightly and securely as you journey next to Jesus in this life. God has given us all things to enjoy. The sunset; the new red radish that mysteriously soaks up nutrients and provides us with a mid summer refreshing bite; the sound of dogs barking in the background while children are laughing and running around; the anticipation of rain as the front flips the leaves up, and the sky grows dark. As I grow nearer to the Lord, I can take more delight in every little gift He has provided in this life. We do not have to wait for eternity in Heaven to choose joy.

The end of a course is always bittersweet for me. I so enjoy the last time the group meets, and we celebrate each member's growth and increased freedom in Christ, but it is the end of one version of a wonderful community. I feel a little bit of the same here as I end this book.

---

[334] Jeremiah 31:25
[335] If this pace concept tugs at you, consider watching the movie "Godspeed." https://www.livegodspeed.org/watchgodspeed

I will share with you what I share with them: This is not the end of your journey with the Lord or the end of learning anything you have learned through this process. This truly is the beginning. It is the beginning of a new life of continually deepening awareness of how much God loves you, our identity in Christ, how the enemy works to entrap, and our authority that comes from Christ.

I believe that any crisis we experience is ultimately a crisis of identity. And when that crisis hits, we recognize that is a time to scrutinize what we are listening to. As you guard that truth of your identity in Christ (see Chapter 3 "Guard the truth" under Open Listening), something powerful can happen in your horizontal relationships. Not only do you bring your more fully integrated self to conversations, but you are also able to bring who Christ is in you. Your partnership with Christ's redeeming work brings light into those interactions, shaping those situations instead of those interactions taking from you. The work in you then has the opportunity to be multiplied into the lives of others. The work that you have allowed Him to do in you will continue for the rest of your life.

Keep abiding in the Lord, sit at the feet of Jesus, and let Him keep teaching you and freeing you. Keep shifting out of the lies when you catch them. Remember that right side column reminds us where rest is found. Receive His forgiveness when you don't get it right, because Christ has already defeated all sin in us and is seated at the right hand of God. Even if you have fallen down many times, hold fast to your confession of faith, for a righteous man falls down seven times but gets up eight. Remember that Holy Spirit is the one working in you. It's okay that you get tired and your giving outruns your filling. Be gentle with yourself in those moments and return to your Source. And remember most of all that you are His beloved. Your faith is deeply personal and eternally alive. The more personal it becomes for you, the more fresh your days will feel, even when the road is dusty and lonely.

My heart is so full that it hurts in a good way. God is expanding my heart to receive more even now. I have prayed for you on my knees, dear reader.

My hands are on your shoulders as I pray this over you: May you live free from the lies that kept you wandering in the desert. May you have the courage to receive Love infinite. May you have the discipline to stand firm on the foundation of Truth. May you serve from a heart of gladness. May you allow yourself to delight. May you take God's rest and life into every cell of your being. May you experience a heart that overflows and a mind that is at ease because it is well with your soul. May you walk in rest and in His peace. I offer this enduring biblical blessing over you. I may not have the robust voice of a worship leader, but I sing this blessing over you with the same fervor, just as I sing it over my grandchildren:

> "The Lord bless you and keep you; the Lord make His face shine upon you and be gracious to you; the Lord lift up His countenance upon you and give you peace."[336]

Shabbat Shalom my friend,
    Cheryl

---

336 Numbers 6:24, Jobe, Kari. *The Blessing.* 2020.

Appendix A: Listening Styles

Listening Style	People Group	With Whom or When Do I Use This Style?	What is the Effect on Others?
• Know it all • Must see it to believe it • Aristocratic considering others to be 'beneath' them • Logic rules	**Sadducees** *Only believed in the first five books of the Bible. Denied resurrection, angels or spirits. Caiaphas was a Sadducee.* **Scripture:** Matthew 16:1,4,6,11,16 Luke 20:27 Acts 5:17, 23:8		
• Steam Roller • Controlling • Give Orders • Avoid conflict through directive approach	**King Herod** **73-4 BC** *Pro-Roman King of Israel. Not truly independent. Crown achieved through bloodshed, power established through foreign weapons from Rome. Goal was to keep internal national conflict at bay through domestic policy, while remaining pleasing to Rome and assured of their continued support.* **Scripture:** Matthew 2, 14 Mark 3, 6		
• Agenda overshadowed everything • Appearances vs. heart of issue • "Should" and "ought" driven - legalistic • Reputation over character • Self-righteous	**Pharisees** *(Separatists) They were also known as Chasidim, which means loyal to God or loved of God. They strictly adhered to the law adding many stipulations to laws.* **Scripture:** Matthew 5:20 Matthew 16:11-12 Matthew 23:2-9		

Listening Style	People Group	When Do I Use This Style?	What is the Effect on Others?
• Naysayer • Pessimistic	**Israelites** *Descendants of Jacob (whose name was changed to Israel and from whom the 12 tribes came). They are the 'chosen' children of God with whom He made a covenant and to whom He gave His Law. (The Mosaic Law is the first 5 books of the Bible, called the Torah by Jews.) Also called "Jews" or "Hebrews". God was with them, but they often contend with Him during their trials and struggled with disbelief and disobedience.* **Scripture:** *Genesis 32:28* *Genesis 35* *Acts 28*		
• Judgmental vs. judicial • Did not take time to confirm • Pushing opinion on others vs. God's truth	**Sanhedrin** *(means "sitting together") Supreme Jewish religious body in Judea during the Roman period. Ancient court system. Caiaphas was the High Priest of Sanhedrin at the time of Jesus.* **Scripture:** *John 10:33* *Mark 14:63-64*		
• Hand-washers • Unwilling to put any "skin in the game" • Detached • Fear of man rather than fear of God • "Go along to get along" mentality	**Pilate** *26-36 AD* *Roman governor of Judea. Responsible for the execution of Jesus Christ.* **Scripture:** *Matthew 27* *Mark 15*		

Appendix B: Barriers

Cultural & Religious Barriers to Promised Land Living Please circle the 1 or 2 barriers with which you most identify.

A. Pat Answers
You may know the answers in your head, but do you know in your heart and realize it in your life?

B. Church Position

Where is your focus – your position in the church or your position in Christ?

C. Protecting My Reputation
If you spend time trying to guard your own reputation, what might it be costing you in harming Christ?

D. One way of doing things.
Whose truth are we operating under – ours or God's?

E. Is what I want "Bad" in God's eyes?
Are you willing to wait on God for Him to decide what your want is going to look like and be fulfilled?

Examples:
David building the temple (I Kings 5:3-5)
Moses leading the Israelites out of Egypt (Exodus 14)
Abraham and Sarah having a child (Genesis 15)

F. "It" has to be hard.
Are you holding onto a certain outcome? Are you holding onto resentment? Unforgiveness?

G. B.U.S.Y. (Being Under Satan's Yoke)
Are you "busy" or is your life "full"?

I. Comparison
God provides everything you need to run your race, not everyone else's.

1. Who are you comparing yourself to right now?
2. What specifically is the comparison you are making?
3. Would you be willing to use that mental and emotional energy in a more constructive way
4. What would you need to tell yourself about you and the other person, going forward?

J. Opinions
In your quest of others' opinions are you delaying making a decision you know needs to be made?

K. Getting it all together
Are you making excuses or getting ready?

L. Self-Sufficiency
Do you feel like you have to do this all by yourself?

Four Questions to Root Out the Impact of these Desert Lies:

1. How have you seen these lies affect your decisions?
2. What changes can you expect by making decisions based on truth rather than lies?
3. How can you begin to make the changes necessary to operate from truth rather than from lies?
4. Where do you sense God wants you to begin this process?

The 7 Step Shift ® from Barriers to Freedom

1. Note the physical symptoms.
What symptoms show up when I am living from the barrier I selected?

2. Ask myself, "What am I telling myself?"
What message is going through my mind – – about me, about God, or about another person?

3. Ask God, "What is the truth?"
Take a moment and consider what the truth is about me, God, the other person and/or the situation.

4. Compare what you are telling yourself to what God is saying to you.
If you are believing a lie, then ask yourself if you will tolerate that lie. If you do not want to tolerate the lie, then confess and renounce the lie in prayer before the Lord, preferably praying aloud.

5. Recite the Truth (the Word of God).
Recite the truth aloud – about yourself, God, or the other person. Declare and decree it with the fullness of His authority. Thank God for giving that truth to you.

6. Ask God what is one step you can take in that truth.
What is my next step based on the Truth? When will I take that step?

7. ACTION: Take the step.

Appendix C: Shift Bookmark

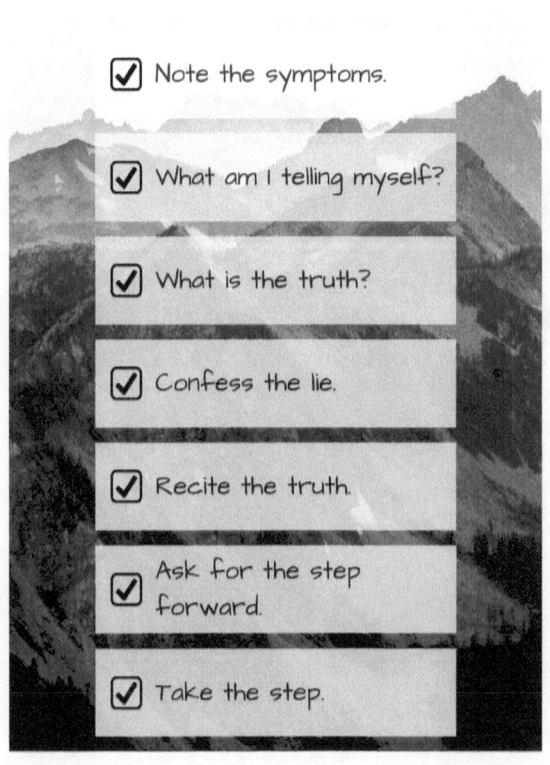

- ✓ Note the symptoms.
- ✓ What am I telling myself?
- ✓ What is the truth?
- ✓ Confess the lie.
- ✓ Recite the truth.
- ✓ Ask for the step forward.
- ✓ Take the step.

Appendix D: Timeline

Event	Year	Age
Nun convo with Mom	1969	4
Lake Geneva Youth Camp prayer and fall from bunk	1974	9
Run away from home	1975	10
Suicide confrontation with Cheryl's Mom and Dad	1981	16
Get married – move from Chicago to NY	December 1985	20
Sell business in NY – move to Florida	1992	27
Sons born in Florida	1993–1995	28 and 30
Elizabeth and Kris enter Cheryl's life and disciple her	1993–1995	28–30
Read Chuck Colson book and have dream	January 1994	28
Cheryl calls her mom and tells her she forgive her	February 1994	29
Tom and Cheryl's first prayer as a couple and subsequent move to NC	March–May 1996	31
Cheryl's Mom diagnosed with Pancreatic Cancer	February 1997	32
Michael faceplants on the driveway – Cheryl surrenders kids	Summer 1998	33

Cheryl's Mom seeks forgiveness 6 weeks before she dies	May 1999	34
Lyme symptoms present waxing and waning until wheel chair and partial paralysis	1995–2003	
Lyme diagnosis – picc line and glutathione treatments	May 2003	38
Cheryl begins her coaching business journey/learn how to walk again	October 2004	39
First Promised Land Living group finishes	2005	40
Tom and Cheryl visit the Healing Room after glutathione treatments are stopped	October 2005	40
Cheryl climbs the stone wall at the state fair and declares healing	October 2005	40
Grace dies – never opens necklace gift given to her by Cheryl	July 2007	42
Tom and David get lost in Pisgah National Forest with Boy Scouts	Sept 2007	42
Father in Law Bill lives with us with advancing dementia	2007–2012	42–27
Michael meningitis scare and 2 week hospital stay in Florida	April 2009	44
Cheryl coaches color guard at kids school while working as assistant to the band director	2007–2019	42–54
Cheryl experiences cardiac tamponade – angry with God moment	Summer 2016	51
Thrown from horse incident – Tom and Cheryl's marriage is confronted in community	December 2020	55

www.ingramcontent.com/pod-product-compliance
Lightning Source LLC
Chambersburg PA
CBHW032031290426
44110CB00012B/754